WHO OWNꟹ
THE FUTURE

TONY KEARNEY

authorHOUSE®

AuthorHouse™ UK Ltd.
500 Avebury Boulevard
Central Milton Keynes, MK9 2BE
www.authorhouse.co.uk
Phone: 08001974150

First published by AuthorHouse 8/5/2008

ISBN: 978-1-4389-0568-6 (sc)

Printed in the United States of America
Bloomington, Indiana

This book is printed on acid-free paper.

CONTENTS

Prologue.. ix
Introduction.. xvi
Preface.. xx
Pre-Note.. xxiii

THE FUTURE OF THE PLANET

A Sustainable Future Isn't Good Enough 3
Save The Planet? You Can Not Be Serious! 11
Where's The Spare Planet? 27
Climate Change? Bring It On!.......................................41
Fossil Fuels Are For Fossils 47
The Caterpillar Effect 61

THE FUTURE OF THE HUMAN CONDITION

The Human Race 67
The Properties Of Being Human 69
The Sustainable Human 73
Population And The Future...89
The Great Culling:Can't Change? Won't Change! 101
9/11 And 11/9 – A Tale Of Two Numbers 111

THE FUTURE OF ATTITUDE

Ownership And Possession 119
Conquest..127
Growth 135
Things Are Not Always What They Seem 143
Make Wealth History 151
Enough 163
Don't Blame Fast Foods For The World's Ills 167

THE FUTURE OF THE PAST

Quantum Evolution 175
The Memory Of Being Human 185
Epigenetics 191
Total Recall 199
Rescue From Abandonment 203
Projection 207

THE FUTURE OF THE UNIVERSE

Space – The Final Frontier 217
Is The Universe An Intelligent Place? 223
Are There Other Forms Of Life In The Universe? 227
Choosing Where To Live In A World Of Non Locality ... 231

THE FUTURE OF LIGHT, TIME AND OTHER STUFF

Light And Dark 239
To Overcome Gravity You Need Light 243
Time 247
The Forces Of Life 255
Smile: You're Having Your Photon Taken! 267
Lights, Camera, Action Smile: You're On Candid Camera ... 275
Coherence And Interference:
I'm Sorry, Could You Say That Again? 281

THE FUTURE OF MEN AND WOMEN

The Future Of Men And Women 291
Men And Women And The Evolution Of Sentiment 303
The Future Of Law And Gender 311

THE FUTURE OF GOD

God: Grow Or Die 319

*This book is dedicated to my wife, Helen,
for 27 years worth of reasons.*

THE FUTURE OF THE FUTURE

Medicine Of The Future..325

The Phoenixing Of The Future.................................331

Projections For The Future...335

The Prodigal Moment 339

The Observer Effect And The Future...........................347

World Citizenship 355

Don't Panic, It's Organic!..361

What Works Best 371

Forgiving And Forgetting 375

Finding A MAP Into An Unknown Future.................381

Welcome To The Beginning Of The Book! 389

Epilogue...390

PROLOGUE

AS A MAN OF A certain age, in recent years I have noticed that the ageing process has a certain challenging effect on one's psychology. This can cause a man to either go into slow down drift on the one hand, or denial on the other. I chose denial, and as a consequence have taken up a series of physical and other challenges including climbing mountains, running marathons, taking part in triathlons plus giving up my life of nearly 25 years as working in London as a lawyer and decamping to Ireland to take up a new life as a farmer.

This may not prevent the ageing process running its natural course, but the rewards certainly seem better than the other options of idle drift on the one hand or numbed comfortability on the other. It was also an opportunity to realise once and for all that I was truly human in facing my own personal limits.

This process of denial began in 2004 when I ran the London Marathon for a charity called Sense that supports children who are both deaf and blind. The children, and their teachers, are truly heroic in the challenges they undertake together each and every day and they made my challenge of running the marathon seem tiny in comparison, which it is.

When I crossed the finish line of the marathon totally exhausted a TV reporter planted a microphone under my nose, said that I was live on the News and asked how I felt. I replied that I felt I now knew how women felt when giving birth! A lot of women have since told me that I would have to do better than that to get anywhere near the pain of giving birth and that running a marathon was small beer in comparison! Ladies, please forgive me!

In January 2006 I attended a conference at the United Nations in Kenya as a facilitator on the subject of Humanity and Gender where the issue of gender relations was being researched as a crucial area in finding a progressive way forward for the human race into the future. This felt like a break-though event for us all, for we could see that unless the genders can reach a new understanding and mutuality then all the old locks in the world would remain in place and that this would make real and meaningful change difficult, if not impossible.

The conference inspired everyone and left us with renewed hope and belief about the future and a vision about the genders working together with renewed respect, value and a dignity about the contribution each can make of their own account and together. We can learn so much from each other's experience when we share the richness of such differences, rather than seeing them as oppositions. After all, opposites are supposed to attract, so this created a sense of optimism about the future.

The stories of the delegates at the conference - especially some of the women - when they talked about some of the adversity they had faced and had or were in the process of overcoming, were very moving. They certainly put some of my problems into perspective.

I wanted therefore to take on a challenge myself that, whilst in no way as difficult as the ones they faced, could help me feel something akin to what they might be feeling. This might help me to empathise more with their struggle in facing issues such as female genital mutilation, forced child marriage and so on.

After the conference ended I therefore travelled to Tanzania to attempt to climb Mount Kilimanjaro. This had been a long cherished goal since having been there 25 years earlier as a backpacker travelling around Africa. I hadn't climbed the mountain then, due to the fact that the cost of doing so would have meant that spending a lot less time travelling around Africa.

I promised myself to return one day to attempt the climb at some point in the future, and so exactly 25 years later, here was another opportunity to climb the mountain and it was too good an opportunity to miss! I knew it was going to require an incredible effort to climb the mountain bearing in mind that I was now 49 and not 24 and that the mountain is nearly 20,000 feet high. Plus there are issues of altitude sickness and lack of oxygen to overcome the nearer to the summit that one gets.

It took all the energy and effort I could muster to get to the summit and there were times when I simply didn't want to continue. When I got to the summit there was not any feeling or sense of having *conquered* the mountain. The overriding sense was one of relief and absolute exhaustion. In fact, I simply collapsed into my guide's arms and burst into tears! This was then quickly followed by a sense of awe and majesty about the view that felt very moving and totally humbling. At this moment I felt more of what it must be like for some of the delegates at the conference, so this deepened my value and appreciation for their endeavours.

The sense on the summit was that the mountain didn't mind me being there, but that it certainly didn't feel conquered or lesser for me having climbed it. I was simply a guest whilst I was there and that it was going to be there long after I was gone regardless of what I made of the experience of being there.

This then caused me to rethink my relationship with the Earth itself, for the same truth applies in that we are all guests on the Earth whilst we are alive. The Earth gives and grants us life from the moment of our very first breath until we breathe our last. How can there be something to conquer or control in such a relationship?

Within that relationship there are things to conquer, or more accurately, overcome in oneself in getting to the top of the mountain. The easily made mistake is to think that one has to somehow conquer the mountain for it and the Earth don't have an issue.

On returning to the base of the mountain I wrote down some of the lessons I had learnt from both from the experience of the conference in Nairobi and also from climbing Kilimanjaro.

They certainly helped in thinking not just about the lessons learnt from climbing the mountain, but also in thinking about the many challenges that the human race faces at this time and the personal challenges in a person's own life.

I share them in case they strike a chord with you too.

1.   To go high in life takes the time it takes and the higher one goes the more it is advisable to go slowly. Rome wasn't built in a day, although it did burn down in three!

2.   You have to prepare properly before you set off. You can't suddenly stop half way up and hope there is a shop to buy something you forgot. As the SAS say, the seven P's are vital in planning any mission and these are – proper preparation

and planning prevent piss poor performance! You can't necessarily predict the unknown, but you can prepare for it.

3. The higher you go the more ultra violet radiation there is and if you are not used to it boy does it burn you quickly. This is analogous to the human development journey in that the 'higher' one goes the more one will be placed outside one's comfort zone. It's a wise person therefore who doesn't assume they can handle the future with what they can cope with at their current level.

4. If you need a guide to show the way then get them on board early and follow their lead as they know the best route to follow.

5. Know your tolerances and work within them. There's no point pretending to be better than you actually are as, if you do, you will be found out at some point well before the summit.

6. Stop regularly on the way and replenish your energy and fluid levels as you go. This is essential, even if you think you don't need to do so, for as you get higher your appetite seems to disappear. It is also good to check progress along the way and reassess the challenge as the journey progresses.

7. You have to acclimatise to each level on the way up otherwise you don't build a platform for the next level. This takes time and cannot be forced or hot-wired.

8. Haraka, haraka, haina baraka - which is Swahili for – Great haste has no blessing. Enough said!

9. If you want to reach the summit you can't focus on simply reaching the summit. You have to set many mini targets along the way otherwise the main goal can be daunting and look impossible from where you are. Many mini successes lead to the big successes in life.

10. Listen to the advice of those who have been up the route before. Use and adapt their advice to suit your own particular circumstances and needs.

11. It's not a race! It's better to start slow and keep up a steady pace rather than starting off too fast and blowing up. This

refers to the story of the Tortoise and the Hare, which applies to mountain climbing and every other kind of goal attaining!

12. Don't be obsessed about reaching the top otherwise you might miss all the many fine things there are to see, observe and enjoy along the way. Fixation and obsession are far more dangerous illnesses than altitude sickness!

13. After the day's hard work enjoy the rest, for tomorrow the journey begins all over again. Each day is harder than the day before, so the quality of rest needs to be better as well.

14. Don't mind if you don't reach the top. The success lies in giving your best, for that is reaching the top of one's own possibility.

15. Any summit attained is only an interim success, for the next challenge always awaits beyond the current one. Do not rest on your laurels as you will become complacent. Each challenge completed, should grow your humility and *not* your ego.

16. Reaching the top is a perilous position because you are then faced with an immediate challenge of getting back down safely. One needs to be on guard against relaxing one's efforts and thinking that the job is done. More people die coming down a mountain than going up because they haven't projected enough energy to do both.

17. Get the right team around you with the right skills. This is essential for any chance of success because it can't be done on one's own.

18. Remember that the effort is not about *conquering* the mountain. Rather the effort is about conquering and overcoming things in oneself. The mountain is the task whereby these obstacles and resistances can be faced and hopefully overcome.

19. Pass on any knowledge or experience gleaned to those who follow you. Why wouldn't you want them not to have to make the mistakes that you have learned from (and also share your successes)?

20.   Never forget that the mountain will be there long after you have gone. This is not a journey of ego or personal vanity, but a struggle to be at one's best.

21.   The best thing about reaching the top is not the fact of getting to the top but the views you get from there. The panoramic views and vistas are simply breath taking and awe inspiring. Here one can really feel close to Creation and therefore oneself, because of the effort put in to get those views. It is this that makes all the effort worthwhile. It will have forgotten that you were even there tomorrow, but maybe you won't have forgotten what it was like to be there!

22.   Finally, but perhaps most importantly, always remember when entering new domains, challenges and levels to take extra toilet paper as you never know what might happen when your tolerances get stretched!

On returning to the base of the mountain I reflected on my experience and also about writing this book and could see some parallels; in particular, the last night before climbing to the summit. Before we set off at midnight I had been suffering from food poisoning and so my energy levels were low, I had had little or no sleep and one of the porters had coughed all night and had to be taken down the mountain due to pulmonary odema! This did not seem to augur well for the attempt to reach the summit! Plus, when we arose at midnight to set off it was a bitterly cold minus 20 degrees and pitch black with darkness.

Thinking back, that was the best time to set off into the unknown. In truth, it wasn't pitch black when we set off, for above our heads there was literally a carpet of stars that radiated the most brilliant, effervescent light. I may not have felt much light within when I set off, but I had not seen as much light outside at that time of night before. This took what little breath I had away! It also encouraged and spurred me on.

Sometimes it is not only safe to begin a journey in the dark, but in fact it is advisable to do so. If we had set off at any other time than midnight then I would not have made it. If we had begun at sunrise I would have been able to see the scale of the task in front of me and knowing this would have made it too daunting to attempt. Somehow there was a safety in not knowing the scale of the mountain to be climbed, so I could begin by placing one foot in front of the other and hope that I would be able to make it.   Luckily, with the help of my guide who was called Good Friend (it's true!) I did.

In a way, the future the human race faces is like that moment at midnight when we know the time has come to make our attempt to climb the unknown mountain. It is a most daunting challenge and will demand a superhuman effort, but we need to try, for the reward of the view of a new dawn will make it all worthwhile.

This book is therefore not an attempt to hide the challenges ahead, and in fact, seeks to highlight them. The main aim and intention within this however is to focus on the reason why we may wish to face these challenges with confidence rather than fear.

It is ironic that the name Kilimanjaro is made up of two Swahili words Kilima and Njaro which literally translate as "shining mountain". This conveys the sense of beauty encapsulated by Kilimanjaro's snow covered peak, yet the decrease in the amount of snow coverage on the peak between 1981 and 2006 was extraordinary. According to current projections all snow coverage on the peak will be gone by 2017.

It is extremely poignant therefore that the peak of Kilimanjaro is called Uhuru which in Swahili means freedom. It was only when I reached the summit that I realised just how fitting this name was. For when I was at the peak, I felt, if only for a moment, the freedom of not actually wanting anything at all. It was enough simply to be there and be with something indescribable and unknowable yet at the same time known.

Freedom is the key to a better future I believe. We have the freedom of choice about which future we want. Let us use that choice wisely. The future demands nothing less.

INTRODUCTION

THERE IS THE WELL-KNOWN EXPRESSION that states that the big always eat the small. Mostly this maxim refers to nature and the fact that larger animals prey on smaller ones. This helps to explain why food chains exist in a pyramid shape, for unless there are plenty of smaller creatures at the bottom and fewer larger ones at the top then the whole food chain will become top-heavy and collapse.

This concept of the bigger being more powerful than the smaller also extends into many spheres of human behaviour where it is often said that a good big 'un will always beat a good little 'un. Examples of this are where large companies will take over smaller ones and big countries exert their power and authority over smaller ones, economically, politically and if needs be militarily.

This pyramid of power explains why there are fewer rich countries than poorer ones and why there are fewer billionaires in the world than there are starving people. By analogy therefore those at the top could be seen as the predators and those at the bottom are the prey.

Nowadays it seems that not only does the saying ring as true as ever, but also that the fast will consume the slow, the rich will consume the poor and if we are not careful we will all consume the future.

Our world has changed dramatically and profoundly during the course of the last 100 years. The breadth and scope of those changes are mind boggling, both in terms of their speed and the implications towards the future of the life of this planet and our lives as human beings on it. Today we have everything from nanotechnology to mad cow disease, genetic engineering and cloning, to poverty and starvation on unprecedented scales, more cures than ever before for all kinds of illnesses and yet more illnesses than ever before. We have greater technology to find and use the Earth's resources yet less of them and more importantly fewer places to share them.

We live in a time of extremes and extremis. The tolerances and balances of life on Earth are acute and given the perilous nature of the times we live in, this suggests that great care is needed in assaying the way forward.

The human race faces an uncertain and unknown future, for the decisions that are made today will determine the railway lines of what kind of future we and our children shall have. The challenges, opportunities and problems we face as a species are monumental. For the first time in history a species can and will determine whether or not it shall become extinct by reason of its own behaviour. Alternatively, it could be a time of a new renaissance of human values and a flowering of talents and abilities on an unprecedented scale.

It is therefore, in short, a time of choices.

We stand at a cross-roads moment in time. Many say that it is too late and that nothing can be done to reverse the tide of things like climate change and global warming. Others say that things can be changed if key decisions are made now about a better and sustainable future.

The latter would seem to be the more likely position for there is still time for us to change our course and follow a safer path.

There is much that can assist the human race in making the key decisions we need to make in order to ensure that we not only survive as a species into the future, but that we thrive and flourish. For never before in history have we been so aware of the reality of our situation, or better informed as to how things work and how they relate to and affect each other. Yet outer knowledge alone is not enough.

It is therefore not a matter of needing more information, science or proof that will help us make the key decisions needed, but rather one of re-evaluating our goals and priorities towards the future, each other and the planet that we live on together.

This is a turning moment in history and we have the power to turn the key in the lock of the future. We can either open up whole new realms of art, science, healing, religion and so much more or we can lock the door and throw away the key and never know what might have been. If we do this then we lock ourselves into more of the same of what went before and where that journey will inevitably take us.

Yet the decisions we need to make cannot be made from where we are. We need to somehow take a giant leap of faith into the future and cast up the vision of what kind of world we want to see for ourselves and for each other. From there we can then backward cascade to now and let that vision tell us what changes we need to make to allow that dream to become reality.

Some say that we cannot afford to make the kind of changes that this kind of vision requires. The more likely reality is that we cannot afford not to make the necessary changes whatever the cost. Piecemeal changes and rhetoric will not provide the answers that are needed.

It is an ill wind that blows nobody some good however. The times and events that we find ourselves in are in fact a blessing in disguise for we cannot continue to hide from the truth for much longer. For it is in times of crisis that real and profound change is possible and it is in such times that true heroes and heroines come to the fore.

This is one of those times.

The human race is looking to find the way of the future and perhaps the future is looking to find its way into the human race?

Time is short, but the irony is that we need to slow down to find what we need to forge the path ahead. Nature has a way of giving things the necessary tools to do the job they need to do, but if we rush too much we won't see them in the blur.

The future needs a volunteer army whose only weapons are their talents and abilities together with their compassion and humanity. Perhaps you the reader are one of those people?

This book is a search for perception, understanding and insight into what the case is and how it might be possible to move forward in a constructive and generative way together.

It is not meant to be a book of answers, but rather a book of questions and starters much in the same way as the future itself is starting each and every moment. Therefore, each chapter of the book ends with a question mark and wonders, not so much whether the reader agrees with what has been said, but what the reader thinks *about* what has been said.

Who owns the future? Perhaps none of us and all of us do? If we consider the future to be an unlimited company in which we are all shareholders with each of us having voting rights as to what the company should do in the future, then that says we all have a say and a stake in what happens. In this election everybody votes, because every thought, idea, belief and action determines what kind of future there will be whether we like it or not.

Some say the future isn't what it used to be. Perhaps that may be our only hope.

PREFACE

The reader may notice that this book does not have any footnotes or references. That is not to say that there weren't any obtained in writing the book – there were a vast number of sources used. So why aren't they cited?

For two reasons:

1. The references and evidences are not something I would want the reader to make their primary focus. Whilst statistics and evidences help paint the background, they themselves aren't the picture or where the focus needs to be. For if the debate is primarily about whether or not the state of the world is truly as the statistics paint it then we miss the point and lose the substance by grasping at the shadow. The issue is not about the quantities of life as portrayed by the statistics, but rather the qualities that we need to find to go forward into the future safely and confidently. After all, if you go to the doctor because you are unwell, you don't need endless hours of commentary and references about your condition, you need to get something that will make you well again. We therefore need to focus on the causes, both natural and unnatural, of our state of affairs and not the symptoms, and that is what this book endeavours to do.

2. Go find your own! Access to this kind of information abounds everywhere from books to scientific literature to philosophy to newspaper articles to film and documentaries to the internet and more. We truly live in an information age and if a person wants to pursue the facts and figures then they can easily do so. I believe the facts and statistics quoted in the book are accurate, but if any are incorrect then I apologise, it wasn't intentional!

However, the point of this book doesn't lie in the facts it cites. They simply give context to the core issues about the truth of our situation and *why* we need to change how we think and what we feel *before* we try and change what we do.

So what is the point then if it doesn't lie in the evidences cited?

Well, hopefully the reader will make up their own mind as to what the point is for them, but here is something from me as to how I view the human situation and what I believe.

I believe that there are carnal, moral and spiritual dimensions to our existence and situation and that the carnal ones (the physical realities) are the easiest to see yet the least important. They are the manifestation of the unseen other two elements of our existence and these are therefore far more important. The crises that we face in the carnal realms come from a deeper crisis that we have in the moral and spiritual aspects of our lives.

If the reader doesn't believe that there are both moral and spiritual dimensions to our reality and situation, then perhaps this book is not for you. However, having said that, there are hopefully enough elements within the book to hold the interest of those who are simply researching the physical reality of our existence and what we can do to improve that reality.

A lot of the book does, therefore deal with the carnal aspects of our current situation but, to repeat, that is not meant to be the driving imperative within it. The imperative lies in the fact that we need to find our humanity, our motives, our values and our vision if we are to find the way ahead.

Can either the moral or spiritual dimension be proven to exist?

No, they can't, and this book doesn't seek to convince or persuade that they do. Nevertheless, I personally believe that they do exist and pervade every fibre of our existence and that they need to be taken into account in seeking to find our place in the Universe and the way forward into the future.

Even if they don't exist, perhaps we should act as if they do anyway for this would in any event lead us to making better and more holistic decisions about the future. This is known as *Pascal's Wager* and suggests that it is better to believe that God exists and act in accordance with that deity's assumed wishes, because if one acts as if such a deity doesn't exist and one in fact does then there has been absolutely no advantage in not believing!

My own view is that one cannot cheat in the University of Life, unless one cheats oneself. So Pascal's Wager is in itself a cynic's deceit. The only thing that works in the long run is to be true to what one really is and be genuine in how one lives one's life.

It is not solutions we need as a first principle; it is perception and understanding as to the meaning of our existence. It is all down to how we relate to our lives and to each other that offers hope to all. If the future affects us all then that makes us all related. The key in finding the way forward lies in how we redefine our relationships at every level.

I passionately believe that the evidence of the meaning and purpose of life is out there in the marvels and clues offered by Creation and Nature and not in the institutions of the world. It may be hidden, but seek and ye shall find.

And don't forget to look inside as well, for there is a huge amount of truth living inside each person if only they care and dare to look.

Finding it or not depends on what a person wants and what they want determines what they see when they look.

PRE-NOTE

ALTHOUGH THE FOLLOWING CHAPTERS RELATE to the planet, the future, sustainability, energy, the environment and more, it is important to note that the author does not believe that any of these issues can be 'solved'. The solutions that are proposed in the world, such as those relating to energy supply and usage, will not, on their own save the day, for they all have their own inherent problems.

For example, assume that suddenly all the world governments decided to convert all cars to biodiesel to radically cut down on CO_2 emissions. If this was done it certainly would cut down CO_2 emissions, but it would cause critical food shortages because the amount of land needed to provide the necessary biodiesel is enormous. In fact, as this is being written, this is indeed happening with food crises and riots happening around the world as the energy 'solutions' create greater food 'problems'. At the level of the problems we face therefore, we are damned if we do, and damned if we don't.

The problems we face are much more fundamental, compounded and interconnected than governments and scientists would have us believe, and this means that they can't be addressed or solved in isolation.

Therefore, if the following chapters seem to suggest that issues like sustainability, energy supply or resource management can be solved, don't be fooled!

The arguments are simply presented to show that at two steps removed from the core of themselves humans are not, and indeed cannot, address the issues in a sustainable way.

Of course, things could and would be a lot better if we did address these issues in a sensible and sustainable way, but we need something far deeper, something much more fundamental, to steer our way safely into the future. Anything lesser can only put off the day of reckoning and is the equivalent of rearranging the deckchairs on the Titanic.

We do not need better and bigger scientific and technological solutions to our problems. Experience tells us, or at least should tell us, that they tend to only make matters worse. Rather, we need to use our moral and spiritual compass to avoid the icebergs of our blinkered vision.

More about that later, but in the meantime let's look at some of these issues simply at the level they bite with a pinch of salt if we can find one!

The Future Of The Planet

The future belongs to those who believe
in the beauty of their dreams.

Eleanor Roosevelt

Man's unhappiness, as I construe, comes of his greatness;
it is because there is an Infinite in him, which with all
his cunning, he cannot quite bury under the Finite.

Thomas Carlyle

The human race is challenged more than
ever before to demonstrate
our mastery — not over nature but of ourselves.

Rachel Carson

A Sustainable Future
Isn't Good Enough

SUSTAINABILITY, IN SIMPLE TERMS, MEANS not using the Earth's resources faster than they can be replaced, either directly by nature herself or with human assistance, e.g., by replanting forests at least as fast as they are used.

At present almost all energy and resource usage is in negative equity, i.e., it is used faster than it can be replaced. In the case of non-renewable energy forms, such as coal, oil and gas, the amount of difference between usage and replacement is quantum. Most people are therefore aware that an energy crisis is looming in the not too distant future, unless another way is found to balance the use of energy with the actual supply.

This awareness of the debit of energy supply has directly led to the rise of what has come to be called the Sustainability Movement, which seeks to research and develop ways in which this deficit between energy supply and usage can be better managed.

The word 'sustainability' has in some ways become tired, clichéd and now has some unfortunate associations to certain stereotypes, such as hippies, eco-warriors and even to groups like animal rights activists.

Whilst much of what the Sustainability Movement proposes is laudable and progressive, it has become primarily associated with the idea of human beings not damaging the Earth and its resources and managing their use in a much more efficient way. This however, is counter to the way things need to be approached, for to stop doing a negative action is, by its very definition, hardly positive!

Such proposed actions can also in their own way be ego based and human centric, for they may assume that human beings have a much greater power and influence in the greater macrocosm than they actually do. This does not advocate for a minute that human actions are not highly influential upon global resources, weather patterns, habitat depletion, biodiversity and so on, but it does suggest that a greater sense of perspective and no little humility is needed if human beings are to change their focus, priorities and behaviour.

It is important to remember that the human race's ascendancy as a species is very recent and incredibly spectacular. It is only in the last 20,000 years that we have, in any real and material way, impacted upon the Earth's natural balances by the way we live and only since the Industrial Revolution less than 300 years ago that our influence has become truly life threatening in a global capacity. This is nano time where the life of the Earth is concerned.

Since the Industrial Revolution the change in the human race's relationship with the Earth has been exponential in every way. During that time most people's direct relationship with the Earth has become more indirect and distant. As an example, only 150 years ago 90% of Americans worked in agriculture and related areas. Today, that figure is only 3%. Our exploitation of the Earth seems to be in direct proportion to the separation and disconnection to it as a life force.

RISE AND DEMISE

An important question to consider, therefore, is whether or not our demise will be equally as spectacular as our rise? We have a choice as to whether or not we shall regulate our behaviour in sympathy with how the Earth works and has worked for countless millions of years; or we can choose to ignore the warning signs and proceed with more of the same. Choices always lead to consequences, and the choices we make now are the most important ever in our history as a species.

At this point it is useful to consider the 'Gaia theory', in which the Earth itself is regarded as a giant self-regulating 'living' organism with the ability to balance and adapt its processes according to what happens on it. The essence of this theory lies in the fact that everything is inter-connected and that every action affects the equilibrium and fine balances that the Earth operates under. It then in turn adapts and changes according to what happens upon it.

The theory stops short of asserting that the Earth is in fact *alive*, but could it in fact be alive in a way that perhaps our human minds fail to perceive? Recent findings tend to give some credence to this possibility. For example, in 1998 geophysicists Kazunari Nawa and Naoki Suda discovered that the Earth has a background hum. This is way below our human hearing, at between 2-7 millihertz at about 16 octaves below middle C. Could this be our own planet's version of the harmony of the spheres? Could it also mean that the Earth is able to give and sustain life in ranges far outside our understanding and that it is truly alive and therefore intelligent?

Humans may assert that the Earth is not intelligent, but its system of self-regulation is far more intelligent than the way humans use these resources, both to destabilise this self-regulating process and to undermine their own future and that of countless other species.

Alongside the question of intelligence, the question is sometimes asked - is the Earth sentient? Most scientists would stop short of accepting such a hypothesis and there is no definitive proof to show that the Earth is sentient, especially in the way that humans measure sentience, which is through emotions and feelings.

Perhaps, therefore a more fitting question is perhaps not whether the Earth is sentient, but is the human race sentient? This may seem to be a ridiculous question, but the point is that the decisions humans make about their lives and their relationship with the Earth suggests that many of these decisions are made in the absence of any kind of sentience. The Earth is treated as a 'thing' rather than a living host and because of this fact, mechanistic and exigency based decisions are sought to be justified. The Earth is never consulted about what happens to it.

It is therefore somewhat arrogant for humans to assume that they might *kill* the Earth, for lest we forget - we live upon it and not the other way around. We depend upon it to survive rather more than it depends upon us. It is doubtful that we can kill the Earth, but we might, however, kill ourselves.

The Earth is our host. The question is; what kind of relationship do we wish to have with our host – a parasitic one or a symbiotic one? By default we currently mostly have a parasitic one.

It is never a clever evolutionary move to damage your host.

A SEARCH FOR PERSPECTIVE

Given the time scales that the Earth works by compared to our own, it is highly probable that the Earth will, over time, heal and cure itself of the human race's wanton and cancerous behaviour should we persist in living beyond our means and damaging the host we depend upon to sustain us. It might take a few thousand or even millions of years for the Earth to recover but in Earth time that is only the equivalent of one of our days in a life span of 70 years. This is less than a mild cold.

This is not so long a time scale when it is thought of in those terms.

Part of the problem seems to be that not only do people take out a mortgage on their houses when they can't afford them, but as a species we seem to not mind taking out a mortgage on the future as well. As with any mortgage, at some point the loan has to be repaid or the property is repossessed. The parallel with our relationship with the Earth is easy to see.

This unconscious awareness may have led to sustainability being linked with stopping negative behaviour or not making things worse.

However, that attitude itself isn't sustainable. We need to redefine our objectives and goals where our relationship with the Earth is concerned. In this regard we should be looking for a symbiotic (mutually beneficial) relationship rather than simply stopping our relationship with the Earth from being parasitic.

It can be done for we have the technology, the intelligence and the resources to do so. It is simply a matter of will.

The word I would therefore use to replace *sustainability* is **BIOGENERATION**. It simply means Bio = Life + Generation.

This model is not something we need to invent, as it already exists. For example, in Scandinavia for each eco house that is built more forest is planted than that which is required to replace it. This is because the quality of the houses is so good that they last much longer than it takes the forest to grow replacement timber, so what is grown exceeds that which is used in the house itself.

These houses are much more energy efficient than regular modular housing. With current technology it is possible to make houses that capture enough energy from geothermal, solar or wind power that they can even give energy back to the national grid. The amount may be small but if many thousands of houses do it then the accumulation of such energy credit is highly significant indeed.

The same principles of responsible use of energy could be applied in areas of the world where energy is just as much a problem as it is for those in the West. Ironically, in many of these places they are better placed to use things such as solar power because they have more hours of sunshine per annum. The benefits of investment in such projects would be massive, but does the West really want these countries to be free from their current dependence for crumbs of aid, and the crippling terms and conditions that come with that aid?

It is a matter of making such an approach not alternative, but rather mainstream. This is of course a huge undertaking, for the current model is ingrained in the Western psyche as the main, if not the only, way to do things. This then comes down to one word and one word only: education. How people are educated about things governs how they think about the issues they face in their life.

IT'S ALL ABOUT RELATIONSHIPS

We need to educate ourselves, and especially our children, into thinking differently about our relationship with the Earth. We can't keep taking without giving back - and we don't have to.

The UK Government talks about possibly having to build many more nuclear power stations to get through the next phase of energy requirements. Yet how much does each nuclear power station cost to build? What if that money was actually invested in *BIOGENERATION* that not only doesn't pollute, but puts energy back into the national grid and helps rebalance the environment?

This is a win-win situation.

It needs us to reset the agenda and insist that those with vested interests do not get to lobby longer and shout loudest to prevent the change that is needed from happening.

We need to incentivise, rather than penalise, people into this way of thinking. People who pioneer this way forward should be seen as leaders of a bold new future of responsible living. Accordingly the governments of the world should be making it easier and cheaper for such integrated solutions to be pursued.

The human footprint need not be one that we are ashamed of. We have a right to be here, but only because our Host allows it and as guests there are certain standards of behaviour that are called for whilst we visit. The Earth is the one home we all share and everything we have is its gift; not ours to seek ownership over.

When the mindset changes from prevention of bad behaviour to one of making things better, then real and meaningful progress is possible.

The way that this will work is from the bottom up and not from the top down. History points to the fact that successful cultures manage their resources carefully. Smaller cultures tend to succeed where they maintain co-operative and non-hierarchical systems of government. In this way everyone is involved in the decision making process, everyone is responsible for their actions, and all look to the future and not just the present.

In larger societies not everyone can see the whole picture, and so there tends to emerge a top down system of government, which often leads to abuse of power and control and autocratic styles of leadership. However, in certain circumstances it can work if the system of governance is benign and for the greater good, not just for the benefit of those at the top of the pyramid of power. As an example, some feudal estates, whilst now seen as totally politically incorrect, worked well with everyone being involved in the upkeep of the estate being cared for. Some Polynesian kingdoms also operate such a system successfully without the need for elections.

What is needed is the best of both systems, for we live in an age of globalisation, for good and for ill, where everything is inter-connected. In this we need to change our perception: that we all live on a tiny planet and that we are all one big tribe or family. We therefore all belong, but we also each need to think of the good of the whole and take responsibility for our actions with this context consciously in mind.

In this way true bottom up power can be released on a global level rather than top down power being enforced. It is said that if every person on Earth stamped their right foot at the same moment, a gigantic earthquake could be caused. Similarly, if every person changes their perception of their role and their responsibilities then the sum of the actions that ensue from such realisations would be equally massive.

We need to grasp the truth that the first astronauts had when they looked back at our island home and felt its extreme beauty, fragility and vulnerability. Such a moment has nothing to do with sustainability. It originates from the pedigree of who and what we are and our relationship to all things, including ourselves and each other.

It's not further information we need, but a knowing.

The question is – dare we remember what we already know?

?

What we call the beginning is often the end;
And to make an end is to make a beginning.
The end is where we start from.

T S Eliot

The earth laughs in flowers.

e. e. cummings

SAVE THE PLANET?
YOU CAN NOT BE SERIOUS!

(With apologies and thanks to John McEnroe!)

THE AWARENESS OF THE IMPACT of human behaviour on the environment is a relatively new phenomenon and the realisation that human activity can and does affect things like global weather patterns is even more recent. It is only in the last 50 years that this concept has even really emerged. This is because the perception was that there were separate ecosystems, each with their own weather and climate patterns. Whilst these evolved over time, they were mostly reasonably stable and self-regulating.

From the middle of the 20th Century scientists began to see that the Earth's ecological balances were much more integrated than previously thought, and that the human footprint had a significant influence on the balances at play. In particular, scientists began to notice the negative effects of things such as greenhouse gas emissions, pollution, deforestation, erosion of natural habitats and diminishing biodiversity as all contributing to the Earth's changing climate in every sense.

Only 200 years ago there was no real perception that the Earth went through different phases and periods in its history because there was no theory of evolution, nor was there any science of palaeontology.

Nor was there any scientific awareness of things like continental drift theory or that the Earth went through different temperate and glacial ages in its history.

The prevailing thought was that the weather was the weather and that some years were cooler or hotter than others and people did their best to adapt to whatever changes occurred. There was no appreciation of global trends over time because people didn't know how to map or analyse such trends. Nor did they have the inclination to study them. Their immediate concerns were simply to find the means to get enough to eat and drink and live as comfortably as possible within their circumstances.

Further, they were not really aware of the impact of their behaviour on their own immediate environment other than in a minor way. 200 years ago there was no appreciation of microbiology and how diseases were transmitted from one person to another. Whilst there was an obvious awareness of not wanting to live in filth and squalor, many people nevertheless did so, and indeed there are many millions in the world today who still do so. Nairobi in Kenya, for example, has a slum that houses 1.7 million people without basic things such as clean water and sanitation. In recently released statistics it has been shown that India has had an increase in people living in slum conditions from 27.9 million in 1981 to a staggering 61.8 million in 2001. This clearly shows the lie in alleging that economic growth helps the poor to improve their basic living conditions. All that really happens is that an elite rich emerges and that the number of poor at the bottom of the economic pyramid increases exponentially.

Today, although there is awareness of the needs for clean water and sanitation, the problem is more a sociological and economic one rather than one of ignorance of the impact of these ways of living.

In the past, all people knew was that if they lived in cities that were overcrowded and dirty then life expectancy was short and it was pretty inevitable that you would get some kind of disease that might kill you. Cures were hit and miss because of the lack of understanding of bacteriology and so remedies were based on a mixture of herbal remedies, trial and error, superstition and old wives tales.

There was certainly no awareness that human behaviour had any major impact on the environment, nor that it might contribute to the

Earth's overall balances and affect, in any way, the weather patterns. Even if they were aware of such an impact, the fact is that before industrialisation the impact would have been much less because the world population was much smaller and the activities being pursued were less damaging than those of today.

Although ancient peoples had less affect on the environment, they still did have a significant impact. Things like deforestation had been practised for many hundreds of years and the forests of Europe and North Africa, for example, were cut back substantially, both to provide room for farming and wood for fuel and cooking - much in the same way that the Third World does today. It is therefore a bit rich for the West to moralise to places like Brazil about not cutting down the tropical rain forests because they have already decimated their own forests long ago. This doesn't excuse Brazil from proceeding in the way that it does either.

THE LEGACY OF THE PAST

The affect of this negative behaviour on the environment was cumulative over a long period of time, and due to the scales involved it is unlikely that this contributed significantly to the CO_2 levels in the atmosphere. Certainly the people involved were not aware of any impact they were having on the climate, other than if they lived in larger cities and towns where they may have experienced smog and breathing difficulties, especially in the winter, due to the burning of these fuels.

Nothing was really done about this direct impact that humans were having on their own environments until the middle of the 20th Century. London, for example, was notorious for its 'pea-souper' fogs in the post-war years of the 1940's and 1950's. These were a deadly combination of fog and smog that could settle for days and even weeks, making it impossible to see more than a few feet ahead, even in the middle of the day. The air became so thick that people found it hard to breathe and hundreds died as a direct result of these conditions.

It was in response to this situation that the Clean Air Act was passed in 1956 in order to try and regulate and control smoke emissions from domestic and commercial sources. The Act was mainly concerned with making the air that people breathed healthier, rather than considering that the emissions upset the Earth's ecosystem.

The aim was to remove the pollution that was caused by coal fires, and this was largely achieved for the amount of pollution produced from this source was significantly reduced over the next few decades. Alongside the decrease in pollution levels from coal there was, however, a very sharp increase in CO_2 and lead pollution into the atmosphere. This was mainly due to the use of fossil fuels for providing energy to the national grid and the exponential rise in the number of cars on the road. The 20th Century was surely the century of the motor car with there being virtually none in 1900 to there being countless millions today, all spewing out pollution on an unprecedented scale.

This has created its own nightmare scenario, and legislation was introduced to eliminate the use of lead in petrol and reduce the amount of CO_2 emissions produced by cars. This has caused some slowing of the process of pollution from cars, but this is more than counteracted each year by there being more and more cars on the road. This is further compounded by an equivalent - if not even greater - rise in air travel. This has an even more damaging impact on the environment due to the fact that jet emissions are made at great height where the effect of the pollutants on the Earth's atmosphere is far greater and lasts much longer.

It was only in the late 1960's and early 1970's therefore that scientists began to look seriously beyond what these activities were causing at local level to what they might be doing at a deeper, global level.

What then began to be researched was whether human activity actually contributed to the changing face of the Earth's ecology and, if so, to what degree. It is only in the last few years that there has been any general acceptance of the principles of global warming. For a long time there was a refusal to accept the truth of the findings of many scientists that showed that human behaviour was contributing to global warming and climate change.

The main reason why countries like the USA refuse to accept the principle of human contribution to these problems is that they themselves *are* the biggest contributors to the problem. They fear that if they admit to this then they will be expected to make significant changes to reduce their emissions and they worry about what effect this might have on their economies. The problem is compounded by the fact that their economies are highly dependent on the use of fossil fuels such as coal and oil. To suddenly start reducing these emissions would have serious knock-on effects on their economies, or so they think.

MOBILITY AND MEANING

Western lifestyles are highly dependent upon the use of the car. The amount of emissions from cars in the USA is not far off being the same as the rest of the world combined. The American culture is built around the idea of freedom and mobility and the car plays a central part in this lifestyle package. People in the USA do not generally regard petrol efficiency and low emissions as being high priority features when buying their cars. They want image and style and cars that reflect their lifestyle needs.

Hence the rise of vehicles like SUVs, RVs and Hummers, which are notoriously inefficient and high polluters, yet extremely popular with consumers. Many people are prepared to accept the inefficiency of these vehicles and absorb the extra cost that this involves because the price of petrol in the USA is disproportionately low compared to the rest of the world. People have no incentive to change their lifestyles because, not only do they not see the need nor have the desire to do so, but the government does not have the will or mandate to tackle the issue directly either.

For a long time the USA has been in denial of the scientific findings regarding climate change and global warming, and indeed has funded its own research to counter the findings. However, even the USA is being forced to face up to the reality of the changes that are happening. This wake-up call was further catalysed in the wake of Hurricane Katrina, which devastated New Orleans in 2005. The irony here is that the USA - as the largest emitter of greenhouse gases - has the most to lose by doing so, for it has the most variable weather patterns of any country on Earth. With such a fragile weather system, global warming is likely to affect it more than any other country, and this can be seen from recent volatile weather changes in the USA.

The USA is by no means the only offender where these issues are concerned. On an emissions per capita basis, Australia is the worst offender in respect of greenhouse gas emissions. They, like the USA, are suffering the consequences of their failure to act with considerable damage being done to their environment and wondrous natural habitats such as the Great Barrier Reef.

Australia's policy is one of pursuing economic growth above all else, and their reasoning is: why should they do anything when countries like India and China are refusing in turn to change their ways and to change would make Australia non-competitive with them?

Such a stance is irresponsible in the extreme, but is unfortunately more the norm rather than the exception.

They are following a template set up by the Western economies since the rise of the Industrial Revolution around 1800. The only difference being that the Western economies, with the exception of coal in the USA, have simply used up most of these fossil fuels in their own countries to such a degree that it is no longer economic to mine them. Ironically therefore, the saying 'coals to Newcastle' no longer rings true, for Newcastle has insufficient coal to economically supply its, or anyone else's, energy needs.

The evidence as regards climate change is so widespread and compelling that the debate is not whether human activity contributes to climate change, but rather how much and whether anything can be done to reduce and even reverse the effects. The difficulty here is in getting any kind of consensus at world level, because climate change is inextricably linked to so many other issues such as economic growth, globalisation and world trade.

As the world governments fail to take meaningful action, the situation appears to drift on. The longer that nothing gets done, the harder it is to take any effective action. The knock-on effect of this inertia increases the other problems of the world such as famine, floods, disease and poverty. This means that the world becomes preoccupied with troubleshooting - dealing with the symptoms rather than dealing with the core issues. With more and more humanitarian disasters occurring due to the Earth's balances being disturbed, more resources are needed to deal with the disasters rather than investing in technologies to prevent or lessen the disasters in the first place.

The longer this cycle continues the worse it seems to get. Current projections are that things will get worse as this century continues, with ice caps melting, sea levels rising, droughts and floods becoming more extreme, disease becoming more widespread, and food and clean water becoming ever more scarce. All this can only be further worsened as the world population continues to soar and competition for resources increases, leading to more conflicts, wars and devastation as a consequence. Sounds like your average night watching the News on TV doesn't it?

LISTENING TO THE VOICE OF REASON

The increasing criticality of the situation that the human race finds itself in has directly led to the rise of many concern groups in the latter part of the 20th century; from Friends of the Earth to Greenpeace and others. They have all, in their own way, sought to raise awareness and consciousness about the crucial issues facing humanity as we venture into a pivotal and telling century, where the future and direction of the human race is concerned.

The clamour for something to be done becomes ever more emphasised. Hardly a week goes past without some new evidence being presented about things being even worse than previously predicted, and the moment of reckoning drawing ever closer.

Much of the effort to raise awareness of the key issues facing humanity is highly worthy and meritorious. The more well-informed people are about the reality of their situation, then the better placed they are to make meaningful and effective decisions about the future. Even more important than the facts of the situation is the context out from which those facts emerge. For context creates a wider and deeper location from which to make better decisions.

It is here that the focus of saving the planet makes a serious error in appreciation of the reality of the situation. The Earth is perfectly capable of saving itself.

As the Gaia theory suggests - it is a self-regulating organism that is able to adjust its workings and balances according to what is needed for its own survival and continuance. This implies that there is some order of intelligence within its working processes, even though human perception of intelligence would generally dismiss such an assertion as being fanciful or mad.

The true form of madness in relation to the Gaia hypothesis would be the human ***antithesis*** version of it as follows:

G   **Greed**
A   **Arrogance**
I   **Ignorance**
A   **Assumption**

These traits are a dangerous cocktail and if taken in any combination lead to human beings being intoxicated with their own self-importance.

The more scientists learn about the Earth and its systems, the more they see that there is at least an order and a balance within how the Earth works and regulates itself. Even at rudimentary level there seems to be a compliance with Newton's law of motion, which is that 'for each and every action there is an equal and opposite reaction'.

How this seems to apply, where the global weather and climate patterns are concerned, is that for all the activities that humans do to upset and destabilise the Earth's balances the Earth seems to do something to counter balance those changes and return to a point of equilibrium and balance. This is not to say that this is the only process at play, for it is clear that the Earth has been through many, many evolving changes throughout its history. However, it does seem that it is able to, and does respond to, what happens in a cause and effect way. The question is: how much does human activity cause or contribute to these changing patterns and response from the planet?

That is very difficult to assess, but the point being made here is that human behaviour is only a factor within the changes occurring and that human beings are not long-term governing, or even probably threatening, to the existence of life on this planet. They are, however, probably decisive in respect of, or at least contributing to, their own viability as a species, and many other species as well, *in the short term.*

The Earth's response to human activity is hardly surprising, for if attacked the natural response of a living thing is to defend itself. The immune system kicks in and it seeks to repel the invader before the invader kills it. The evidence suggests that the Earth's immune system is probably stronger than our self-sabotage, virus tendencies.

Perhaps this is where the human race needs to apply Newton's second law of motion, which is that 'once an object is moving in a particular direction it will continue to move in that direction until another force acts upon it causing it to change direction'. At present the human race is heading in the direction of what appears to be a cliff in front of it; accelerating as it approaches the abyss. What is the force that is needed that will cause the human race to change direction? This question needs to be addressed and quickly, before it is too late.

THE PATIENT HAS TO WANT TO GET WELL

The human race is clearly not the only contributor to the current changes that are happening on the planet at this time, but they are a destabilising factor within those changes. As such, the human race could tip the balance of the naturally occurring changes in an unfortunate direction, where their own quality of life is concerned, and for the planet itself. However, the planet's ability to recover and heal itself should not be underestimated either.

One of the main problems here for the human race, alongside that of context, is getting the right perceptions. Perceptions govern and condition what people think their situation is, and how they should therefore respond to it. If people do not regard the Earth itself as being a living organism, they will not regard it as being capable of self-regulation or any kind of intelligence. Therefore, either consciously or subliminally, they will regard themselves as being more intelligent and think they are able to control nature and its forces and powers. This is a grave and naïve mistake.

It is not being definitively claimed here that the planet is intelligent, but rather suggested that we consider that it might be; and if so that it might even be more intelligent than we are. It certainly appears to show signs of intelligence in its behaviour and ability to adapt to changing situations. It gives us everything we need to live, from food to water to resources, yet we seem to pay it back by exhausting what it gives us and polluting it as a way of saying 'thank you'.

To definitely assert that the planet is not alive is arrogant, and to behave as though it is lesser than ourselves and subject to our whims and fancies is compounded arrogance.

This means that the human race tends to overestimate what it knows and underestimate what it doesn't know. This is done by limiting and not taking enough account of what may be unknown and making over confident assumptions about what known. This then governs attitudes and behaviours and causes humans to justify their actions according to what they *think* they know. In this scenario humans arrogantly assume that the Earth is neither alive nor intelligent, and this then justifies them in treating the Earth as a commodity.

This arrogance is further compounded by the lack of connection that humans have with the planet they live on. This is illustrated by people mostly regarding themselves as living *on* the planet not *in* it. This may sound like a pedantic point, but it is key to thinking differently about our relationship with the Earth. Otherwise all we can hope for is a damage limitation process where the future is concerned.

What is needed is a shift in consciousness and awareness about the relationship with the Earth so that people start to become aware that they *are* the Earth. We and everything else that lives on the Earth are together one living thing and everything that people do ultimately affects themselves, for they are part of everything else. We currently don't live *on* the Earth we live *off* it and that is neither moral nor sustainable.

Humans wouldn't consciously breathe in carbon dioxide if they had the choice, yet in effect that is what they choose to do by reason of the actions they take.

Unless a holistic and integrated consciousness exists about our relationship with the Earth, we can only become unwelcome guests in our own home.

Humanity needs to realise that the Earth can survive perfectly well without it. It has managed to survive without us for several billion years and can probably do so in the future. It is estimated that well over 99% of the species that have ever lived on the planet have not been able to adapt to meet the changes in ecology and climate. Why should the human race be any different?

Given that human beings have only existed as Homo Sapiens for about 150,000 years out of the Earth's 4.6 billion years, to say that we have the power to end the life of the planet is somewhat over-egging our importance. Recent studies have estimated that it would only take 200,000 years for all trace of human beings ever having lived on the Earth to have disappeared.

What follows is a timeline of what would happen if the human race disappeared today:

- Immediately: most endangered species start recovering
- 24-48 hours: light pollution ceases
- 3 months: air pollution (nitrogen and sulphur oxides) lessens
- Within 10 years: methane in the atmosphere gone.
- Within 20 years: rural roads overgrown; GM crops disappear.
- Within 50 years: fish stocks recover; nitrates and phosphates in water gone.
- Within 50-100 years: urban streets and buildings overgrown.
- Within 100 years: wooden buildings overgrown.
- Within 100-200 years: bridges collapse.
- Within 200 years: metal buildings collapse.
- Within 250 years: dams collapse.
- Within 500 years: coral reefs regenerate.
- Within 500-1000 years: organic landfill mostly decayed.
- Within 1000 years: most brick, stone and concrete buildings gone.
- Within 1000 years: all signs of humans having contributed to climate change will have gone.
- Within 50,000 years: most glass and plastics degraded.
- Within 200,000 years: man made chemicals disappear.
- The only thing that would remain after this time is some nuclear waste, which can remain deadly for up to 2 million years.

This is a revealing list, as the longest surviving evidence of our having been here is both the most damaging and also, supposedly, the best evidence of our so-called technological advancement. That seems somewhat paradoxical at best.

Whatever the case, the Earth can recover from our brief but highly damaging reign. To assume otherwise is egocentric arrogance.

There have been previous periods in the Earth's history when there have been natural surges in greenhouse gases and the Earth has simply adapted and moved on. Current human activity could therefore be regarded as being an artificial booster to the current levels of these gases in the Earth's atmosphere, and the Earth will simply react and adapt as necessary.

Learning From The Big Changes

It appears that the Earth is going through one of those times of profound change naturally and that human activity on the Planet is simply a contributing and accelerating factor within those changes. To say that human activity is the primary or only cause of climate change and global warming is probably as erroneous as asserting that human activity contributes nothing to these changes whatsoever.

What is important is that human activity is a material and unnatural contribution to the changes that are occurring. With the Earth's balances so finely poised, these activities could tip the balance in an unfortunate direction, or trigger a domino series of changes.

Whilst nothing is guaranteed, the Earth appears to be very resilient and able to meet the challenges that come its way. The challenge it faces in dealing with the consequences of human behaviour appears to be far less than those it has faced in the past. Nevertheless, the planet already seems to be using measures to deal with these challenges. If human behaviour continues on its current course, then it is highly likely that the Earth's counter measures will themselves increase in response.

The main question seems to be not whether we can save the planet, but rather whether we are able to adapt in time to meet these challenges and change our behaviour in order to save ourselves? Not only do we pollute the air we breathe by increasing the levels of CO_2 in the air, but we also compound the problem by chopping down the trees that can turn the CO_2 into the oxygen that we need to breathe.

It is almost as though the human race is living in a hermetically sealed jar that it has built for itself, not able to see that it is slowly killing itself by polluting the jar it lives in.

The planet itself operates over much longer time scales than the human race and it therefore has an ability to counter any destructive behaviour perpetrated by the human race. In fact the Earth seems to allow human behaviour to be what it is because within such behaviour the human race produces its own toxicity to destroy itself.

With this kind of self sabotage it really doesn't behove the human race to assert that the Earth isn't in any way intelligent or even sentient. Whilst human beings can accept that perhaps a dog can hear things outside the range of its hearing, and that a goldfish can see things outside their visible spectrum, they do not seem able to consider the possibility that there might actually be things in the Universe that are more intelligent than themselves.

RISING TO THE CHALLENGE

This is compounded by the human race operating at a far lesser and more dangerous level than they are capable of acting. Because of this there is little coherence in how the human race addresses its situation, as it keeps thinking at the problems rather than thinking inside the reality of the situation.

The question is often raised as to whether the human race can actually do anything to stop the trends of things like global warming and climate change. Perhaps a better question is not what can be done, but rather: how did we end up like this? How did we get to the stage where we came to regard such destructive behaviour as being acceptable? How could such incoherent and illogical behaviour come to be the norm?

Perhaps the cause of the problem lies outside of ourselves and we are simply the victims of a time of change, where the Earth is concerned and there is nothing that we can do? This may, to one degree or another, be true, but to simply rely on this line of argument would appear to be folly, for we are at least contributors to the situation we find ourselves to be in.

Perhaps Shakespeare had more than just a passing insight into the human condition, where this is concerned, when he has Cassius say to Brutus in Julius Caesar:

> *"Men at some time are masters of their fates:*
> *The fault dear Brutus is not in our stars,*
> *But in ourselves, that we are underlings."*

Without a true appreciation of our place in the Universe, we can only make foolish and short sighted decisions about the future. In default of there being a coherent and comprehensive understanding of the way that things truly work, and an appreciation of the human race's proper place in the reality of things, there can only be a scramble to rearrange the chairs on the deck of the Titanic where the future is concerned.

Coherence comes from sameness.

Appreciation comes from humility and gratitude.

We are the same as the Earth not different.

It will go on.

Will we?

The choice seems to be ours, but maybe not ours alone.

Finally, to return to John McEnroe for a moment. His now infamous line of "You can not be serious" came from a tennis match he played at Wimbledon some years ago. There was a dispute between McEnroe and the umpire as to whether the ball was in or out. The ball hit by McEnroe was called 'out', and this caused him to go into a rage that led to his now famous statement.

However, he also said: "The ball was on the line."

Perhaps the ball we live on is *on the line* too?

Maybe like John McEnroe we need to keep things in perspective, lighten up a little and get on with the game, trying not to forget to enjoy it whilst at the same time playing the best game possible in the hope that we win through!

After all, the next point we need to win is more important than the last one.

Perhaps this point is the realisation that we *are* the planet and it is us.

Without a doubt, this would revolutionise all thinking about the issues and the future that we face.

So the next time someone says to you they want to help save the planet, maybe remind them that the planet has already been through at least 5 great extinction events in its history and survived and indeed flourished. We haven't been through any yet so who needs to save who?

?

Even God cannot change the past.

Agathon

All things bright and beautiful.
All creatures great and small.
All things wise and wonderful.
The Lord God made them all.

Mrs Alexander

WHERE'S THE SPARE PLANET?

A KEY ISSUE FACING HUMANITY today is that of the distribution and use of the Earth's resources. This is particularly so given that within literally a few years many of these resources will have run out. Plus, there are parallel and directly related problems, such as global warming and climate change, that are exacerbated by the use of many of these resources such as oil and coal.

Latest scientific estimates indicate that we may only have about 10-15 years in which to prevent global warming from running out of control. This is due to the fact that CO_2 levels are building up in the Earth's atmosphere to such a degree that they could be self-sustaining by 2026. This means that fossil fuels will need to be replaced within the next 10 years as a primary source of energy supply and then another 10 years would be needed to bring Carbon levels under control.

Unless this is done then by 2026, CO_2 emissions will reach 440 parts per million in volume, and this is the point where global warming becomes self-sustaining and thereafter rises exponentially. Until 200 years ago these levels varied between 180 and 300 parts per million. They are now more than 380 parts per million and rising fast.

With the world's oceans becoming saturated with CO_2, and therefore no longer able to absorb some of the surplus, this figure will accelerate throughout the course of this century as more and more CO_2 is released into the atmosphere.

THE POWER OF THE FEW

Many of the world's countries have sought to address the use of such resources, in conferences such as Kyoto, but with little or no consensus as to how to agree and enforce any necessary changes. The problem manifests itself primarily in there being an apparent direct conflict of interest between economic growth on the one hand and a limiting of use of these resources on the other. In particular, the USA is reluctant to sign up to any limitation on the use of the Earth's resources and / or the regulation of CO2 emissions.

The reason for this is that, as the world's only Superpower, they regard any such compromises as being a limitation upon their pre-eminent position in the world, both economically and militarily. After all, it is estimated that the USA spends nearly the same amount on its military budget as the rest of the world combined, and this requires a massive use of the Earth's resources and this has side effects.

The USA regards the war on terror as being their main priority in the wake of 9/11 and therefore they channel huge amounts of money and resources into this battle. In doing so they fail or refuse to see that there is a much greater form of terrorism: the one that they (and others) wage on the environment.

The USA is by no means the only offender where this environmental terrorism is concerned, but it is setting the example that others are following. If countries like China and India succeed in adopting and applying this model - which they are clearly setting out to do - then the world will really be in deep trouble, for together China and India have a combined population that is seven times that of the United States.

BAD HABITS ARE CATCHY

India and China are adapting the Western economic model to suit their own local circumstances in order to compete successfully in the world markets. For example, China exploits (or at least plans to exploit) its resources in a more damaging way to the environment than any other country, whereas India is, according to the UN, the worst country for exploiting its people with something between one and two million children sold into bonded labour - or as it is known by its more traditional non politically correct name, *slavery*. These children are paid virtually nothing and are not in any real sense of the word, free. Nor do they get any education other than how to be an economic unit in the wheel of exploitation.

There is no such thing as a free lunch, and the question is: does the end justify the means? The answer has to be, no it doesn't.

These actions are sometimes sought to be justified in the name of progress and growth and raising the standard of living. This is a denial of the true reality of the situation because the long term damage and cost far outweigh any short term benefits.

Whilst materialism may advance and there are short term apparent gains, the uncomfortable truth is that such so-called gains are made at a terrible cost and impact to the host that provides the possibility for these gains to be made in the first place, i.e. the Earth.

The human race is therefore killing the goose that laid the golden egg.

Because of this refusal to compromise on what is seen as being a lessening of their standard of living, the First World countries, and those of fast developing economies, face the huge converging challenge of dwindling resources on the one hand and global warming and climate change caused by the excessive short term use of those resources on the other.

DENIALS DON'T CHANGE REALITIES

This is compounded by a full or partial denial of the truth of the issues that humanity is facing. For example, the scepticism and even denial that issues such as global warming and climate change have been scientifically proven, or that the use of fossil fuels is a contributing cause.

The continued use of such resources at the rate they are currently being used means that alternative sources will have to be found as the demand is increasingly outstripping supply. This means that foreign policy is becoming influenced by these needs in ever more desperate and cynical ways. The invasion of Iraq is a clear example of this with the USA acting on the pretext that Iraq had or was in the possession of weapons of mass destruction (WMDs). The clear evidence is that Iraq did not have such a programme.

Coupled with this was the government's attempt to link the invasion of Iraq with the 9/11 attacks in New York. Again, there is absolutely no evidence to support such a claim. However, the government spin has clearly worked because well over 50% of people in the USA believe that there is a direct link between the regime of the late Saddam Hussein and the 9/11 attacks.

What many people don't realise is that control of the Iraqi economy, and more importantly its oil production, has been passed into the control of the USA. Not only that, but also the awarding of lucrative contracts for the reconstruction of Iraq's infrastructure is also almost exclusively controlled by the USA with almost all contracts being awarded to USA companies. This is a stealth way of not only obtaining the wealth from the inherently rich Iraqi economy, due to its large amount of oil reserves, but also of obtaining control of the resources themselves.

This information is diluted or hidden from the public as much as possible. If people were truly aware of the real reasons that the government acts in the way that it does, then there would be a much greater demand for accountability than there is.

This is not likely to happen as people are unwilling to surrender their standard of living and oil is the key driving force of this economic model. However, the government cannot afford to take any risks and therefore proceeds with its campaign of disinformation.

None of this means that regimes such as that of the late Saddam Hussein are in any way legitimate or worthy. All it does mean is that the reasons or methods used to depose them were no more altruistic or legitimate in themselves. For they too seek to plunder the country's resources for their own benefit and not the genuine interests of the people or the country at large.

ALL WRONGS ARE WRONG

The bottom line is that there are not enough resources to satiate the world's lust for energy and the gap between supply and demand is ever increasing, particularly as the point of Peak Oil is being reached.

This is partly due to the diminishing production of oil, but also to the ever escalating use of energy and the failure to devise and develop new forms of sustainable energy to cope with the demand.

The USA is not the only offender here by any means, but is an example of what many countries are doing as they face an uncertain future over energy and climate change issues.

It should also be emphasised that it is the policy of its (and many of the world's) leaders that is being called to account and not the people themselves. These policies have developed and evolved over the latter half of the Twentieth Century and into the Twenty First Century.

The USA of today has become departed in large part from its declared sentiments of the Declaration of Independence:

"We hold these truths to be self-evident, that all men are created equal; that they are endowed by their Creator with inherent and inalienable rights; that among these, are life, liberty, and the pursuit of happiness..."

With nearly 2.5 million of its own citizens locked up in prisons, (the USA has the highest percentage of its population in prison of any country in the world) there is a strong smell of irony about those words.

The USA Constitution sought to guarantee certain freedoms, including the right to bear arms, but it did not make such a right mandatory and there is nothing to prevent its citizens from electing not to carry or bear arms either against its own citizens or those of other countries, should they so wish. The USA makes a better friend than it does an enemy.

Perhaps the policy makers in the USA could do well to revisit the words of one of their former leaders, Woodrow Wilson, when he said:

"I would rather belong to a poor nation that was free than to a rich nation that had ceased to be in love with liberty."

The USA has so much to offer the world in terms of knowledge, leadership, expertise and skill if it can be channelled as a force for good rather than a force of self-interest. In this regard America would be far better to simply help the world rediscover awe about the future rather

31

than using 'shock and awe' tactics to suppress its so called enemies, as it did in Iraq.

The sentiments on the Statue of Liberty have welcomed many a lost pilgrim to its shores when they had nothing left but hope:

"Give me your tired, your poor, Your huddled masses yearning to breathe free, The wretched refuse of your teeming shore, Send these, the homeless, tempest-tost to me, lift my lamp beside the golden door!"

This is something the USA can still offer the world when it remembers what it stands for and not what it has become. As Winston Churchill once aptly said: "The American people generally do the right thing, after first exhausting every available alternative." Surely, now is the time to do the right thing.

Abraham Lincoln encapsulated the true sentiment of what America can offer the world in his Gettysburg address when he said:

"This nation, under God, shall have a new birth of freedom, that government of the people, by the people, for the people, shall not perish from the Earth."

Since that time there seems to have been a retreat from these principles to it being one of; government of the government, by the government, for the government.

The core principles of the the USA ideal remain however, like Liberty herself, a crown to reach for and a goal than can be achieved.

Whether it will remains to be seen, and it seems that this lies more in the hands of its people than its leaders. Already this change from below is appearing and this offers grounds for hope and belief that real change for the better is possible.

Meanwhile China, to its shame, has embarked on a course of growth that could dwarf the USA's influence on the planetary ecology. Based on current projections of growth, China will soon eat two thirds of the world's entire global harvest and burn 100 million barrels of oil a day - or in starker terms, 125% of the current world total oil output. Considering that oil supplies are currently dwindling at an ever-decreasing rate, this can only be a recipe for disaster.

However, the situation is likely to be even worse than that for, based on current models of prediction in relation to climate change, if temperatures continue to rise then China is likely to face the problem of having to feed 200 million more people than it currently has on only two thirds of its current food supplies. This is because more and more of China's land will become unsuitable for farming due to the intensive farming methods used and the environmental degradation caused by its resource mismanagement and abuse.

Intense farming only serves to make matters worse. For example, it is estimated that the use of pesticides in the USA kills 67 million birds per year. Such a statistic cannot be relegated as a necessary, but unfortunate side-effect. It is a total disaster and a criminal act that totally undermines any claim that the pesticide industries are helping farmers and the environment.

Or if that statistic doesn't do it for you, consider the fact that the Aral Sea (once the world's fourth largest source of freshwater) has lost 11,000 square miles of its area due to the need to irrigate surrounding, thirsty cotton fields. That is bad enough on its own, but the problem is more than doubled by the fact that the remaining areas of the Aral Sea have been so polluted by the run off from the use of pesticides on the surrounding cotton fields that now no marine life can be supported.

Yet the short-term policy making continues unabated.

Within these issues new theatres of policy are being tested and developed in case they are needed at a later date. As an example, the USA is currently considering whether to authorise carrying out energy exploration in its protected wilderness areas. This policy is regarded by many environmentalists as the thin edge of the wedge where the future of energy usage is concerned. If and when energy is found in such areas, who is going to be able to object to these energy reserves being harnessed, especially when energy supply becomes critical?

The bottom line is that gaining access to and control of Iraq's oilfields or finding oil in its National Parks will not solve the USA's energy problems. If anything it adds to the complacency that there is enough to go round and therefore nothing is done to curb consumption. This means that other sources of energy supply will need to be found, and already the USA is looking at Iran and other countries as potential sources of supply, and developing its foreign policy accordingly.

This is not that difficult to do, for often the existing regimes in many of these countries are totalitarian, repressive and brutal in how they treat their own people. Therefore with a sufficient campaign of preparation a disinformation a case can always be made out to justify interventionist action on the grounds that it is either to liberate the oppressed people of the invaded country, or that is in the interest of the invading country's national security that it takes the proposed action.

WHO REALLY IS THE VICTOR AND VICTIM?

The USA has started to manifest the traits of the regimes that it itself finds so abhorrent. These trends are worrying indeed for many reasons.

The USA has itself become fundamentalist in how it addresses the rest of the world by seeking to impose its will and dominance through economic and military means. At the moment it is partly able to do so as it is the strongest country in both areas. But for how long?

The USA paradigm and mindset for dealing with the problems to be faced is summed up in one word – *growth*. Growth is perceived as being the way out of all the problems. This simplistic approach fails to recognise that the model within which the growth model is based is itself finite, as the resources upon which it is based are limited and dwindling fast.

The rate at which this growth is proceeding is inversely proportional to the amount of resources left, i.e. the faster the rate of growth the quicker these resources will run out. The evidence indicates that this crisis is approaching at an exponential rate. The technology to exploit these resources has developed out of this lust for growth to such a degree that we have accelerated our own rendezvous with the consequences of our own profligacy.

If the whole world used the Earth's resources at the rate that the USA does then it would need five Earth's to sustain everyone living on it. If the analogy were applied to Western Europe then it would still require three Earth's. The fact is, however, that we only have one.

Another way to look at these statistics by analogy is that in any given year the USA effectively lives off its own reserves and resources for only January, February and part of March. For the rest of the year it relies on the reserves and resources of other countries because it can't produce what it needs for itself. It is therefore living four times beyond its means. If the same equation is applied to Western Europe, then it manages to do a little better by surviving on its own reserves until the end of April before effectively relying on reserves from elsewhere.

This is a recipe for disaster and shows the classic signs of the collapse of previous cultures due to over population and failure to maintain sustainable environmental policies. The difference today is that, due to globalisation, all cultures are to one extent or another connected to and influenced by each other. Therefore, if one collapses probably many will.

YOU CAN RUN, BUT YOU CANNOT HIDE

Despite what NASA and other science disciplines might tell us, Mars is not a viable option due to the fact that our bodies could not sustain living in such alien environments long term. In the absence of Earth's gravity the human body quickly begins to deteriorate. Astronauts on long-term missions risk losing up to half their bone mass, their blood volume decreases by up to 22% and their muscles atrophy. On a lengthy trip to Mars these problems would be further compounded to the point of complete non-viability.

In any event, even if we could travel to such places, how long would it be before we polluted the environment there to such a degree that we would have to look for another place to live?

With this in mind it is hard to see any way in which any further expenditure on space travel can be justified. In reality much of the public face of space exploration is a smokescreen, for the real agenda that drives it is to do with military and defence systems, which is where much of the funding comes from.

We are designed to live here on planet Earth and it is our home. There is plenty to go round if the human race decides to act responsibly and in sympathy with the ways and laws of nature.

As Gandhi said:

"There is enough for everyone's need, but not for everyone's greed."

Greed creates the impression that there is not enough to go round, and this in turn fuels a primitive survival and competitive urge to ensure that one does not miss out. When this happens, the fight for these resources will be reminiscent of an African water hole when all the animals desperately try and get the last drops of water before it evaporates.

In terms of water itself, experts estimate that there are some 2 million cubic miles of water underground. This is sixty times the amount stored in all the freshwater lakes and rivers in the world and is a mind boggling amount. But, as with fossil fuels, we are using these fossil water supplies far faster than they can be replaced.

This then poses questions such as: do some people have more of a right to existence and therefore the Earth's resources than others, and as such can they impose their will on others to suit their own needs and requirements? Whilst most people would probably answer 'no' to these questions, the answer is tailored by the luxury of having water coming from the tap when it is turned on. If and when that situation changes then the real answers to the question will start to emerge.

The real answers are not academic, for they are already appearing and manifesting in how countries are preparing to face the issues of energy and resource shortages in the future.

With the world using resources faster than the Earth's ability to replace them, it is inevitable that clashes over resources will increase exponentially over the next few years. Governments will look for excuses and justifications for their actions but, as the situation worsens over time, it is likely that increasingly the pretence for such actions will disappear and it will be less a war over ideology, but rather a direct conflict over the resources themselves.

For example, with Iran it won't be difficult for America to be able to find reasons to use interventionist actions, should it decide to do so. It already has a track record there having been heavily involved in the deposing of the ruling regime in the 1950's that wanted to nationalise its own energy resources for the benefit of its citizens. This was an unacceptable position for the West, so they backed a coup that disposed of this democratic regime, replacing it with the despotic Shah of Iran who in turn was overthrown by the Islamic Revolution.

The mantra of 'freedom of the people' hides the real truth of the matter as the clamour for energy resources escalates into ever-increasing crises.

These are the forces that will govern and shape foreign policy over the coming years.

What is clear is that no matter how successful and effective these policies may be in the short term, in the long term they are doomed to fail. This is because they are based on flawed economic theory in that demand will exceed supply until such time as the supply runs out.

IT'S NOT JUST ABOUT OIL

This does not simply apply to matters of energy, for fairly soon many developed countries, will start to know what it feels like in many third world countries when their reserves of water begin to run out. Most of these countries are not able to live in a sustainable way from the rainfall they receive and they therefore have to supplement the water supply from underground aquifers. These supplies of water took millions of years to form and are used at a far greater rate than they can be replenished. As such, an imminent crisis over water is looming.

The USA uses about 340,000 million gallons of water per day, of which domestic use only accounts for approximately 1%. Whilst any savings of such a precious resource is to be applauded, it is clear that any domestic savings on usage of water can only literally be a drop in the ocean as the vast majority of water usage relates to agriculture and industry. Given that it takes 1,000 tons of water to produce a single ton of grain, it can be seen that, despite the vast reserves of water underground, it won't take long for these resources to be depleted. It takes 20,000 litres of water to make 1 kilogram of coffee, and 11,000 litres of water to make one cheeseburger. This demand for water compounds as one goes up the food chain, for it takes up to 60,000 tons of water to make a single ton of beef. Next time you have a steak for dinner, perhaps think about how much water it took to put that steak on your plate.

Will the oil crisis peak before the water crisis, or will some other shortage face us down first?

It seems that the world is heading for a tipping point moment where the issues of supply of resources and the consequences of misuse of them all compound into a crisis of unforeseen magnitude.

It is at this point that economic theory will become replaced by evolutionary theory, in that natural selection will clearly favour those humans who have been able to adapt to their changing environment. Those that don't will either be wiped out or forced to live in very reduced circumstances.

Some may say that this view is fantasy or a long way off. The facts suggest otherwise, for the issues facing the human race are not singular, but ones of compound criticality and the evidence points to an earlier rather than later point of culmination.

What can be said of politicians who fail to address the real issues facing humanity when countries are allowed to exceed their CO_2 emission quotas - providing they balance the books - by buying quotas from other countries that do not exceed their quotas? This ostrich-like approach to the problems is compounded by the fact that it is possible for such quotas to be traded on the stock market.

Individual companies are given quotas of emissions that they are allowed to have, and if they exceed their quota they then have to buy up unused quotas from other companies who do not use all their entitlements. This kind of trading is now one of the most lucrative on the stock market.

Is this really the way to tackle the issues of the future? Do so-called free market opportunities justify continuing abuses of the environment? Are we therefore avoiding the real battle?

Perhaps the battle of Armageddon is therefore with ourselves?

?

Everything flows and nothing stays.

Heraclitus 500BC

There is a tide in the affairs of men,
Which taken in the flood leads on to fortune.
Omitted, all the voyage of their life
Is bound in shallows and in miseries.
On such a full sea are we now afloat,
And we must take the current when it serves,
Or lose our ventures.

William Shakespeare (Julius Caesar)

CLIMATE CHANGE?
BRING IT ON!

WITH ALL THE CHANGES HAPPENING in our fast moving and kaleidoscopic world, climate change has risen up the agenda of possible Armageddon issues facing the human race. It leaves things like Y2K as merely a distant and insignificant memory.

This Armageddon syndrome is something that is engraved deep within the human psyche. It has haunted the human race for thousands of years with everything from soothsayers predicting the end of the world to possible nuclear holocaust to comets striking the Earth and everything in between.

To date none of these predictions have come true, but that doesn't mean that one of them might not occur at some point in the future. In this regard it would seem that climate change and global warming - and the spin-off threats – could be a self inflicted Armageddon unless something is done about it and soon.

The focus today, therefore, is not so much whether climate change is real and happening, but what can be done to prevent it.

However, this chapter suggests that climate change is exactly what is needed to preserve the future viability of the human race.

The climate change needed is not one of external weather patterns, but internal ones of attitude and sentiment.

It is the wrong internal climate change that has led, in large part, to the problems we now face where external climate change is concerned.

If the human race hadn't become so consumed with progress, profit and greed then many of the problems we face today wouldn't exist to the degree that they do - if at all.

Motive governs behaviour, and in the last 10,000 years there has been a seismic shift in the attitude of the human race towards its relationship with the Earth. This in turn has contributed to a shift in the climate of the planet on which we live. This is particularly so since the Industrial Revolution and the leap in technology that occurred at that time. Since then the governing motive has been to get more energy to allow more production to obtain more profit.

The side effect of this growth in technology has been to release massive amounts of greenhouse gases into the upper atmosphere and this now seriously threatens the human race's future due to increased global warming, pollution and - most dangerously of all - an exponential increase in population. In this cycle of positive feedback it is population increase that drives the need for increases in energy and resources, and this leads to exigent decisions being made as to how to supply these needs. This in turn leads to increases in pollution and global warming. And so it goes on.

The whole situation is a vicious circle based on a false premise of the human race assuming a level of importance and success that is unsustainable. This attitude has manifested and expressed itself in many ways through history, from greed to religious dogma, with the human race assuming a God-given right to exercise dominion over the Earth and all other forms of life that exist on it, including at times each other.

This attitude has led to humans exploiting the Earth's resources to the cost of countless other species by using them for everything from vivisection to showing them off in circuses to hunting them for the perverse pleasure obtained from killing another living thing.

These attitudes reveal a warp in the human psyche and this has led to the problems that we now face. The good news is that many people are beginning to wake up to the true nature of the crisis that we now face and are seeking to find ways to minimise and even reverse these effects. The bad news is that a lot of negative things have happened whilst we have been asleep and we awake to find ourselves in deep peril.

WHERE TO THINK FROM

The difficulty is that the human race mostly tries to solve the external problems that it faces from the external parts of themselves.

One of the climate changes that is needed, therefore, is for human beings to redefine who and what they are, what their relationship is with the Earth and, perhaps most importantly of all, what does it mean to be successful as a species.

In simple Darwinian terms success can be defined as a species living at optimum numbers within their ecology. When a species is successful its numbers grow and the range of territories that it occupies also grows. It then becomes the dominant species within the environments that it lives. In reality, no species ever actually becomes that dominant because it forms complex relationships with all other species in the same environment and the Earth itself.

Nature operates a system of checks and balances on all species, and if a species becomes too dominant it becomes vulnerable due to the excessive demands it places on supplies and resources. The same principle applies when a species becomes over specialised. For example, the Giant Panda is in grave danger of extinction because its sole diet is bamboo leaves. If something were to happen to the bamboo trees then the Pandas would surely die out, as they would not have enough time to adapt to an alternative form of diet.

The evidence suggests that the most successful species are those that are the most suited to their environment yet are able to adapt as their environment changes.

The irony for human beings is that they are, in fact, one of the most adaptable species on the planet, for they have managed to adapt to almost every kind of ecology on Earth. They can be found everywhere from the frozen Artic north to baking deserts to wild jungles to cities teeming with millions of people. Despite this obvious adaptability there appears to be an increasing inability to change its attitude to its relationship with the Earth. The human race regards this relationship as being a master and servant one, with the human race viewing itself as being the dominant partner.

COMMAND AND CONTROL

Most people would say that they do not view the relationship in such terms, but actions speak louder than words and the collective actions of the human race demonstrate that this is the case. Most modern societies adopt this attitude by using a hierarchical system of governance with the dominants at the top and the recessives at the bottom. Such societies work by a system of command and control whereas long term successful societies function by a process of connection and co-operation.

The human race also seeks to implement this system of command and control in its relationship with the Earth. Despite the obvious short-sightedness of such a policy, and the countless examples that Nature offers to show just how much we are subject to its forces, humans do not seem to be able to change this view in themselves.

There can only be one possible outcome in such a battle and that is that the human race will lose out to Nature.

This is because the solutions that the human race seeks to implement inevitably make things worse in the long run. Within a command and control structure the human race can never see the bigger or integrated picture and so they implement partial and segmented solutions. This is why, in the short term, they delude themselves into thinking that they can beat nature with things like dams, chemicals and genetic engineering.

If humans did see the bigger picture, then they would see that the solution lies not in command and control technologies, but in wisdom and understanding. All cultures who have thought they were better or more powerful than nature didn't live to tell the tale.

Surely this is something we should be teaching in our schools and in the boardrooms of all companies, institutions and governments. Nature gives us everything we need. What do we wish to give her back in return?

?

If you want to go quickly go alone.
If you want to go far go together.

Old African Proverb

They claim this mother of ours, the Earth, for their own
use, and fence their neighbours away from her, and
deface her with their buildings and their refuse.

Sitting Bull

FOSSIL FUELS ARE
FOR FOSSILS

ONE OF THE MOST VITAL issues facing the human race, where the future is concerned, is the supply and use of energy. We are currently using energy at a far faster rate than it can be supplied and the gap is ever-increasing as the world population soars and demand continues to increase.

The main factor in this ever-increasing crisis is that the vast majority of the world's energy supplies come from non-renewable sources of energy such as coal, gas, oil and, to a lesser degree, wood. Trees are often used as a source of energy in Third World countries at a rate far faster than they can be replaced, much in the same way that the West uses coal and oil so in that way wood is their equivalent of a fossil fuel.

Fossil fuels literally means that the energy sources come from things that were once living and have now condensed into a form that can be harnessed by combustion to create energy. What is often forgotten is that it took millions of years and millions of organic lives to live, die and gradually change into what we now see as coal or oil. In fact it is hard to imagine that the lump of coal on the fire or the gallon of petrol in the car was once a living thing.

However, this is the case, and it was quite a number of living things because it takes a large amount of life to produce the end product energy that is used. This type of energy usage is therefore very inefficient when compared to other forms of renewable energy.

There has been a huge amount of this fossil energy stored by the planet and it has been reasonably easy to access, but the human race has taken advantage of this supply to maximum effect and continues to do so. So much so that it has created a danger of becoming too reliant on these forms of energy for their use, as well as not diversifying enough into other forms of energy.

George Bush, in his 2006 State of the Union address, openly stated that the USA had become 'addicted to oil'. This was the first such admission from the USA government for previously it had, to one degree or another, refused to face up to hard reality where its use of energy was concerned. This is compounded by the fact that having been able to supply much of its own energy requirements in the past, the USA has increasingly had to rely on foreign supplies of oil as its own oil fields dry up.

This dependency on oil creates a huge problem for the USA as it sees that much of its supply comes from what it perceives to be volatile Middle Eastern states. The USA consumes 25% of all the oil produced worldwide and to support this demand it has to import 20 million barrels of oil a day. Because its own oil fields only account for 3% of all known oil reserves, it has to obtain oil from other sources.

The point here is that more and more people are competing for less and less amounts of these ever-dwindling supplies of finite resources. Plus the yearly use of them increases exponentially to the point that most experts regard 50 years as being an extremely optimistic estimate for the amount of time left for these resources to last.

The chilling reality is that, despite the upbeat noises many oil companies make about their ability to find new sources of oil, the fact is that for every new barrel of oil discovered that can be added to known reserves, five existing barrels are being consumed. The resource is therefore being depleted five times faster than it is being replaced, which curiously enough is the same rate at which the USA uses all resources beyond their ability to be replaced. This depletion is put into stark relief when one considers that the world consumes oil at the rate of 1,000 barrels a second. Yes, that is correct – 1,000 barrels a second!

Ireland is even more dependent on oil than the USA for its energy supply on a per capita basis. Despite the fact that it is a tiny country with a small population, it is the 9th most oil dependant economy in the world. 90% of Ireland's energy supply comes from fossil fuels, of which 95% are imported. If it does not wean itself of its own dependence on fossil fuels for its energy supply then the Celtic Tiger might not even be able to raise a meow in a few years time.

This creates a Catch-22 situation for the Irish government. Like many other countries it has embraced the American mantra of economic growth as being the key to prosperity. Yet every 1% of economic growth requires a 2% growth in the use of oil.

A case of damned if you do and damned if you don't? Well not necessarily because Ireland has one of the richest potentials for development of alternative energy with wind and wave power sources that are unsurpassed anywhere. The average wind speed is one of the highest in Europe and the waves of the Atlantic pound the continuous shoreline with constant, yet mostly untapped, power. Yet investment in these energy systems is minimal at best.

A BAD IDEA HAS LOTS OF BAD EFFECTS

Alongside this wanton wastefulness of these energy sources, the use of fossil fuels also has a negative side effect in that they are dirty, i.e. they produce greenhouse gas emissions that not only cause pollution, but also add to the ever-increasing problem of climate change and global warming.

The dependency on the use of these types of non-renewable sources of energy continues and if any so called alternative is proposed then it is either mocked or dismissed as not being viable. What is clearest of all is that this current dependency is the least viable option of all because it relies on finite and fast dwindling supplies of fossil fuels.

Why does it continue?

Part of this is to do with money. With the rise in use of these types of energy there was a huge increase in industrialisation, and as a result great profits was there to be made. This continues today and the large oil companies, for example, make ever-increasing profits despite the supplies of crude oil getting smaller and smaller. Profits in the order of £35 billion were posted recently by Shell and BP in the UK for the past year alone.

Another reason why this addiction is hard to break is the fact that governments themselves do not want to break it. After all they obtain massive amounts of tax revenue from the sale of these non-renewable sources of energy with the vast majority of every gallon of petrol, for example, going to the government. With nearly 70% of every gallon of petrol that is sold being taxation revenue that's a rather large amount of money isn't it?

Governments therefore have a vested interest in not upsetting the status quo where the supply and use of these forms of energy are concerned. They may pay lip service to the need for change, but they fail or refuse to grasp the nettle because they themselves are locked into the culture of dependency that has been created.

The oil companies have a huge amount of political influence, both in terms of lobbying government and because they employ so many people in their industries. They know that anything that overturns that system could cause a major economic collapse and depression. As a result, decisions about the reality facing the human race are fudged and blatantly ignored.

As an example, China as an emerging world economic power has seen the need to step up its energy usage if it is to fulfil its target of becoming a world economic superpower. Whilst it is looking to invest in some forms of renewable energy, it is certainly not doing so at the cost of ceasing to exploit its vast supplies of fossil fuels.

China is planning to develop over 500 new coal mines over the next decade and the consequences of the use of these fossil fuels can only add to the world's growing problems where climate change and global warming are concerned. It can also only add to the World's and China's own already severe pollution problems, for China already has 16 out of 20 of the world's worst polluted cities with Linfen in the coal rich northern province of Shanxi having the dubious honour of being the world's most polluted city. By opening an average of one new coal mine every week for the next 10 years this pollution problem will become even more extreme.

The side effects of pollution are beginning to bite as well. For the number of babies born with birth defects is rising at an alarming rate with an increase of 40% per year since 2001. This means that a staggering 2 million Chinese children are born each year with some kind of birth defect and many of these birth defects can be directly attributable to this increase in pollution. The level of increase in birth defects is actually higher than 40% in the more polluted areas of the country.

Recent World Bank estimates indicate that about 460,000 Chinese die prematurely each year from breathing polluted air and drinking dirty water.

The costs of dealing with these problems therefore far outweigh any benefits obtained from the 'magic bullet' of economic growth and can only get worse as the problems become ever more exacerbated.

IT'S HARD TO GET OFF A SLIPPERY SLOPE

The use of fossil fuels such as coal means that more CO_2 is released into the atmosphere. This in turn means that the Earth's atmosphere continues to warm at an ever-increasing rate, which in turn will accelerate the rate at which the Earth's ice fields (particularly those in Greenland) will melt. This is what is known as a system of positive feedback and means that the more these negative effects occur the more they compound exponentially until total collapse is caused. This will lead to rising sea levels, which whilst potentially catastrophic on its own account, more importantly will lead to huge releases of methane gas that lie beneath the ice fields.

Why this is significant is that methane is a much more powerful agent in contributing to global warming than CO_2 - about 23 times more powerful, in fact. There is far less methane in the atmosphere than CO_2, but such a release from under the ice fields will have a disastrous effect on the rate of global warming.

Continuing down this road of developing rather than limiting the use of fossil fuels is not only folly; rather than simply shooting ourselves in the foot it is more like shooting ourselves in the head just to make absolutely sure that there is no chance of survival.

Once a country has become dependent upon the increased use of energy from finite resources it is very hard to get it to lower its expectations. This is where the real problems will happen; when the supplies dwindle and nations will start to compete for what is left, more than they do already. This will inevitably lead to an increase in war and conflicts as too many people will be competing for too few resources.

It is clear that the use of fossil fuels is grossly inefficient. They take millions upon millions of years to form and they only take minutes to use. Any businessman worth his salt will say that that is not a good long term business plan.

Secondly, these forms of energy are not *alive*; they are made up of dead organic matter that can now be used as energy. However, it takes a lot of effort to get this energy and as supplies of it run out and are harder to find, then more effort needs to be expended to get it.

Thirdly, almost all - if not all - of the energy we use on this planet is derived from the Sun, which is a *live* source of energy. The Sun provides the fuel for all living things, for without it - either directly or indirectly - all organic life on this planet would die. Its supply of energy, in relative terms at least, is infinite if humans can find the ways to effectively and efficiently tap into it.

THERE'S PLENTY TO SHARE

The Sun is a burning source of heat that can be easily converted into usable energy forms by using things such as solar heat panels. This is a very efficient form of energy supply with the desirable side effect that it doesn't pollute or add to global warming. The Sun provides a huge source of energy as every second it converts 5 million tons of matter into energy by way of nuclear fusion reactions where hydrogen is turned into helium.

The Earth only gets a small amount of this energy, but the amount that does get here still works out as an average of 1400 watts of power for every square metre of the Earth's surface per second. This is an incredible amount of untapped energy source, which we would do well to harness by developing the technology involved.

It also is meritorious to seek to harness the Sun's energy because it can be used either in large scale projects in places such as deserts, or on small scale projects such as individual houses to supply much, if not all, of their energy needs. It is hardly practical, on the contrary, to have an oil rig or a nuclear reactor in one's back garden!

The same points can also be made in favour of other forms of renewable energy such as wind and wave power.

The argument against them is often that they create an eyesore on the landscape and they can't supply the amount of energy required.

In respect of the first point, compared to what the use of fossil fuels does to the landscape and the environment, such concessions to aesthetic beauty are tiny. Coal mines and nuclear reactors are hardly things of beauty themselves!

With investment these renewable forms of energy could become more efficient, and with large and small-scale prototypes the load could be spread and a solution is possible. But not without integrated thinking and joint effort.

As regards these forms of energy being inefficient, the facts don't support this assertion. The human race has inherited this vast bulk of ancient stored energy and hasn't had to pay for it. However, the amounts of these forms of energy are finite and ever more difficult to extract. This means that the net cost to harvest these forms of energy is much higher than developing renewable forms of energy. The renewables look more expensive because they require initial capital investment to set them up from scratch, whereas the fossil fuel forms have already made much of this capital investment and therefore much of the cost is hidden.

However, even with these hidden costs renewables still compete very well and will do so on an ever-increasing basis in the future as the costs of extracting fossil fuels escalates as supplies run out. This is already being found with the latest oil recovery projects such as the ones in Canada where oil is being extracted from huge sand deposits. The cost of extracting the oil from the sand is nearly prohibitive; plus there is the massive environmental damage that is caused by carrying out such work.

If one takes into account the cost of cleaning up after the use of fossil fuels due to pollution and environmental damage, then there is no contest. The already incurred costs of the use of fossil fuels is enormous and bound to increase exponentially as climate change and global warming increase due to their use.

BEWARE OF WRONG SOLUTIONS
MASQUERADING AS RIGHT ONES

As regards the possible use of nuclear energy to fill the gap, then in the long term this really is the nightmare scenario. Not only does it have huge capital cost to set it up, it also itself has finite sources of 'fossil fuel' that it needs to keep it going. Nuclear reactors need Uranium to power them and the supplies of Uranium are already scarce and becoming even more so.

Not only is that the case, but the waste from the use of nuclear power plants is highly radioactive and extremely toxic for hundreds, if not thousands, of years. If the number of nuclear power plants increases significantly then the amount of radioactive waste increases proportionally. The chances of a nuclear accident or terrorist attack increases as well and one has to only remember the relatively minor disaster of Chernobyl and the continuing after-effects to realise that the so-called solutions to the energy problems could, in fact, create a much bigger problem than any solution they propose to make.

As this is being written Britain is deciding its future, where energy use is concerned and the political consensus is swinging towards returning to using nuclear energy. The argument being put forward to justify this move is that nuclear energy is 'clean', in that it produces no carbon dioxide emissions and this will enable Britain to meet its obligations where the lowering of CO_2 emissions is concerned. This argument sounds attractive to some, but it is a deceit upon the truth.

Not only does nuclear power leave a much greater polluting footprint than any other form of energy, in that the waste by products take thousands of years to clean up, but such energy pollutes of its own account. Nuclear reactors need Uranium in order to produce nuclear power and if numerous more nuclear reactors were produced to fuel the need for energy then the supplies of Uranium would dwindle very quickly; to such a degree that supplies of premium grade Uranium would be depleted within 10 years, thus making the reactors redundant not long after their manufacture.

There are lesser grade Uranium stores left, but these are less pure and would have to involve sophisticated extraction techniques, which are themselves polluting in nature. In fact, the pollution caused by the extraction of such lesser grade Uranium would far outweigh any benefits gained by using the so-called 'clean' form of energy that nuclear power is supposed to be.

HOW CLEAN IS CLEAN?

Despite what the nuclear industry would have us believe, nuclear energy is not clean in terms of what it releases into the environment. For example, Sellafield in the UK still pumps low level radioactive liquids into the Irish Sea making it the most polluted sea in the world. Some of this pollution has been found as far north as the Arctic and whilst such polluting is due to be phased out over time, it is not due to cease until 2020 at the earliest. However, despite the fact that this low level waste pollutes the sea to the level it does, the fact remains that most of this low level waste stays on the land and is compacted and stored somewhere waiting for a home. Sellafield stores this waste at a place nearby called Drigg, but this site will be full by the middle of this century and then another storage facility will need to be found.

At present the UK has enough nuclear waste to fill 5 Albert Halls, yet it only has 1 Albert Hall and there are currently no known plans to put any of the nuclear waste in that Albert Hall! In fact it doesn't have anywhere to put it.

Therefore, the argument that nuclear waste with a half-life of many thousands of years doesn't count as waste because it can be sequestered away somewhere (although such places aren't yet known of) is an arrogant lie and a curse upon future generations.

With regard to the claim that nuclear energy is safe, one can easily provide a one word response to this arrogant assertion; Chernobyl.

Further, governments claim that over the long term nuclear energy is probably the cheapest form of energy to provide. This again is being less than economical with the truth because it fails to take into account the decommissioning costs in respect of closing redundant nuclear power stations.

Current revised estimates indicate that the decommissioning costs for all of Britain's 19 nuclear power stations (they will all have to be decommissioned at some point) will be in the order of £75 billion. This figure is regarded as a very conservative figure and as of writing it has been suggested that the cost is in fact going to be much higher. This money could go a long way towards developing sustainable energy solutions if it was invested proactively at the implementation end, rather than at the clean-up end.

The real reason the governments shy away from offering real solutions to these real problems is twofold:

1.   Because they are heavily lobbied by the energy companies who have huge weight and clout in the decision making process.
2.   The political cost of taking such tough, but necessary decisions would, in their view, be catastrophic.

In part this is a circular problem because politicians sell the public a dream of what life could be like if they were elected. People buy into this dream and therefore if someone then tries to tell them they can't have it they will vote for someone else who will give them the standard of living they demand with as little cost as possible.

At some point this house of cards has to collapse, if for no other reason than because the resources upon which this dream is built are finite.

In the long term renewable sources of energy are cheaper, cleaner and more sustainable. However, to accept this path of action requires a change of mindset and behaviour for all concerned. This change is one from being a consumer to being one of a responsible player in the greater dynamics of inter-relationship and inter-support between the Earth and the human race.

Let's be clear here. A change of how we get our energy supplies alone isn't going to save us. The problems are much deeper than that for they involve matters of attitude and alignment that have compounded over thousands of years. The short term resolution of the problems cannot be found inside the same exigencies that created them.

PRINCIPLE OR PRINCIPAL?

These issues transcend politics to a massive degree. Some may still argue that renewables cannot supply all the energy requirements needed and with current demand levels this may be true. Therefore, alongside changing energy supply policy there also needs to be a change in energy use policy.

The way energy is used is just as inefficient as its supply method. This is again where empowerment of the individual can be effective, for if everyone becomes more aware of the situation and informed of the positive choices that can be made to lessen energy demand, use and waste, then it is possible to reduce energy consumption to manageable levels.

Finally, as regards fossil fuels, there is the most important of all fossil fuels for human life. That fuel is water for it is the most vital thing that humans need to sustain their survival. The fossil aspect of water is the fact that much more fresh water lies below the ground in the water table aquifers than above it in lakes and rivers.

This underground fossil water takes millions of years to form up, yet the rate at which this water is being used is on average twice as fast as the rainfall that falls on the surface of the Earth above. We are therefore borrowing water from inside the Earth, but do not have the ability to repay this debt. This excess of use over supply is bound to worsen in the future as the world population increases and the demand for water also increases.

The problem is exacerbated both by how much water is wasted and by its inefficient usage. In particular meat production compounds the demand for water, as this is the most inefficient use of it in any food production chain.

If the whole world were vegetarian, for example, then the demand for water for food production would halve. If the use and distribution of water were made more efficient then this would lower demand as well. However, the demand for water looks like increasing rather than decreasing as the world's population continues to soar and economic growth continues to drive demand for all the Earth's resources.

This can only get worse as countries like China continue to industrialize. Currently China has 22% of the world's population, yet it only has 8% of the world's fresh water. Despite, or perhaps because of, initiating the world's greatest engineering projects to construct dams to try and regulate water flow and usage, China simply doesn't have enough water for its needs.

In fact China is now beginning to admit that rather than helping to solve its water and energy problems its flagship project, the Three Gorges Dam is actually causing more problems than it is solving.

People in the West mostly think that water is a limitless and free resource and that you simply need to turn on the tap and water comes out. People in the Third World know only too well that this is not the case. However, people in the West are becoming more aware of the importance and value of water as they themselves start to face increasing droughts and shortages.

It would therefore be wise to regard water as being the top of the list where fossil fuels are concerned, for without it nothing else can work. It is a gift from the planet, but like all the other fossil fuels it does not come from a limitless supply. Accordingly, we need to treat it with respect and value because if not then it, like all the others, will run out. The others we can do without, but without water there is no future.

The same principles also apply to the air that we breathe, for no air - no life. Because it is more 'unseen' than water it is easier to take it for granted. However, when we think that 99% of the mass of the Earth's atmosphere lies within 18 miles of the surface of the Earth itself, then we can see just how fine the balances are. Yet into this wafer-thin membrane we currently pump all sorts of pollution - and then we breathe it back in!

If that isn't madness the dictionary definition needs rewriting!

All air is recycled anyway and the chances are that your last breath contains molecules once breathed by Jesus Christ, Mohammed, the Buddha, Attila the Hun, Adolf Hitler, Mother Teresa and the Virgin Mary! This fact may help explain why you have not been feeling quite yourself recently! Somehow the planet has a way of recycling the air and keeping it fresh, and this is something we could learn a lot from.

The world cannot continue simply being driven by market forces and globalisation. These forces are competitive rather than co-operative by nature, and so there needs to be developed a much greater degree of mutual co-operation and forward thinking if real solutions are to be found.

ACTION VERSUS INACTION

Analyses have been undertaken to show that it would only cost 1% of GDP for the USA to comply with the Kyoto Protocol. Even this figure is probably high for the figure assumes that there is no net benefit in such a cost, but clearly there is because applying investment into such alternatives actually creates jobs and benefits the economy.

The stick is that if the human race doesn't decide to develop these ways of dealing with their energy needs then we ourselves run the risk of becoming fossils ourselves. The carrot is that with the right amount of co-operation and will things can be turned around and made better.

With this being the age of mass communication we truly do live in a global village. It is time for the human race to actually realise this at a deeper level and start treating the Earth as a village and not it and each other, as commodities.

In a village everyone knows each other and everyone is looked after and has a role to play. If energy were invested in building such a global village then the returns on that investment are bound to be manifold.

Why should the future be any different?

*No man is an island, entire of itself every man is
a piece of the continent, a part of the main.
If a clod be washed away by the sea, Europe is the less, as
well as if a promontory were, as well as if a manor of thy
friends or of thine own were any man's death diminishes
me, because I am involved in mankind and therefore never
send to know for whom the bell tolls it tolls for thee.*

John Donne

*There is enough for everyone's need in the world,
but not enough for everyone's greed.*

Mahatma Ghandi

THE CATERPILLAR EFFECT

THE TITLE OF THIS CHAPTER comes from the well-known principle called the 'Butterfly Effect', which states that a butterfly flapping its wings in South America has an affect on the world's weather patterns. This is because it creates a slight breeze by flapping its wings and as the Earth's weather systems are interconnected this slight disturbance changes the weather to a small degree.

The amount of that affect is minuscule and probably not measurable in the bigger scheme of things. Nevertheless it does have an influence, as do the countless billions of activities that occur every day on the planet amongst millions of species of flora and fauna life as they process force and energy.

Even thinking can change the world's weather patterns, for before mankind carries out any activities that alter the balance of the world's weather and other patterns they have to first have an idea of what they want to do before doing it.

Before any wind farm was ever built someone had to conceive the idea and come up with the plans as to how one could be built. Once built it, like the butterfly, affects the balance of the Earth's weather and ecosystems.

This is where it is important to examine another view of the Butterfly Effect before going back in time to examine its predecessor, the *caterpillar* effect, for the seeds of any events are sown before they are ever seen.

ALL AFFECTS ALL

In the Butterfly Effect the primary premise is that every action however small, affects every other life force on the planet. The obvious - but hardly ever mentioned - corollary to that position is that the butterfly itself is therefore affected by and influenced by every single action carried out by every other organism on the Earth. Nothing exists in isolation, and everything is joined in a dynamic flow and exchange of energy.

It is the state of disconnection from this truth that deceives humans into thinking that things are separate and that the consequences of any action are limited or can be ring fenced or isolated. This is clearly not the case, for every single action is like a stone falling into a pond with ripples going out to affect every single corner of the pond.

In this analogy it could also be asked what caused the butterfly to flap its wings in the first place? In this state of interconnectedness it is not always clear as to where causes and actions begin and end and how they inter-relate in the unfolding reality of life here on Earth. This principle applies to the whole Universe for the Earth itself exists within other dynamics from the Solar System to the Milky Way and beyond.

THE UNIVERSAL WEB

The whole Universe could be seen to be such a system with each and every part connected to every single other part.

The current theory as to how the Universe began is that it occurred with an event called 'The Big Bang'. At that moment the whole Universe existed as one incredibly dense mass concentrated in a space infinitely smaller than the dot at the end of this sentence. It was all in the same state of definition, which is why it is called 'The Great Singularity'.

The whole Universe is therefore related to every other part, it is just that the number of generations that have to be travelled back through to find the common ancestor is rather large! Nevertheless this gives added impetus and significance to the assertion that every action affects each and every other part of the Universe.

As *Newton's Laws of Motion* state; 'for each and every action there is an equal and opposite reaction'. This further confirms the reverse of the Butterfly Wing effect, for every time the butterfly flaps its wings it causes a reaction from each and every other part of not only the Earth, but also the whole Universe! This may seem to be far-fetched or even silly, but the laws of physics bear this out.

It also relates to certain principles within the Bible where it says: "Do unto others as you would have them do unto you." For what a person does unto others they do unto themselves. In other words – what goes round comes around.

THE CATERPILLAR EFFECT.

Before the butterfly emerges from its chrysalis it is a caterpillar. In its caterpillar stage it eats as much as it can and gorges itself until it can't eat anymore. It then weaves its cocoon and enters a stage of complete meltdown where it dissolves its previous form and slowly starts to change into a butterfly.

This process is both miraculous and breath-taking and the analogy to the human condition is apparent at many levels.

Like the caterpillar, modern industrialised living can be seen to be gorging itself on the rich fruit of the Earth's generosity. This gorging process applies to the use of the Earth's resources and also at the individual level. Over 50% of the population of the USA is described as being clinically obese and it is an increasing problem, not only in the West, but also in developing countries such as China. Obesity is caused by not only eating too much food but also by eating the wrong kind of food with the wrong kind of ingredients in it.

The proposition here is that the human race has to, like the butterfly, go through a complete process of metamorphosis and emerge into a completely different future. There is no point in trying to adapt the caterpillar behaviour of gorging on its environment as that will not save the environment or the caterpillar itself.

A complete change is needed and this means that we have to completely reinvent ourselves and approach the future with a completely different set of ideas and ideals.

The excellent news is that like the butterfly we have within our genetic coding all we need to meet the new opportunities and challenges ahead. This requires us to surrender the old form whilst at the same time trusting the process of the new form appearing. If the individual and collective talent of the human race is collected and harnessed into a state of concentrated consciousness, then not only can the problems be faced, but a brilliant future can be realised.

It all begins with realising the need to stop going on in the way of the old form. The gorging needs to cease.

THE PROCESS OF CHANGE

The solutions to the world's problems lie in the promise of what could be, what hasn't yet appeared.

Potential is something that all things possess. Potential energy is something we all share. Who knows what might happen if human beings agree to change their patterns of behaviour?

Finally it is important to note that the butterfly flapping its wings changes the weather patterns of the *future* and not the past. The future is where the winds of real change truly come from, not from reacting to the problems of the past.

This suggests that any pain from the change is well worthwhile enduring because of the long-term gains that could be achieved.

Finally for this chapter a joke!

Two caterpillars are sitting on a leaf gorging themselves when suddenly they look up and see a butterfly flying overhead. One caterpillar then turns to the other and says: "I don't care what they say; you'll *never* get me up in one of those!"

THE FUTURE OF THE HUMAN CONDITION

The end of the human race will be that it
will eventually die of civilization.

Ralph Waldo Emerson

If a man could have half of his wishes,
he would double his troubles.

Benjamin Franklin

Koyaanisqatsi   - a Hopi Indian word meaning:

1.   *Crazy life*
2.   *Life in Turmoil*
3.   *Life out of balance*
4.   *Life disintegrating*
5.   *A state of life that calls for another*
     way of living

THE HUMAN RACE

THIS IS HOW HUMAN BEINGS describe themselves. Yet this very description begs many questions, such as:

Since when did it become a race?
A race from where to where?
A race between whom?
Why race anywhere in the first place?
Where's the finish line?
Aren't there winners and losers in races? Is that what human beings are about as a species?
Should humans not rethink how they label themselves?

Labels such as this are accepted for a reason and they give telling insight into the perception humans have about themselves and their psychologies.

Perhaps it is time to change how we describe ourselves?

?

Man is the only creature that refuses to be what he is.
Albert Camus

Man - a being in search of meaning.
Plato

Powaqqatsi - a Hopi Indian word meaning:
An entity, a way of life that consumes the life forces
of other beings in order to further its own life.

The Properties Of
Being Human

IN THIS SECTION A BRIEF exploration will be made into some
of the unique properties that identify human beings as being what we
are. In particular, those *'higher'* qualities that distinguish us from other
forms of organic life on Earth. For just as every piece of matter has
particular chemical and physical properties – human beings have their
own unique and particular properties that signify who and what we
are.

What then are the properties of being human?

Here is a list of some of those properties that might qualify:

Reason
Intelligence
Honour
Sensitivity
Compassion
Love
Dignity
Kindness
Hope
Belief
Warmth
Value

Generosity
Humanity
Respect
Patience
Humility
Care
Trust

The more that these properties are present in a person, the more they can truly call themselves a human being. The reason for this is that the word 'properties' is actually:

PROPER TIES

Qualities such as those stated above are the *proper ties* to aspire to have if we are to realise who and what we are and thereby earn the merit to call ourselves truly human. These qualities have a long range, permanent and indelible sense to them.

They are not based in profit seeking, greed or gain and loss, and they appear, to all intents and purposes, to be totally sustainable and have the added benefit of having no CO_2 emissions, and are non-toxic non-carcinogenic and non-polluting!

In an age of strategic alliances about the future, we would do well to form allegiances to these most human qualities, for each person has within them a veritable unlimited source of each and every one of them. It is these things we need to trade in with each other on the international market, because if we do then the other finite resources we have, would be better and more sustainably and equitably managed for the benefit of all and the future.

On the other hand, there are features which mark out the negative behaviour that humans often perpetrate which, in their own way, all have these negative side effects. These behaviours could be called *'improper ties'* and are things like:

Hate
Envy
Greed

Lust
Vanity
Control
Suppression
Spite
Destruction
Violence
Murder
Slavery
Revenge
Torture

These activities besmirch the human condition and are below the line of what is acceptable in terms of the properties of being human. The common denominator in these behaviours is that they occur where people regard themselves as being their own criteria rather than measuring what they do against some external authority that is greater than themselves.

The question this raises is: who and/or what should that external criteria be if we are to go forward safely into the future?

Humans merely share the Earth. We can
only protect the land, not own it.

Chief Seattle

He who knows that enough is enough will always have enough.

Lao Tzu

THE SUSTAINABLE HUMAN

LIFE FOR EVERY LIVING CREATURE on this planet works within incredibly fine balances and tolerances. The finesse with which the Universe works is truly remarkable. This applies at all levels for think about the countless systems that are involved in keeping a person alive. The body has so many working parts that it is not really possible to fully understand both how they work individually on their own account and how they work together. Imagine what is actually involved in getting up and making a cup of tea, then think about having to actually consciously carry out each and every movement involved.

Consider how the lungs work in relation to breathing and the environment. Humans breathe oxygen in and carbon dioxide out whereas trees take in the carbon dioxide and release oxygen back into the atmosphere. It is amazing that the lungs know how quickly and deeply to breathe so that we end up with just enough oxygen in our system. The oxygen is then magically transferred to every cell within the body to support their processes. Miraculous!

These balances can be upset quite easily and this is what human beings are currently doing, both in terms of how we live individually and collectively as a species.

The technologies that humans are using, particularly since the start of the Industrial Revolution, are threatening the life-support systems of the Earth. The issue therefore is whether humans will soon reach the position where life on this planet may no longer be sustainable for themselves and many other species, or whether they will stop, pause, reflect and change their lifestyle processes in order that a new level of sustainability is reached to secure the future of our species and many others.

Human beings have evolved certain attitudes, abilities and technological advancements in a multitude of areas, but it is questionable whether they have developed the maturity and responsibility to match their technological advancements. The mind has not evolved in sympathetic alignment to the physical advances; hence the reason why humans are at such a dangerous cross-roads for life on Earth.

One example where this has happened before is Easter Island in the remote depths of the Pacific Ocean far from any other land. Archaeologists have long wondered about the statues on Easter Island and what happened to the culture that had previously lived there, for it appeared that the island had mostly been abandoned. Recent research has thrown quite a different light on what may have happened to the inhabitants of the island.

It seems that Easter Island was originally a lush island with many different types of trees. Gradually over time, the people on the island used the trees up for things like housing, firewood and making fishing boats. The problem was that they used the trees faster than they could be replaced by nature. Things therefore became increasingly desperate as the trees disappeared. This then led to wars between the different tribes on the island and eventually the island culture collapsed because they had reached a point of unsustainability. (The processes of how this abuse of trees occurs is also marvellously described in a book by Dr Seuss called *The Lorax*).

Easter Island today has none of its original trees. The only things that remain are the eerie statues, almost mourning what has been lost. These statues can therefore teach us a lesson.

Most people think the Easter Island statues are on the shore looking out over the vast expanse of the Pacific Ocean. In fact they look inwards into the island. Rather than looking out across the ocean for help and salvation, they are looking back in on themselves as if to say: "What have we done?"

This could be a lesson for us all.

In fact, the lesson of Easter Island doesn't quite end there for it after the near total collapse of the island in the 17th century it appears that by the time the first Western explorers, the Dutch, arrived in the 1720's the population had stabilised and was living a sustainable existence again, albeit without trees. However, thanks first of all to the Westerners bringing syphilis to the island later that century, the population plummeted again. Then in the 19th century slave traders raided the island and transported about 1500 people (about 1/3 of the island population) to work in terrible conditions in mines in Peru. After 1 year all but 12 of them were dead and so these 12 were taken back to the island to be with their kin. But unfortunately, (why does that word keep appearing?) they also took smallpox back with them so that by the 1870's the island population had dropped to a mere 112 individuals. Thank goodness for civilization huh?

Easter Island is a tiny speck in the Pacific Ocean and in relative terms, is not far off being in direct proportion to the size of the Earth as the Earth is to the rest of the Solar System. Could it be that if humans are not careful then life on Earth for them too inside the bigger picture of the Solar System, will become unsustainable, just as the Easter Island culture became unsustainable?

How close are humans to this position? Some say even now it is too late, for the situation is analogous to that of a person who is gravely ill with kidney failure. If this condition gets too far advanced then what happens is that all the other organs get put under pressure and often collapse from the strain. It certainly appears that human life is very close to this because there is so much strain on the planet's resources from food to water to pollution to exploitation of resources to deforestation to loss of ecosystems to species extinctions to lack of biodiversity, social alienation and much more.

WHO CAN MAKE THE CHANGES?

No real change can be made by the world's governments, because the rich countries will not agree to the kind of changes needed; to do so might mean lowering their standard of living. This would in turn lead to economic decline, recession and unemployment and so on.

It is therefore the issue of paradigms that is the crucial one to focus on here. All the moralising and obscurantism about the problems we face are based upon the paradigm of what is wrong. The only real and meaningful change that can happen occurs when there is a paradigm shift out from the old thinking patterns and actions into a new set.

An essential blocker to any real change is the Western mindset of 'putting off the evil day'. This is illustrated by the rise of the credit card culture. What this essentially says, in psychological terms, is that a person can have what they can't afford to pay for. However, the condition is that they will have to pay back more at a later date. This then reflects powerfully into the issues regarding the depletion of resources, i.e. that if humans use them now they will have to pay more later.

This concept doesn't exist in nature, for lions don't go up to zebras and say "I'll have three now and run around the equivalent of catching four zebras later as interest."

Nor does anything pay interest on its investment, because the way nature works is that if something does something with what it is given then it gets continuance.

Because of technological advances made by humans in the last 500 years, they have been ever more able to live beyond their means; in that they have been able to exploit the planet's stored energy reserves far beyond the planet's ability to replace them. This in turn gives humans an unrealistically high population base that is not sustainable long term because these resources will soon run out.

This will lead to wars over resources of every kind from oil to minerals to food and even water. With recent scientific findings showing that currently 25% of the world is suffering moderate drought conditions, the tensions over the supply and use of water are bound to escalate. This can only increase as current projections indicate that, due to the influence of global warming, by the end of this century this figure will rise to 50%. This is further compounded by the fact that the number of places suffering extreme drought conditions has risen from 1% in 1950 to 3% currently. This figure is also set to rise throughout the course of this century.

This problem will be further exacerbated by the fact that much of the rest of the planet will suffer increased flooding. In other words this century will see much more extreme weather and therefore extreme consequences.

Despite this inevitability, the politicians of the world do not seek to make any meaningful changes because firstly they are not allowed to by the people who hold the real power and influence in the world, and secondly because they know that they can't actually do anything in a short-term, vote catching way. They therefore keep putting things off and praying for a miracle.

Surely the best minds in the world can get together, read the runes of what all this is saying and begin to admit to the truth? This doesn't happen and can't happen whilst all the talk is of quotas, tariffs, subsidies, economic growth, blame, recrimination and denial.

Whilst the topics are limited to quotas and emissions the real issues remain hidden and unreachable. If the talk is of the world's finite resources, such as oil and coal and rainforests, the ever-approaching reality is that these resources will run out soon and then there will inevitably be conflict over them. The very resources that can help humans with their problems are in fact limitless and environment friendly with no toxic waste. These things are qualities; things like respect, value, wisdom, compassion, responsibility, care, sharing, humility, courage, kindness, generosity and many, many more. It is here that rescue and relief can be found and not in quotas.

What humans have is a compound set of problems that conspire to place them in the perilous position they find themselves to be in. These exist in every realm, from ecology to resources to social, economic and political systems to religion, education, health and more. Ignorance, fundamentalism and misalignment are like wildfires in the tinder dry forests of tomorrow.

SEEING THE UP SIDE

The way things are in the world today is in fact not a great problem, but a great opportunity. It is often said that real change can only happen when things get really bad or close to the edge. This is the story from the Bible of the Prodigal Son who throws away his inheritance and then reaches the lowest of the low; then at the last minute swallows his pride and foolishness and returns to his father's house to seek forgiveness and change his ways.

Can humans see how that parable applies to their situation today?

No matter how well intentioned all the aid packages in the world are - and the wonderful people who serve selflessly in the help of others less fortunate than themselves - the truth is that such programmes do not lead to fundamental change.

Whilst there are such concepts as ownership, possession, exploitation, nation states, territorialism, war and so on, there will also be the belief that there is not enough to go around. Protectionism is developed out of fear and nothing fundamentally changes.

The truth is that there *is* enough to go around if humans simply decide to share and be responsible. The fear that prevents this happening is that others may not reciprocate.

The change needed begins at individual level, first of all with a change of mindset. The first thing a person can and must do is to change their own perception and thereby their own reality. This doesn't require a person to DO anything as a first principle. This requires a different kind of discipline, for people are trained to solve problems by trying to *do* something about them. This is often precipitous because the first thing in causing real change is to change the location that a person is approaching the issue from. The stronger the location the stronger and more resilient the change of action will be.

This doesn't mean not to do the many small actions one wishes to do to help and assist wherever possible. It simply states that the real power of any change begins not in the seen, but in the unseen. The energy for real change begins in the beliefs of the person inside their connection to the reason for their existence.

It is important not to expect things to change overnight towards rightful alignment. This is not only impossible but dangerous, as any mother weaning a child will know.

Touching The Presence

This need for slow adjustment applies to changes at physical level, but if changes are made from the higher part of human beings then the effect can be much more rapid. Danger occurs when people try and change too many physical things too quickly when the mindset is the thing that needs to be worked on first. The changes that need to happen begin in the mind and heart.

Compassion and reverence are far more important features in any sustainable development plan rather than statistics that paint the gloomiest of pictures. It is therefore far better to have an action plan rather than a *re*action plan.

The necessary action begins inwardly with greater consciousness. Mostly people in the world aren't really conscious of the bigger picture of their situation. Whether exploiter or victim the consciousness of a person is generally consumed and subsumed by the local view of things which mostly is to do with exigencies of living. If consciousness can be raised in respect of true human spirituality and the human race's integrated role then real, meaningful and immediate change can be effected.

What is needed is a transcendent solution and not simply a logistical one.

The answer already exists in the unseen. The key lies in each person discovering who and what they are and why they are here. The more that this is done, individually and collectively, then the more humans will change their behaviour. Not because they ought to, but because they cannot not. Therein lies the real power to change the world. When things reach a critical mass then it only takes one small event to cause the irreversible process of change to onset.

Now is the eye of the needle moment: whichever way the human race decides to go over the next very short period of time will determine whether it becomes the first species on the planet to become extinct primarily by its own hand rather than by external forces. On the other hand, will there be a true renaissance and reconnection to the beacon of true human spirituality and purpose?

Primitive people may have been wiped out and marginalised in the ever harder quest for progress, but perhaps humans can learn a thing or two from them in terms of respect and values in formulating policies for the future. Look at a map of the world and see how it is divided up into countries and states. Then fly over the planet and see that the only unnatural boundaries that exist are those put up by human beings with fences or barricades. Then it is possible to see how senseless and mindless some of the human race's actions can be.

Was Chief Seattle expressing the thoughts of a savage when he spoke these words?

"Tribe follows tribe, and nation follows nation, like the waves of the sea. It is the order of nature, and regret is useless. Your time of decay may be distant, but it will surely come, for even the White Man cannot be exempt from the common destiny."

Wisdom doesn't live in space programmes and nuclear reactors, nor in the patenting of genes or cloning. It lives in people and is born out of experience. It certainly doesn't appear to live in multi-million dollar space programmes, which state, for example, that the most constructive use of a spaceship at the end of its journey is to destroy it by crash landing it into the surface of the Moon or some other planet including our own.

The key decisions today are made in abstract places of power such as the stock exchanges of the world, in tall buildings and behind closed doors. Often the people who make these decisions spend weeks and sometimes months without ever touching the Earth itself as they travel in planes and cars round the world and walk only on tarmac and red carpets. They attend opulent world summits to supposedly address key issues facing humanity yet never get to grips with the real issues.

It was said in the sacred texts of Ancient Egypt that the greatest crime there was at that time was that of hypocrisy – to say one thing and mean another. To commit such an act was deemed to be so serious that it was regarded as being a prevention of the person obtaining any possibility of immortality in the after-life and it would condemn them to eternal damnation.

Perhaps we would do well to adopt such an attitude towards our own modern day cultures?

HAVE YOU THOUGHT OF YOURSELF AS A RESOURCE?

When looking at the core of the issue where sustainable development is concerned, there is one key word above all to look at and that is: *resource.*

We humans need to reconnect to the *source* from which all comes. Is that which gives life not the same for all? What is more, the source from which all are blessed and benefit is itself unlimited. It is only when humans block the flow by their attitudes of greed, control, tyranny and power that the supply gets cut off.

Rhetoric and recrimination are signs of failure to read the runes and take responsibility.

There is no spare planet after humans have finished using this one, yet the speed at which they are using up the resources of this one says another one will be needed within the next 30 years or so. The chances of achieving that are infinitesimal.

If humans do not change their processes then the planet's immune system will attack them as alien invaders and seek to eliminate them so that it may continue its own evolutionary and life affirming journey.

Humans are but children in the Universe, yet they have the technology to either bring light and healing to the world or blow themselves up.

The damage humans have done is nearly irreversible; therefore they need to better understand the meaning and understandings within the word *consequences*. Rather than looking at their situation through the hazy light of right and wrong, it is far better to examine the truth through the neutral eyes of the consequences of choices that are made. Hidden within this word are two simple but profound adjacencies:

The first is that it is a *con sequence*. This means that everything people consciously do sets up a sequence of events that cannot not happen, for the Universe is not an arbitrary place. If it is true that the greatest gift to the human is consciousness, then it must also be true that the more conscious they are the better informed their decisions and actions will be. If they become more conscious then they cannot become anything other than more responsible for what they do. CON also stands for Carbon, Oxygen and Nitrogen – the building blocks of the Universe. In terms of sustainable development these three elements are the most important in considering the delicate ecosystem balance humans face in looking towards the future. How humans treat these substances and use them sets up a sequence of events that impacts heavily upon their future as a species.

The other aspect of *con sequences* lies in the vernacular meaning of *con*, which means to trick or deceive. Humans do this in using propaganda and misinformation to hide the truth. This is what those who stand to gain most in the short term do. Yet the truth is that in the long term the natural laws and natural order of things cannot be conned. The payback time may be delayed, but that kind of avoidance ultimately leads to the pain being greater and harsher. Far better that humans admit to the reality of their situation and set up conscious sequences of fundamental change rather than delude themselves that all is well and that science and technology (the new religion) will save the day.

Deeper clues lie in better understanding of the mechanics of the Universe and the processes at play. All life on this planet ultimately derives its energy ultimately from the light and heat of the Sun. In simple terms, the equation for this planet is, no Sun, no life. The Sun radiates its warmth and light onto this planet and causes it to spin (much like the ovaries of a woman) and thereby give birth.

Humans need to develop more of a feminine response to the processes of the planet on which they live. Piecemeal solutions are not needed but rather humility, awe and wonder, together with a healthy dose of context and perspective.

Human capability has advanced massively in the last 250 years since the Industrial Revolution. Yet it is also a very short period of time when compared to the great culture of Ancient Egypt which thrived and flourished for over 4000 years. This culture is less than 250 years old and, by all prognoses, is threatened with erasure within the next 50-100 years. There must be something to be learnt from our ancestors before launching forward into yet another crisis.

The truth is that humans are doing more and more about less and less. Yet, as people know, there are lies, damned lies and statistics. As an example, scientists say that ten times more people today are being cured of cancer than there were 50 years ago with the advanced treatments now being used. What they won't say is that 100 times more people are getting Cancer. The battle is therefore currently being lost not won. They also conveniently neglect to point out that medical treatment itself is the third highest cause of death in the USA after heart disease and cancer. So you'd better think really, really carefully before next seeking medical help, because although it might cure you, it also might kill you!

SOMETIMES THE SOLUTION IS WORSE THAN THE PROBLEM

The public is also being told that genetically modified foods are the answer to the world's hunger problems. Anyone who is against this is deemed to be some kind of anti-progress Luddite who doesn't know what they are talking about. The truth is that the scientists don't know what they are doing, for what is being proposed makes Frankenstein look like a nice uncle. The possible repercussions are enormous. The real question is why are humans doing it? Why is it needed? How did it get to this point? Why, after the CJD disasters of a few years ago, are scientists telling us that it is OK to feed cattle animal products in their food again? Actions like this make one wonder whether the scientists themselves already have CJD!

In any event, why have the Luddites got such bad PR? Were they so bad after all, or did they simply fall foul of the same process as countless minority cultures who were judged and marginalised and whose names actually came to mean a negative attribute?... the Stoics, the Cynics, the Barbarians, the Vandals and its more general term, 'the savages' of any primitive culture. Or such labels as the 'Third World'. These all reach into the human psyche and unconscious thought patterns and condition people's thinking and responses. The Third World, after all, has been populated much longer than the New World of modern cultures, and often more successfully.

The Luddites had a serious point to make about where this obsession with progress was heading. The point they, like many others, were seeking to make was that the human race as a species was losing the sense of who and what they are by placing priorities in things outside of themselves. They could see that the fast changes in history are the ones that do not last, but rather set the clock of evolution backwards. Nature has a law, which is: soon ripe soon rotten.

There is a spectrum of issues for humans as a species to consider in deciding any course of action where the future is concerned. Mostly humans have elected to respond from the red end of the spectrum, which is the *doing* end; the end that men in particular are more prone to react from. It is little wonder therefore that there are so many wars. The violet end of the spectrum, on the other hand, is to do with genetic change its wavelength is shorter and finer.

Whilst humans continue to treat the planet and everything on it as commodities, then nothing can change at fundamental level. If they do not love the fact of their existence, the magnificence of the planet and that they are part of Creation then it is quite likely that people will see the planet and everything on it as being part of the resources market.

Why is it that human beings are so obsessed with using up and dealing in the planet's resources? All technological advances in this area seem to be towards developing better systems for extracting and using up these finite resources as fast as possible. Humans as a species do not seem to want to deal too much in the infinite resources that Creation has to offer, such as respect, compassion, generosity, kindness, warmth, value, honour, patience, and so on. If they did then they would not pitch so much at this 'more and more about less and less' culture that seems to have them imprisoned in a vice like grip.

The word *resource* suggests to *re - source* something. This implies that not only have humans gone off course, but that they have lost contact with the source itself. This is why they keep looking for solutions outside themselves and thinking that better and bigger technology will save them.

It will not, and will only accelerate the process of demise that they are already locked in. Rather the journey needs to be back inwards to rediscover who and what we are and why we are here.

The memory of what human beings are as a species lives not in *doing* as a first principle, but *being*. After all, *being* anagrams to *begin* so surely that is the place to start.

The research into finding the way forward into the future therefore needs to begin with considering the key elements that constitute our being human beings.

HUMAN BEINGS BEING HUMAN

It is noteworthy that humans describe themselves as Human *Beings*. This suggests that before they do anything they need to BE something.

What does it mean to be a Human Being? From that search people can begin to find themselves and each other. This requires a redressing of the human race's engagement with the Universe.

An imagery that goes with this is very much that from the film *Close Encounters of the Third Kind* where people who are picking up the same signal are driven by it to such a degree that they all find themselves at the same point where the UFO has landed. How did they get there? They just did. Something got in to their being that caused them to be in a place in themselves where they were compelled to respond.

Humans therefore need to resist pre-emptive doing in the first instance in response to the problems they face. They first need to relinquish control. For example, in the Alexander Technique in dealing with back problems one of the first techniques is to listen to instructions given but not to try and "do" them; rather let the body do them.

We need to listen.

Whilst there is obviously a time and place for doing rather than prevaricating, nevertheless for the deeper and more profound issues it is necessary to resist this doing psychology and locate a deeper place to respond from.

This doing feature is a brain-governed response, and in evolutionary terms the brain is like a young child. Whilst it has phenomenal abilities and talents, it is nevertheless immature in its growth and development. Like the new kid on the block it tries to assert itself and appear all found and all knowing, whereas clearly it isn't. When it gets hold of new toys it can get wildly out of control as can be seen from such things as nuclear weapons and power, exploitation of planetary resources, genetic engineering, cloning and all the rest of it. The brain wants its satisfaction and thrill and is often unable or unwilling to face up to the long-term consequences of its actions.

The brain is like a giant computer in that it can be programmed to respond in certain ways and that is mostly how it is trained. But the question is: trained for what?

A computer programme works by the principle that it is only possible to get out of it what has been put in to it. The brain works by feeling in its higher parts and calculation and logic in its lower aspects;

or in terms of the two sides of the brain: the creative, imaginative, intuitive side and the analytical, logical and practical side with the former more to do with being and the latter to do with doing. This suggests that it is good to meditate on problems as this trains the brain to wait and feel things before responding.

The right kind of being naturally leads to the right kind of doing. It doesn't work the other way around - at least initially. Doing is the means by which being is anchored or secured.

There is the well-known expression that 'a thought without an action is an empty thought'. Conversely an action without a thought is a dangerous one. The wrong kind of doing causes people to work to deadlines, whereas the right kind of being will lead them to necessary lifelines. If humans find their true place in the natural order then they would genuflect a little, apologise a little and reform from their errant, childish behaviours and take instruction from the greatest teacher of all - which is not a person but nature herself.

If people respond more from the Human *Being* of themselves then not only will their actions be much more natural, but they will also be much more effective and powerful.

It is important to emphasise that this is not saying that doing is bad and people should therefore stop all doing and just be - a lot of what people are doing is helping and keeping things open for change to happen - yet there is an over emphasis in modern culture on doing and that balance needs to change to there being more being inside what is done, for that is where the real fulcrum of change lies. If people are genuinely moved inside what they do then that is a tide of change that cannot be resisted.

MAKING A RESOLUTION FOR CHANGE

If there is a marriage between Being and Doing the plasma that links the two aspects inside a commonality of purpose lives in *Resolve*.

The human race has become largely fixed in wrong processes in terms of attitudes, responses and behaviours. The coagulation of the human spirit needs to be freed and the way to do this is for people to *Re - Solve* themselves, i.e. to make things fluid again.

Solve and coagula are the processes by which Creation "invents" itself and keeps itself refreshed and renewed. For example, rock is turned into molten lava by the super heating processes of a volcano. It is then ejected when the volcano erupts. Over time the lava is turned into soil or sand by the processes of wind, rain and sea action.

A constant and renewable energy supply from the planet to itself is thereby created. Much can be learnt from the planet's mechanics where renewable energy supplies are concerned rather than depleting long term energy investments. Whilst humans are absorbed with doing they will use what they have as quickly as possible to make a profit rather than see that that is not sustainable and thereby look to other forms of energy such as solar, wind and wave power.

It doesn't take a genius to know that that kind of profit motive ultimately leads to the principle of there being no principal assets left. Humans cannot spend their inheritance twice.

It seems that a large part of what has become lost to humans as a species is the awe and wonder to be found within their existence and circumstance. Awe is not a property that is in danger of being used up, for its source seems to be endless. Nor does it harm the environment or pollute rivers; rather it causes union inside a state of affairs that has a much greater resonance and power than any of the problems that people might think they face. The solution does not lie in more disconnected schemes of quotas and carbon sinks. It lies in better location and reconnection to what the situation actually is.

Awe and wonder are good places to start for they are guaranteed to give people a different set of eyes to look at the situation through. They also have a marvellous side effect (not all side effects are bad!), which is to cause integration – harmlessly, painfully and naturally.

Integration is needed both in terms of perception of the human race of itself as a species, and out from that place, in looking at the issues to be faced and how to go into the future. One thing that integration can bring as a natural consequence is regeneration and that is what is desperately needed at all levels of human and planetary existence.

?

Population, when unchecked, increases in a geometrical ratio. Subsistence increases only in an arithmetical ratio.

Thomas Malthus

The hungry world cannot be fed until and unless the growth of its resources and the growth of its population come into balance. Each man and woman, and each nation, must make decisions of conscience and policy in the face of this great problem.

Lyndon Baines Johnson

POPULATION AND
THE FUTURE

AT SOME POINT VERY SOON the issue of population growth has to be addressed by the human race, for the longer it is avoided the greater the problems will be in the future.

Although in theory there is enough for all to live on the planet in relative comfort to an acceptable standard, if all the resources were harnessed and shared in a responsible and sustainable way; the truth is that with 6.5 billion people - and rising – there is an incredible strain on the Earth's resources. The problem is bound to get worse as current projections suggest that the Earth's population could be in the order of a staggering 12 billion by 2050.

Once upon a time to say to someone, "You are one in a million," really meant something. Today it could be construed as almost something of an insult as it means that there are at least 6,500 other people somewhere on the planet who are exactly like you! Who knows, maybe even some of them are better at being like you than you are!

The issue of population growth was addressed by Thomas Malthus over two centuries ago when he expressed the theory that population growth was always going to outstrip the ability of any society to produce the food and resources necessary to cater for the increase in population. In effect what he was saying is that whilst the propensity for populations to increase was exponential if given the chance, the ability of any society to increase its productivity was only arithmetic.

This means that while population grows by a multiplication factor, food production only grows by an additive factor.

Therefore, the greater the increase in population, the larger the deficit in food and resource production. In the long run, societies that succeed are those that tend to have stable rather than growing populations, although there are many variables to take into account.

This theory is much debated and disputed, but in recent times with the world's population accelerating at an ever increasing rate towards 7 billion, it is finding more favour than it had 20 or 30 years ago when it was regarded as being over simplistic. Today it is its very simplicity is that makes it attractive to some analysts.

Whatever the case, the truth is that societies tend to become over-populated to the point where they are unable to produce enough food for their members and this makes them prone to collapse. The perverse irony is that without net immigration, wealthy societies tend to have stable populations, whereas poor societies tend to suffer from an exacerbation of their shortages by the fact that their population numbers increase making them even more vulnerable to things like famine and disease.

Action needs to be taken as regards world population numbers as part of an integrated approach to addressing the needs of the future. Whilst there is in theory enough to go round, the human race is a long way away from this theoretical position because there are more people in the world that do not have enough than those who do.

As an interesting side note, statistics show that there are far more overweight people in the world than there are starving people – 800 million people with not enough to eat compared to 1 billion who are eating too much. This is a staggering figure that most people think should be the other way around but it isn't. Any incredulity there may be about this statistic highlights the perception problem there is about the reality of the situation.

Neither figure is acceptable or in fact necessary, especially if those who eat to excess share this surplus with those who haven't enough. We therefore cannot tackle one problem without considering the other.

This rapid increase in obesity poses its own set of problems where the future is concerned for dealing with obesity drains resources just as much, if not more, than helping those who are starving particularly as can be seen from the above statistic that there are more of them.

Obesity is mainly a First World problem and therefore people in these countries are much more likely to get medical treatment than people who are starving in the Third World. This means that money is channelled towards treating obesity and its side effects, which in turn means that less money is available for foreign aid. For example, every year 300,000 people die in the UK directly from the causes of obesity. The costs of dealing with obesity are, if you pardon the pun, huge with estimates suggesting, that in the USA alone, the estimated figure is $100 billion per year. This is money that could be better used elsewhere.

Obesity is also spreading as developing and Third World countries seek to adopt a Western life-style including eating western style unhealthy food, drinking alcohol and smoking cigarettes.

At the other end of the spectrum, every year there is a famine somewhere in the world that threatens millions of lives and the way that this is mostly dealt with is for aid to be sent to the affected region to help people through the crisis.

Whilst this is laudable and clearly important from a humanitarian point of view it is no long-term solution to the overarching problem that there are just too many people sharing too few resources in too small a space. Coupled with the added issues of rubbish and waste disposal this makes for a cramped and over crowded planet that is creaking at the seams.

OBESITY AND GREED

This is compounded by resources not being shared equitably. This is evidenced by the fact that the world's 3 richest people are worth the same as the poorest 600 million in terms of what they earn in a year.

That means that three people - yes three people - earn as much as $1/10^{th}$ of the total world population.

Is there any way that that can be justified? Or the fact that 20% of the world's population consumes 86% of its resources, or that only 12% of the population uses 85% of the water?

With this being the case, giving aid in crisis situations just makes the problem worse, if that is all that is done, for it simply means that more people are alive when the next crisis occurs and therefore more misery is created as the problem compounds.

This is not saying that we should suddenly cease all aid to affected areas of the world, for to not help is cruel and uncaring. What it is saying is that the focus of help needs to change from keeping people alive to one of improving the quality of people's lives, making them less dependent on hand-outs, giving them back their integrity and dignity and empowering them to be self-determining and self-sustaining wherever possible. In short, giving them an informed and relevant education, to help them make better decisions about their lives.

This must however address the fact that the world's population is increasing at an exponential rate towards 12 billion by the middle of this century. Where are they all going to live, and what are they going to eat and drink? No country knows this problem better than China for it already has 160 cities that have a population of 1 million people or more and has massive infrastructure problems from housing to pollution to treatment of sewage to providing clean water and so on. China already has to spend $170 billion per year on the clean-up costs incurred as a result of pollution and environmental degradation. There is something unnatural about this surge of human population for nature normally has a way of controlling and regulating its species. No doubt it will do this to humans if we do not do it ourselves. Humans are the only species that are directly aware of their situation where their population levels are concerned and can do something about it before a solution is forced upon them.

We also have the technology in place to facilitate this need to control our numbers, i.e. by better sex education to include advice on family planning and contraception, yet we are not doing so and therefore our numbers continue to grow at an ever alarming rate. The Earth seems to creak under the weight of all these people and their demands for living.

If nothing is done then a tipping point will be reached where the consequences of too many people competing for too few resources will lead to a complete breakdown of not only law and order, but also the human immune system where disease and famine are concerned. It is not hard to see that already many of these features exist in the world and the signs are that it is only going to get worse.

The problem is not one that can be looked at in isolation from all other issues facing the human race at this time for the problems are all linked. There are however some key features that can help provide understanding as to how this situation developed and what might be able to be done about it in the short, medium and long term.

Many of the problems regarding population stem from when humans moved from being hunters and gatherers to farmers. While humans were hunters and gatherers nature determined their numbers for when there were years of plenty their numbers rose and when there were years of shortage their numbers declined accordingly. In this way humans were in tune with the changing patterns inherent within nature and modified their behaviour accordingly. In times of shortage they would not have children because they knew that there was not enough food to feed them and that the children would be allowed to die if there wasn't enough food to feed everyone for a child was easier to replace than an adult. When there were times of plenty they would seek to replenish their population again.

When humans discovered how to farm and domesticate animals and crops then the relationship with nature changed. Humans now had means of controlling the forces of nature and by doing this they were able to produce larger yields of food (e.g. by irrigation) and they were able to sustain larger populations.

When times were difficult, or the populations outgrew the ability of their culture to supply everybody's needs, then either they would have to get additional supplies from somewhere else (which led to conflict) or they would suffer hardship and famine and thereby have their populations reduced. They, like modern humans, also suffered from things such as climate change for there are countless examples throughout history of humans living in settlements, sometimes for hundreds of years, but then abandoning them suddenly due to things such as drought, flooding, or the food resources being exhausted.

NATURE ALWAYS HAS THE FIRST AND THE LAST WORD

Although humans have found ways to regulate nature's processes they still have to live within the natural order of things. This means that if demand is greater than supply it must at some point lead to population controls being imposed by nature.

This natural law is compounded in the human situation because humans have the ability to tap into nature's storage vaults e.g. underground water supplies, to obtain the resources they need. By robbing the bank in this way humans are able temporarily to sustain population levels that are artificially high against their own viability. Therefore, unless huge changes are made in their lifestyles the problems of today will be minuscule against those yet to come.

When the supply of these resources dries up then the reality of both the artificially high population levels and the acute shortage of necessary resources will crescendo into an apocalyptic nightmare.

In such a scenario it will be a battle for survival and there will be an escalation of conflict in the world. If there is nothing to eat and there are too many people in the world then what will people do - eat each other? This is obviously abhorrent and many would say that as a species we would not resort to such actions. That remains to be seen, but the human race's actions where its relationship with the planet is concerned, could be seen to be cannibalistic already.

In 1969 there was a smash hit pop song released by a one hit wonder duo called Zager and Evans. The name of their song was: ***In the year 2525***. The song projects into the future and considers how the future might look if the human race continues on its current path. The only thing perhaps naïve about the song is that the writers - if anything - grossly overestimated how long it would take for some of these things to become reality.

One of the verses towards the end of the song is:

In the year 6565
I'm kind of wondering if man will still be alive
He's taken everything this old Earth can give
And he ain't put back nothing.

And later in the song it says:

In the year 9510
If God's a comin' He ought to make it by then.
He'll either say I'm pleased where man has been
Or tear it down and start again.

The way things are at the moment, with population levels increasing as fast as resources are diminishing, the chances of the human race surviving until the year 9595 are not that great. This is based on the current modes of human behaviour continuing unchecked.

We may choose to introduce population controls ourselves voluntarily, or if not then nature will at some point impose them herself by way of famine, disease and even war. It might seem strange to regard war as being a natural phenomenon, but in a sense it is because it mostly results from the fact that there are population tensions due to there being limited territory or resources for members competing populations to share. Animals compete for territory all the time and by doing so ensure the best of their species gets carried forward into the next generation.

The difference with humans is that it seems to be the worst of their number that compete for territory and this then gets carried forward into the next generation where the problem is compounded. Accordingly, attitudes such as selfishness and competition get carried forward into the next generation. Those who are dominant in such times succeed in surviving in the short term, but in the long term all lose out due to lack of foresight, planning and responsible action.

RISING ABOVE THE BIOLOGICAL URGES

The difficulty in dealing with an issue such as population control is that trying to check the inexorable rise of the world's population is counter intuitive to the human race's biological drive. Within every species there exists this urge to thrive and flourish and the clear signs of that urge are progeny. After all, a successful parent in nature is one with lots of offspring.

This attitude exists within the human race and especially in men for it is a natural urge within the males of any species to spread their seeds and genes as far as possible. In many cultures an important ingredient of a man being a success is that he has many children as proof of his virility. He would also hope to have male children for they continue the blood line. In royal circles it is often said that a king needs to produce an heir and a spare – i.e. two sons in case one dies. Nothing is said about how many daughters he has to produce which actually says a lot!

This desire to produce as many children as possible is a throwback to the human race's early history where mortality rates were much higher. Despite mortality rates lowering this urge for progeny and particularly male progeny continues.

Ironically this may help to sort out the population problem. In many countries now there is a positive discrimination against having girl children and many are even aborted or killed at birth. This then leads to the situation that many countries now have a much greater male population than a female one. In China alone there are nearly 50 million more men than women. In India nearly 11 million girls have been given up for adoption at orphanages because they are not wanted by their parents.

This means that there aren't enough female partners for all the men due to the parents wanting male children. Therefore many children won't be able to continue the family line because they won't be able to find a partner to have children with! This may in time lead to further reductions in the population as men begin to compete for partners and start killing each other for the privilege. This may sound like an extreme analysis, but it is already happening.

Many cultures in the past had very high infant mortality rates due to the prevalence of disease and due to life expectancy rates also being much lower. They therefore needed a high birth rate to keep their population levels up.

Today, with the advent of improved health care and technology, it is possible to lower the infant mortality rate and increase life expectancy. Whilst this is obviously good for the people it affects, it means that the population starts to reach unsustainably high levels because the birth rate remains the same or more likely increases. The same number of babies are being born as before, but the death rates have gone down. Many of these babies then grow up to have babies of their own.

This means that the delicate balance that was maintained before is upset and, as such, there are more people, but no more resources than before - in fact there are far less. This can only lead to more misery and famine for more people. This in turn leads to guilt for the richer nations then give aid to the suffering nations so they can continue to expand their populations beyond unsustainable levels. Thus each time a disaster occurs it is worse than the last time because there are more people living on the margins who will be affected.

The problem is that humans have not updated their attitudes to the times they live in. Nor have the institutions of the world, particularly those that hold sway and power over many of these people. Many of these institutions that seemingly help people are actually controlling their lives in many different ways including attitudes to sex and population via political, social, religious, economic and education methods.

NOT ALL HELP IS HELP

Many of the church groups that help in the poorer countries of the world do some amazingly helpful and important work where health and education for the people are concerned. However, they also bring their own moralities to these people and often this includes a ban on contraception because it is immoral or against the will of God. The conscious or unconscious agenda behind this is that it means the numbers of that particular faith grows as well.

It is therefore a similar attitude to that which causes individuals to think that their legacy can only continue if they have many children to carry their genes forward into the next generation. This is dangerous especially when further growth threatens to undermine the continuance of one's species unless steps are taken to moderate the population numbers. Animals know this perfectly well, for when their numbers get too large then either a natural kind of birth control kicks in where no more offspring are produced until environmental conditions change, or alternatively a migration to new territories begins to ease congestion.

The position for the human race is that there are no real new areas for people to migrate to because just about everywhere is overcrowded and stretched to the limit as it is. Many of the wealthy countries of the world are now facing a growing crisis in dealing with the problem of illegal immigrants as they flood from poorer countries to those they see as offering some kind of hope for a better future.

This only leaves one realistic and viable solution, which is for some kind of population control. However, the main controllers of education are often people who want the population to grow or do not offer methods of sex education that would help these populations to better regulate their numbers.

Many of these church groups often peddle the view that the use of contraception prevents creating another life and is therefore a sin. If anything is a sin then surely it is encouraging children to be born into a world where they and their families have no realistic chance of having any kind of life other than one of misery and suffering.

Further, these groups often say that the prime if not sole reason for sex is for procreation and if people do not wish to have children then they should simply practice abstinence until they do want to have children. This teaching is either naïve at best or cruel, for people like to have sex and it is entirely natural to do so. To suggest that it is wrong to have sex without trying to make a child is to completely fix sex as being something far less than it actually is.

Whilst self-restraint is no bad thing, for contraception is not a substitute for education, nevertheless it could help alleviate much of the growing population problem. At the same time it could help in the prevention of transferable diseases such as Aids and thereby improve the quality of life of those alive today.

There is no substitute for people being better educated about the truth of their situation because this leads to better decisions being made. However some of these attitudes take time to change.

The West itself is not immune from these population issues although the ones they face are of a different nature. Here the issue is not one of exponential population growth, for with the exception of the USA, most of their populations are growing relatively slowly. In fact without net immigration more of them, like Italy, would have negative population growth.

The issue for these countries lies at the other end of the spectrum where they all face a situation where they have an increasingly older population. With families tending to be smaller, better health care and medication and lower mortality rates, people are living longer. Each year the average age for death increases, and this means that there are more old people in all these societies than previously.

These people all need health care as they get older, and because there are less people in work than retired by proportion each year, this places an increased strain on the existing work force to look after the ageing population. Not only that, but increased financial strain is put on the economic system because pension funds aren't able to cope with the payments they have to make to pensioners who often live on well into their 80's and 90's.

The financial models upon which the pension funds were originally calculated were based on projected life expectancies at the time and those figures are seriously out of date due to longer life expectancies. More people will be expecting pension payments from funds that will become depleted of their assets due to these increased demands.

Ironically the world economy is put under tremendous pressure because more people are surviving birth and cheating death. It is not that birth rates themselves are actually going up very much or at all. As a result of this improved survival rate (especially infant mortality rates, because those who survive themselves grow up to have children who also survive to grow up and have children, etc.) the human population has increased from about 500 million just over 100 years ago to more than 13 times that figure today.

If nothing is done voluntarily then nature will impose a solution. Some might call it the planet's revenge, but the planet clearly isn't vengeful, it simply responds to what happens on it. Revenge is something that unevolved and undeveloped human beings do to each other and to accuse the Earth of such baseness underestimates its life giving and life affirming properties.

If there are too many people depleting its resources then the Earth will adopt measures to control the human population. The early signs of this can already be seen with things like the spread of Aids and the increase in global and climate disasters from famine to war to tsunamis and even war and terrorism.

With too many people using up too much of the Earth's resources urgent action is needed.

With 6.7 billion people on the planet it is not that anyone need be lonely and people might begin to realise that it is no longer necessary to have large and unmanageable families simply to prove virility or continue a genetic line.

The human race is its own genetic line and its viability is on the line. In this everyone is responsible for the changes that are needed.

So what are the changes that are needed where population is concerned?

I sent my soul through the invisible some letter of that afterlife to spell and by and by my soul returned to me and answered "I myself am heaven and hell."

The Rubyiat of Omar Khayam

"It was the best of times, it was the worst of times, it was the age of wisdom, it was the age of foolishness, it was the epoch of belief, it was the epoch of incredulity . . ."

Charles Dickens (A Tale of Two Cities)

THE GREAT CULLING:
CAN'T CHANGE?
WON'T CHANGE!

HAVING SPOKEN ABOUT POPULATION IN the last section, this one considers the possible consequences of failing to address the issue of ever increasing population growth.

It is often said that we live in and on a world that gets smaller every year. This is literally true, for each year with global warming and climate change the sea levels rise and therefore a little bit more of the Earth's land mass becomes submerged and disappears from view and use. So, not only is there increasing pressure on the land with the galloping increase in population levels, but this is also compounded by the fact that each year there is a little less land for us all to share. With the punishing use and stress that humans put the Earth under, so does the quality of that land diminish also.

At present these changes are relatively small, but they are incremental and projections are that, as this century wears on hundreds of millions of people will be affected as sea levels rise by possibly 5 metres or more. If this is the case then many millions of people will have to be evacuated from around the coastlines of the world's vulnerable places - but where will they go? The rest of the planet is pretty much full up with more than enough people already and with hundreds of millions of people on the move this will create an intolerable pressure and burden on already over-stretched resources and infrastructures.

Hurricane Katrina was an early warning sign of things to come when it breached New Orleans's flood defences with devastating consequences. Imagine what it would be like if, instead of it being a one-off event, it and countless other cities were affected by the ceaseless and remorseless rise of sea levels all around the world. The evidence suggests that this is happening faster than anticipated.

This creates massive logistical problems for the human race, for it means that there will be less and less time to prepare for and respond to the Biblical type changes that look likely to occur in the lifetimes of those being born today.

When the stories of the Bible, and especially those of the Old Testament, were first written most if not all people believed them to be literally true and many people continue to believe in them. Some say they are the direct word of God and cannot be challenged and must be accepted as articles of faith. This includes the stories that God created the World in 7 days and that Noah and his kin were the only survivors of a great flood.

In recent times science has challenged many of these stories and shown that clearly the Universe wasn't created in 7 days and that it is a lot older than the Creationists view of it being 6000 years old.

LEARNING THE LESSONS OF OLD

Recent new scientific discoveries however tend to suggest that some of these stories may be based upon real events in human history. The story of Noah and the flood has even earlier origins in stories like the epic of Gilgamesh. It appears that such events may have actually occurred in the past in other times of rapid climate and / or environmental change and that these stories relate to these events.

With Noah the theme of the story is that God was unhappy with the people and threatened to wipe out the human race unless they changed their ways. Noah tried to persuade God not to do it but the human race didn't change and so only Noah, his immediate family and two of every animal made it on to the Ark to survive.

Putting on one side the question of whether Noah actually existed and whether the story is literally true, nevertheless the analogy and parallel to our situation today is striking. Then and now the cause of the environmental disaster was human behaviour. Then it was wicked human behaviour that caused God to make it rain for 40 days and 40 nights and thus make the sea levels rise. Might we too be causing the weather to change to our disadvantage by our own errant behaviour?

Many cultures have developed stories and explanations for environmental changes and have developed all kinds of ceremonies and rituals to appease the Gods from offering them gifts to ritual sacrifice of other humans. They thought they must have done something to displease the Gods and needed to do something to placate them. Yet the fact is that none were sufficiently technologically advanced to have had a major impact on their environment in a way that could directly affect the weather patterns. They could clearly affect their ecology by exhausting their resources locally and this is what many of them did. However, any climate changes that they suffered were in all probability due to natural changes rather than caused by their own actions.

The difference today is that humans are contributing to climate change in a significant way. In an eerie way the stories about floods haunt our experience because we keep ignoring the warnings about what changes global warming and climate change will cause.

The problem is that the consequences of such actions are gradual enough for people not to take effective action over them. In this sense global warming for the human race is a bit like cooking a lobster. The lobster is put in warm water and, as the temperature of the water is increased, the lobster goes to sleep and as it does so it starts to be cooked without ever knowing what happened to it. The difference between the human race and the lobster is that the human race is turning up the temperature of its own pot.

Global warming and climate change are not the only issues facing the human race where these matters are concerned, for everything is inter-connected and inter-dependant. This can be likened to a domino effect where one action can have many and compounding affects on other seemingly unrelated and disconnected events.

If global temperatures continue to rise then one of the side effects is that habitats and ecosystems of the world will change accordingly.

103

Some species will become extinct and others will move into the spaces thereby created.

What this means for the human race is that it will come under threat from such things as diseases becoming more powerful and prevalent. With global temperatures rising diseases like malaria will be more widespread. Therefore rather than eradicating malaria, the struggle will be to prevent its spread into previously malaria free zones.

Some prediction models estimate that if temperatures continue to rise as forecast then by the end of this century malaria could spread into the UK and deep into the USA. Not only that, but many other diseases will develop stronger, mutated strains and create an ever-increasing threat, much like the Bubonic Plague in the Middle Ages and the Influenza epidemic of 1918-1919 that killed over 40 million people.

With overcrowding and international travel, conditions are ripe for such diseases to spread rapidly in a way that has never been seen before. Certainly there have been many scares where this is concerned, from Ebola to Asian Bird Flu, and the likely scenario is not whether such an event might happen but when. All it needs is for something like an airborne disease like TB to become mutated with a near 100% mortality rate disease like Ebola and then the Bubonic plague could be made to look like a small outbreak of a minor disease.

The human race is like any other organism in that a species has two ways in which to respond to huge environmental changes if it doesn't want to become extinct. Either it adapts or it migrates.

Where the human race is concerned migration doesn't appear to be a realistic option for its success as a species means that there is not really anywhere else for it to migrate to that isn't already occupied. Despite countless billions being spent on space programmes, any plans to colonise other parts of the Universe are misguided in the extreme for our bodies couldn't adapt to the migration quickly enough as we have evolved over millions of years to live here.

ESCAPE OR ADAPT?

This suggests that adapting our behaviour is the only hope we have to ensure that we have a chance of surviving the coming changes.

Failure to adapt increases the likelihood that the changes will threaten our chances of survival as a species due to having made our own habitats uninhabitable. With too many people and not enough clean water and food and increase in disease, conditions will be ripe for a culling and plague of Biblical proportions.

This therefore makes the human race itself much like a plague of locusts that eats everything in their path until there is nothing left and then they face a mass culling as there is no food left to sustain their population level.

The important thing to note about a plague is that it cannot thrive unless conditions are right for it to do so. The Black Death spread because human beings lived in crowded and dirty conditions that enabled disease bearing rats to pass the disease on to humans via the fleas that lived on the rats.

Malaria can only exist because the malarial bearing mosquito is able to live in swampy, warm conditions. With global warming therefore the likelihood is that the range of conditions that malaria can exist in will expand. As global warming makes life more threatening and challenging for some species, for others it will be an opportunity to thrive and flourish as conditions become more favourable for them.

Because of the way that humans live and our sheer numbers, we are creating favourable circumstances for other organisms to exploit these conditions. These organisms will then adapt and mutate to suit these conditions and then exploit them to the full against us. When this happens none of the existing drugs and vaccines will be able to cope with these new strains of diseases.

The situation is already tenuous in the extreme. Many existing antibiotics and vaccines are becoming less effective as many strains are developing resistance to these cures. Only those organisms that are able to adapt to these changes quickly will be able to survive.

Likewise there is no guarantee that human beings will survive unless they can modify and adapt their behaviour.

The point here is that human behaviour is significantly contributing to the changes that are happening in the planetary ecology. We could therefore minimise the amount of adaptive behaviour required later when the environment undergoes large changes by changing our behaviour now.

Negative behaviour patterns that undermine a habitat or ecology require more drastic remedial action the longer they are left unchecked. Many cultures in the past have suffered from this due to perhaps cutting down all the trees, using up all the water supply, overusing the land until it became infertile, over-fishing, exhausting the food supply, and so on.

With so many people now sharing this tiny planet, and with projections of the population nearly doubling over the next 50 years, there is also the question of what to do with all the rubbish? We already can't cope with the volume of rubbish being produced so the thought of the amount of rubbish doubling within 50 years conjures up a nightmare scenario of drowning in our own waste and excrement.

The problem here is that the more rubbish we produce the more places we have to find to put it, but the more places we find to put it means there are less places for the burgeoning populations to live and fewer places for them to grow food.

Bit of a circular problem really, isn't it?

DROWNING IN A SEA OF WASTE

As a raw statistic, each person in the UK on average throws away the equivalent of 4.5 times their own bodyweight in rubbish per year. That is just what they themselves throw away and to this figure must be added the amounts that manufacturers, suppliers and energy producers throw away as well. The true figure of what is discarded as landfill rubbish every year is the equivalent of each person throwing away 200 times their own bodyweight, or 20 tonnes each. This means that in net effect every 2 days each person throws out the equivalent of their own body weight.

The UK isn't the worst offender where the disposal of rubbish is concerned, even though it is bad enough. After all, any country that produces 450,000 tonnes of plastic bottles a year and only manages to recycle 5% of these cannot be accused of pioneering the way forward where efficient waste disposal is concerned. In the European Union Greece, Portugal and Ireland all have worse records in disposing of their waste. Ireland is in fact the dirty man of Europe as it sends 69%

of its waste to landfill and the average annual waste is a massive 869kg per person! The Celtic Tiger is swiftly fouling its own habitat, and with no effective means of disposing of this waste the rubbish is piling up fast, particularly given that Ireland is a small country with a steadily growing population.

Some countries try and hide their poor records where disposal of waste and recycling are concerned by exporting such waste - much of which is often highly toxic and therefore dangerous - to third world countries for disposal. China is now the major depository for such waste. The Chinese government turns a blind eye to the environmental problems it causes because of the money it brings and Western governments turn the other blind eye to their failure to dispose of their own waste effectively.

The Basel Convention is a UN treaty that was drawn up to ensure that hazardous waste is not exported from one country to another. This is often flouted and the USA is the only country not to have signed up to the treaty at all. No surprise there, then.

It seems that we are determined to undermine our future at both ends of the spectrum. Not only are we grossly negligent and profligate in our use of energy to provide for our needs, but we are also equally culpable in how we deal with the consequences of our use of that energy.

The problem here has always been lack of foresight and planning and / or lack of will to implement any plan to work with the environment and its balances.

Because of technological advances and population growth we have reached a critical threshold where such behavioural patterns are no longer local in their effect but global. We need to think globally and in an integrated way to address the changes needed. This requires people not to be selfish, which sounds easy, but in fact has always been the human race's Achilles Heel.

This is because the human race has a dominant genetic print of being tribal and local in its aspirations. This is to one degree entirely understandable because before now the effects of human behaviour have mainly been local and limited. In the last 200 years however these effects have increasingly become global and this trend is incremental and exponential. Hence the urgent need for greater consciousness and awareness.

Never before has the human race so needed to rise above local and parochial interests to see that only by looking to the needs of all can the needs of self be addressed.

In times of shortage everyone else is seen as a potential enemy and competitor for the ever-dwindling resources needed for survival. Somehow humans need to defy this way of thinking and not put one's own personal desires first.

The subpoena in this is that if something isn't done then a mass culling of the human race is much more likely. In the short term of the Anthropocene period (the period since the rise of human beings as a dominant species) we have become far too successful by using short-term methods that are not sustainable in the long term. If we don't curb this behaviour voluntarily we will make our various habitats unliveable due to food and resource shortages, water shortages, pollution, disease and desertification.

It doesn't really need any kind of prophet to read the runes of the coming shock if we continue to evolve in the current self-destructive way. It is one thing not to adapt to changes in the environment caused by external changes, but it is quite another thing to actually cause the changes that one cannot adapt to. If ever a definition of madness were needed then this would be a good one to use!

Human beings know about culling for they often do it to other species whose numbers grow too large to suit their requirements in their particular ecology. They even do it to each other and the names for these activities are war, genocide and ethnic cleansing. Perhaps a new name for how we foul our own planet could be *Planetocide*?

Humans themselves have also experienced such cullings in the past, although they have probably interpreted them as being Acts of God or simply unfortunate events. Today they are better able to interpret these events of the past, but that doesn't mean they can prevent similar and possibly far worse disasters happening in the future.

Prophets were historically ignored and they will be again in the future for their problem is that they see the future and not the present.

Those who live for now compound the problems by being so short-sighted.

It does require a mindset shift.

Either a person is a prophet or they are after a profit.

One sees the future and adapts before it happens. The other wants its share now and that kind of profit must ultimately lead to an even bigger future loss.

Which one are you?

?

I keep six honest serving-men
(They taught me all I knew);
Their names are What and Why and When
And How and Where and Who.

Rudyard Kipling

You cannot simultaneously prevent and prepare for war.

Albert Einstein

I have principles, and if you don't like
them I have other principles!

Groucho Marx

9/11 AND 11/9 – A TALE OF TWO NUMBERS

FOR AN AMERICAN AUDIENCE, AND indeed most of the world, 9th September 2001 (9/11) represents a very significant milestone in human affairs. It marks the day when the USA came under attack from the so called 'forces of terror' when the World Trade Centre and the Pentagon were attacked by Al Queida. Thousands of people lost their lives as a result of these attacks and it marked the beginning of the USA and its allies launching a counter offensive which has since be termed 'The War on Terror'.

Whilst such acts as those of 9/11 can never be justified against innocent civilians, if indeed justifiable at all, the response to these actions cannot be justified either.

For America has pursued its own particular form of fundamentalist vengeance in response by setting up places such as Camp X Ray, Guantanemo Bay and Abu Grahib prison, carrying out rendition flights to transport terrorist 'suspects' around Europe to various CIA camps where they are allegedly tortured on occasion (or as the US military would have us believe that don't use torture but they do use 'enhanced questioning'). Further, there are allegations from Iraq of the US military carrying out violent attacks against the civilian population and murdering or torturing prisoners in their capture.

However, this chapter seeks to examine a deeper issue than the rights and wrongs of the foreign policy of the USA and its allies and any hypocrisy in its implementation. For beyond a wrong leading to an equivalent wrong there lies a more fundamental issue of tracing the causes of actions to the source of their arising.

This is where the tale of two numbers becomes relevant, for whilst most people know what 9/11 relates to, not many remember what 11/9 relates to.

Yet by a strange quirk of fate it was on 11/9/1989 that the Berlin Wall that separated East and West Germany came down. This was a hugely symbolic event and marked the beginning of the collapse of Communism in Europe. In the West this was seen as a moment of liberation for the people in Eastern Europe from the dark and oppressive forces of Communism.

In part this was true for it led to democracy, or at least a version of democracy, appearing in many places east of the Berlin wall. This in turn led to a sense of optimism and even euphoria in the West and a renewed hope that the collapse of the Berlin Wall might lead to a new world order, free from the dark days of the Cold War.

However, in reality it did not lead to a spread of greater freedom from the West to the East, but it led to the spread of Capitalism to the East. This continues apace not only in Russia, but also in other states, such as India and China. With this unleashing of capitalist forces, coupled with the rise of advanced technology and globalization, new tensions are being created not only between the different peoples of the world, but also between the peoples of the world and the planet they share.

Further, somehow the tensions between these two apparent opposite states of Capitalism and Communism managed to keep the worst of each other in check during the Cold War years, although at times matters came perilously close to a nuclear war; for example during the Cuban Missile Crisis.

After such near misses the major players in the Cold War - the USA and the USSR - came to realise that any such nuclear war could not be 'won' due to the capability both sides had of destroying the other with retaliatory strikes, and so they came to rely on a policy which was understood by both sides as being 'MAD'. This was literally true, for MAD was an acronym for Mutually Assured Destruction, which meant that if one side launched a nuclear strike on the other then a retaliatory strike would be launched to cause equivalent damage. In this way the world's two great superpowers managed to keep each others imperialist ambitions in check, at least to some degree.

As a side note here the USA, in particular, seems to indulge in much sabre rattling about other powers in the world developing nuclear energy programmes and nuclear weapon potential. Why is that? Because they already have them of course! This gives them a position of supreme advantage over everyone else if and when push comes to shove. Their rhetoric speaks of needing to police other rogue states to ensure world safety, but would you really want to place world security in the hands of the one state that has used nuclear weapons in anger not once, but twice against totally civilian populations? Does this set a precedent? Yes it does; and not one to feel comfortable about.

For who is one meant to trust in this nuclear debate; those that have them or those that don't? The answer is easy; neither, for as Einstein said you can't simultaneously prepare for and prevent war at the same time. The inevitability is that once weapons are produced they will at some point be used.

VICTORIES ALWAYS END IN DEFEAT

With the fall of the Berlin Wall Capitalism won the war and thereby managed to spread its sphere of influence less by military influence than by economic power. In this way the war today is more an economic one - the battle for wealth, power and influence - as people realised that with the collapse of the Communist regimes massive profits were to be made and economic rather than military empires could be built, although by no means has the military option been abandoned.

At first this was thought to be an entirely good thing, for capitalism and democracy were perceived as bringing freedom and emancipation to the people's who had previously been subject to the suppression of their communist rulers. Suddenly the people seemed to have some choice and control over their lives as Western investment poured in.

The truth is however that one kind of exploitation replaced another and the cold reality is that the lot of most people in these countries has improved little, if any at all. Some individuals have made countless billions as a result of the Berlin Wall coming down but the average citizen mostly only sees the same struggles as before with a slightly different face to them.

This in turn has led to its own tensions, for 11/9 led to the forces of capitalism being able to expand in quite a dramatic way. There was now only one world Superpower and it could achieve some if not many of its imperialist ambitions through economic rather than military means, and this is what it now sought to do.

In doing so it came to replace the previous oppressors and in this way the trace of the origins of 9/11 can be seen in the events of 11/9.

Without anything to resist it, the forces of capitalism were able to expand and for many of the countries that they supposedly helped liberate they became the new 'enemy'. Alongside the alleged desire to set the people of these countries free came an equally if not stronger desire to expand their own sphere of influence politically, economically and also in relation to its own need for resources.

In pursuing these policies the USA in particular was, and is often insensitive at best to the local customs and beliefs of the countries and states that they deal with as they vigorously pursue a policy of what is best for the USA. They are not alone in this, but being the world's only Superpower they are able to pursue this policy more aggressively than most due to the power and influence they are able to wield.

Once the Communist regimes influence in these territories weakened then the adversary for the fundamentalist groups in those territories became the so called liberators themselves. Prior to this the West had often funded these terrorist groups in an attempt to undermine the power base of the territories involved. Having managed to achieve their initial goals this left a large number of factions armed and free to pursue their own agendas in the pursuit of furthering their own ideologies, and often this meant biting the very hand that fed it.

Osama bin Laden is a case in point, for prior to becoming a world known figure he had been funded by the West to carry out his own terrorist counter insurgency in Afghanistan and surrounding territories. However, once many of the desired goals of undermining Russian influence in the area had been achieved, bin Laden refused to defer to his capitalist masters and began with his followers to pursue a jihad against the 'other' imperialist infidel: the USA.

In this regard therefore there is a curious connection between the events of 11/9 and 9/11. Although they are nearly 16 years apart, the seeds of one were in many ways sown in the events of the other.

It is not being suggested here that 11/9 was the only thing that led to 9/11, for world events are an extremely complex matrix of interconnected forces. Nor is it being suggested that the perpetrators of 9/11 were in any way heroic in their actions in somehow teaching the imperialist West a lesson.

All the wrongs in the world cannot combine to make a single right.

The evidence suggests that the lessons haven't been learned and the events of 9/11 were used to justify a furthering of rhetoric and imperialistic ambitions. This coupled with a deliberate campaign of disinformation, such as seeking to link the events of 9/11 with the invasion of Iraq, has led to a hardening of both the foreign policy of the Western Allies and also the forces that seek to oppose them.

After 11/9 the myth that developed was that somehow the war against Communism was won. This failed to see that new forces would arise to take their place.

What the West has failed to see is that they themselves have unleashed many of these forces into the world. To a large degree it is a case of chickens coming home to roost, and if further proof of this is needed one only has to examine the links between the Bush and bin Laden families prior to the events of 9/11. Power and greed have a funny way of making strange bedfellows and enemies.

If even further proof of this fact were needed then by another coincidence on the 11th September 1973 the democratically elected government in Chile of Salvador Allende was overthrown by a USA backed military coup led by the fascist dictator General Pinochet. The crimes against humanity committed by this regime are legion, yet the USA backed the change even though the Pinochet dictatorship was about as far from true democracy as one can get. The point being that the USA backed what it thought would further its own interests in the area regardless of the political status of the regimes involved.

This has been a consistent and prevalent policy of the USA (and some of the imperial aspirations of other countries such as Great Britain, France, Russia and China) particularly since the Second World War.

With the USA having backed over 50 insurgencies and bombed 30 countries since the Second World War it can hardly claim it is the only, or indeed worst, victim of terrorism or the bastion of freedom and righteousness it seeks to portray itself as being. That is a very advanced case of the 'pot calling the kettle black'. It seems that there are far more pots than kettles where world governments are concerned.

What goes around comes around and in a way what this shows is that numbers influence every part of our lives.

The only regular shape that doesn't have any number of sides is a circle, so this suggests that it is best to take on board the full 360 degrees of any situation before taking any action. Anything lesser can only lead to problems further down the line.

The question then remains; what is the full 360 degree context of any issue? It may not be possible to answer that question in any given case, but it is important to at least ask the question before proceeding, as assumption and vested interest are dangerous bedfellows where the future is concerned.

THE FUTURE OF ATTITUDE

Love does not cause suffering: what causes suffering is ownership.

Antoine de Saint-Exupery

What do I think of Western civilization? I think it would be a very good idea!

Mahatma Gandhi

OWNERSHIP AND POSSESSION

THIS CHAPTER IS CONCERNED WITH how people are caused to see temporary things as being permanent and permanent things as being temporary. With this in mind the concept of ownership can be seen to cause people to put wrong priorities on things.

A person may own a house, a car, a stereo, clothing, a computer, a TV, a yacht, a bike, a watch, a fishing licence, a TV licence, a pen and countless other things that they could list. They might even say that they own a pet. Or how often do people introduce someone by saying: "This is *my* wife / husband / son / daughter."? Innocent possibly, but is it? Language reveals much about how people think and perceive things to be at conscious, semi-conscious and unconscious levels.

A person cannot really own things at fundamental level. They may exercise influence and a degree of control over them, but they do not own them, nor do they possess them.

Take the car that a person might say that they own. Everything in it will ultimately decompose and change form into some other kind of energy. Everyone will have seen abandoned cars in fields or junk-yards slowly decomposing. It may take some parts hundreds of years, but in Universal time scales that is merely the blink of an eye.

Or what about owning the land on which a person lives? The Earth has been around for a lot longer than human beings have, yet humans have this strange idea that they can own bits of it. (That is providing they don't have a mortgage, in which case the bank has a proprietary interest in it even though the bank isn't a person!)

So what is this concept of ownership and how did it evolve?

In the natural world it is easy to see that all species need an ecology or territory within which they can live, feed, grow and reproduce. Within this there is a Darwinian element of natural selection, for only the adaptable succeed in ensuring the continuance of their species.

This is very different to the concept of ownership, which is a particularly human development that seems to have emerged out of and alongside human evolution.

Early humans were hunters and gatherers, and so in being mobile and itinerant and having to follow the seasons and their food, they did not need to develop a concept of ownership. Indeed this persists today in many so called primitive cultures where they do not have the idea of ownership over such things as land, sea and sky. It is noteworthy that most of these cultures are sustainable.

It is ridiculous to say that a person can own the airspace above their house, infinitely into outer space! Or the land beneath it, technically to the other side of the world! What happens to the claims from people coming from the other side of the world when they meet somewhere in the middle? Who is going to police the border?

Not long ago I met some young children aged between 6 and 7 and showed them some of the amazing pictures of the Earth taken from Space. I then asked the children who owned the Earth and they all said that no one did, it belonged to everyone. However as I showed them photos that got closer and closer in to the Earth the children could begin to identify countries and they got to the point where they could identify the USA and said that it was owned by the Government and people of the USA. This was quite revealing for it showed that the concept of ownership is a matter of perception. The more local the perception the greater the concept of ownership grips. This is because the person relates all of their experience to themselves.

The other example is to do with space travel itself and the human race's determination to conquer and colonise other space bodies, presumably so that we have somewhere else to go once we have used up all of the resources on this one. One of the first acts the astronauts did when they landed on the Moon was to plant a Stars and Stripes flag on it in what can only be interpreted as an act of possession. The latest plan from the USA seems to be to spend approximately $1 trillion to try and land a manned mission on Mars. Maybe a flag will be put there too?

THE GRASS IS GREEN WHEREVER YOU ARE

The best possible riposte to this desire to conquer Space could lie in something that happened when I was cycling around Ireland in 1980. One day whilst seeking directions for the next part of the journey I came upon a quintessential Irish farmer at the crossroads of somewhere to somewhere else and asked for directions to the next planned stop. Most people have heard the story of the Irishman pausing and reflecting and then saying "I wouldn't start from here if I was you!" or the alternative "You can't get there from here!"

This was even better, for after pondering for a few moments on what was the best route the Irishman paused, looked me in the eye with a firm gaze and said: "What's wrong with here? Why don't you like it here? It's great here. You've got everything you need here, why would you want to leave?" He wasn't joking, and for him it was true!

This point holds valid for the human race's view of the planet on which they live and everything on it.

There is absolutely nothing wrong with the Earth other than what human beings have done to it under the misguided perception that they own it and it is their pleasure to do with it what they will.

Until that perception changes then humans will continue to look outside of themselves to fulfil their need to consume resources rather than look inside themselves and see that they are in fact overflowing with every resource they will ever need. This is providing they are prepared to share what they have rather than abuse what they use.

Returning to the whimsical Irishman for a moment, he wanted for nothing and because his life was simple it was more complete and more fulfilling. There was a sense that he didn't need to go to another place physically because he was himself where he was.

This sounds simple but is rare because many people spend their lives journeying to try and get some kind of understanding as to who and what they are yet forget to look at who and what they already are.

From this standpoint travelling to Mars doesn't make any sense whatsoever. If humans need to find out who and what they are then all the clues they need are right her on Spaceship Mother Earth and not one rocket needs to be built to begin to find the answers to those most searching questions such as:

> Who and what are we?
> Why are we here?
> Where do we come from?
> What is our part in the unfolding Universe?

Once humans started to develop an agrarian culture it meant that they no longer needed to travel and so they could begin to tailor and condition their environment to suit their needs. To do this they would then look around for prize land upon which to use their newly acquired farming skills, and no doubt there were fights for the better quality of land as it got scarcer.

At some point this concept of territory evolved into one of ownership and all the side effects that this has left humans with today. This is bizarre because the costliest real estate in the world today might be somewhere like the Empire State Building which occupies less than 10 acres in area and yet is probably worth many billions of dollars. Yet the land on which it resides produces no food or water or minerals of any kind whatsoever!

IS YOUR LIFE REALLY YOUR OWN?

This concept of ownership is in many ways delusional. It causes people to identify with things that they think they have possession of. They think according to what they place around themselves and what they regard as being important. This then extends even further into less obvious realms such as things like who owns a person's life?

> Do they?
> Does the government?

Does the Earth?

Does God?

In thinking about who owns a person's life the one crime that a person until recent times could be convicted of attempting to do but not for successfully carrying out was suicide. Consider also Euthanasia and people claiming the right to end their own lives to prevent undue continuing suffering due to debilitating illnesses. The law is very confused about these issues and the argument comes down to questioning who ultimately has control over a person's life?

After all, does a person think they own their own body? Does it belong to them? Is it even *them* in the first place?

Or is it on loan to the person whilst during this phase of their journey through the cosmos?

When its time of service is over, the person as Shakespeare said, "shuffles off this mortal coil." and it goes back to the factory, i.e. the planet from whence it came.

Because humans think they are their bodies they often think that when they die that is it. But is that true? Or is it simply a case that, like the hermit crab, when they no longer have use for the shell they have been living in they shed it and move on to the next stage of their life? The hermit crab isn't its shell and when a person 'dies' the shell (the body) is still there but the person isn't. Like magic, their life force has disappeared into the ether!

A person is the sum of their experience and not their physical body. The body is the medium through which experience is had whilst 'the person' is here.

Yet even after death a person is not necessarily free from the long arm of the law of the secular authorities. For example, China has recently announced that as part of its control over Tibet that no one is allowed to reincarnate without state permission! Now this may sound insane, or at best incredible, and it is clearly both. For an atheist state is stating that people can't do something that the state doesn't believe in without their consent!

Further, the Chinese authorities do not offer any specific guidance as to how someone is to get permission. Are they to ask someone in this life before they die and do they have to give full details as to how, when and where they shall reincarnate, or should they ask someone when they are being reborn? Or is there some halfway house place where they can check in with the authorities before choosing who they come back as? The lack of clarity is something of a problem and it is with great anticipation that further details of how this will be policed are awaited. If it weren't part of China's rigid controls of another sovereign state it would be laughable.

Similarly the Russians have recently decided that because they have the technology to plant a titanium flag directly underneath the North Pole at 2 ½ miles under the surface of the ocean, that somehow this legitimises their claim to 'own' the land and mineral rights over the whole area. The reasons why they have done this are clear in that the area is blessed with an abundance of energy and mineral resources and the Russians think that because they have put a flag there first then it's theirs. Clearly the world of politics has not evolved greatly from caveman attitudes of grabbing and possessing territory by whatever primitive methods possible.

Unless these attitudes evolve and update soon we are all in deep trouble, regardless of who 'owns' the North Pole and whether or not the Chinese authorities decide that we all need to get their permission to reincarnate. Are Tibetans allowed to reincarnate as Italians? Are Samoans allowed to reincarnate as Tibetans? And what do you do with bluffers – how do you test their claims? Do the reincarnation police reincarnate backwards in time to check out the veracity of any claims? How will they know whether to go forwards or backwards in time and what will they do if someone else reincarnates backwards in time and kills their father when he was a boy so that he never marries and fathers them in the first place?

Gosh, it's all very complicated isn't it?

Finally, here is a curio to end this particular chapter.

The more a person wants to, or thinks they can, *own* things the less they are living in the *now* because they are forever looking to what can be *won* rather than shared.

Ultimately things do not belong to anyone for they simply belong where they belong. Everything returns to the source of its arising and so it is wise not to become too attached to material things.

Conversely, it is prudent to become attached to higher things because that is where a person's future destiny lies. The way a person becomes attached to higher things is by being useful to them rather than trying to own or possess them.

This raises an interesting question which is: what is it that a person wishes to be useful to and for and why?

The 'control' of nature is a phrase conceived in arrogance, born of the Neanderthal age of biology and the convenience of man.

Rachel Carson

The conquest of the Earth, which mostly means the taking it away from those who have a different complexion or slightly flatter noses than ourselves, is not a pretty thing when you look into it too much.

Joseph Conrad (Heart of Darkness)

CONQUEST

ONE OF THE SERIOUS MISALIGNMENTS within modern cultures lies in the development of the attitude of conquest. This seems to stem back to the time where humans changed from being hunters and gatherers to agrarian cultures.

Slowly over time the view developed that nature could and should be conquered rather than humans following nature and its seasons in how they lived and arranged their lives. With the new found ability to produce more food than they needed, populations grew but conflicts inevitably arose when shortages occurred. To compensate for this, fresh conquest of new territory was needed, both in terms of nature's resources and other cultures to obtain their territories and resources.

The defeated were then usually put into some kind of bondage, slavery or reparation in order to serve the needs of the victorious culture. However, this growth by conquest cannot be sustained as new territory runs out. When this happens the empire created collapses in on itself.

Anything that thinks it can conquer something or someone else doesn't know itself.

Such attitudes can only be a self-defeating for ultimately it is only that which does not have mastery over itself that would try and conquer someone or something else.

The psychology of conquering comes from an 'us and them' mentality. Whilst there must be certain processes undertaken for survival and continuance, this does not naturally lead to the idea of conquering or greed. In ancient cultures they knew that the principle of oneness needed to be respected otherwise the natural order of things would be upset.

Modern cultures do not understand this principle and therefore they think that problems can be conquered by such things as better technology and scientific advances. The chimera here is that for a while it seems that this is true because the new technology in things such as food production gives bigger yields initially over a period of say up to 50 to 100 years. This time scale is tiny in evolutionary terms but nevertheless gives science a seemingly plausible mandate for the argument that humans can use technology to get themselves out of trouble and provide what they need.

Such things as Genetically Modified foods are therefore seen as a way of solving world hunger problems and people are told that they should trust the scientists because they know what they are doing. Instead of trusting God and the Church, as per 500 years ago, they should now trust Science as the new God of the future.

All this misses the point in two fundamental ways: firstly the more removed from themselves human beings are the worse the solutions become, thus the situation becomes increasingly perilous because each time a bigger and more powerful 'solution' is proposed the greater the ultimate payback will have to be. These solutions are therefore nothing of the sort. They are avoidance technologies for they fail to address the real issue, which is that humans are trying to conquer what they are no longer connected to - which is themselves.

The second and more fundamental way in which this thinking misses the point is that it comes from arrogance and not humility. Anything that thinks it is more intelligent and more powerful than Nature and Creation makes a serious and potentially damning mistake. The laws of Nature cannot be beaten or broken or conquered, and things that try to operate outside these laws eventually get reaped. If the 4,500,000,000 years of the life of this planet were compressed into one calendar year then the human race only appeared on the planet 3 minutes before midnight, i.e. at 23:57 hours. The Industrial Revolution only happened 3 seconds before midnight and everyone alive today was born less than a second ago. The laws of nature however have been present the whole of that time.

Human beings have done tremendous damage to the planet, themselves and the future during their 'three minutes' by way of their conquering mentality and it pervades all aspects of modern life.

LIES, DAMNED LIES AND STATISTICS

This conquering attitude is full of deception and self-justification and often masquerades as freedom, holy wars and free trade. It can be quite subtle and deceptive at different levels. For example, it is commonly believed that Columbus discovered America. He clearly didn't because it was existing quite nicely before he got there! Secondly there were already many people living in North and South America at the time. Recent estimates suggest that there were up to 100 million people in the whole of America and that the plagues and diseases brought by the Europeans wiped out far more people than was previously thought.

Consider also how the Christian Church conquered the so-called ignorant savages of the world and brought them their version of God and plenty of diseases as well. Or how the USA government continues to support the herding of Native Americans into ever smaller reservations and forces them to forget themselves to such a degree that they end up either having massive social problems or running casinos!

Further, consider the use of conquering language by calling them 'Native Americans', or calling black people 'Afro Americans', as though that changes anything. It is deceiving people into thinking that they can change the reality by changing the labels of things.

This applies to governments trying to put pressure on their people to accept non-sustainable 'solutions' such as GM foods by calling these non natural processes things like biotechnology. In fact, in the USA the food labelling doesn't even require the producer to state whether the food is GM modified or not.

Humans have certainly become unconscious to many things over the millennia, for how else could so much damage and destruction be done in the name of progress? Humans have become desensitised to the pain they cause themselves and the planet.

Unless a person can see a bit of themselves in everything they look at they are lost to themselves and they will look for solutions to problems outside of themselves. Whilst they do that they will try to conquer what they perceive to be adversaries when in reality there are none other than ignorance, fear and lack of perception.

This point is illustrated in the film *The Silent Flute* (co-produced by Bruce Lee before he died) where a great martial arts expert seeks to fight the true master so he can prove himself to be the best. He fights all these other people on the way and finally gets to the castle of the true master and earns the right to see the book of truth. He opens the book and on every page is a mirror where all he sees is his own reflection. He is at first angered by this, but then sees the absurdity of his quest to conquer everything outside of himself. He sees that all the battles he had were in fact with himself and with the fears he had projected outside of himself.

Fear plays a huge part in this conquest process, for fear leads to insecurity at all levels.

That which knows itself needn't have fear for it is aware of the way things work. This is why the ancients said: 'to know the human study the Universe; to know the Universe study the human.'

Therefore the quest of conquest is just that - a Con Quest. It is a con, an empty shell and a sign of developing wrong priorities due to a warp in attitude.

It is noteworthy that all the great teachers throughout the course of history have not been primarily concerned with the material things in life. They have sought to place the right balances on things with a deeper emphasis on the spiritual aspects of life. As Jesus Christ said, "Give to Caesar that which is Caesar's and give to God that which is God's."

In truth, nothing worth having can be owned for who ever heard of someone conquering kindness or compassion? Or that freedom has been isolated in a lab in Geneva? Or that love has been successfully crossed with maize to yield better crops? Higher things cannot be possessed they can only be processed, but not in a can.

The only way to have kindness is to give it away.
The only way to have love is to love.
The only way to earn respect is to show respect.
The only way to have enough is to share.

The only way for a person to know is to admit that they don't know.

The only way to find the right answers is to ask the right questions.

The only way to help others is to let them help.

There is no college course or diploma in genuineness.

There is no secret mine in Siberia where humility is quarried.

There is no shortage of humanity, just a shortage of volunteers to process it.

There is a saying that 'love conquers all.' That may be the biggest oxymoron of all time! Love conquers nothing otherwise it wouldn't be love.

Love simply loves without condition for it sees the pedigree of what something is unto itself and the promise of what it could be if it were allowed to be.

People don't fall in love they simply need to connect to it. There is a big difference.

So instead of *conquest* what is needed is for the human race to *connect* to who and what they really are.

This pathological need of the human race to colonise things is dysfunctional and it is misaligned human thinking that believes there is a hierarchy in the way that life is ordered with humans at the top.

The principle of what goes round comes round is a natural truth. This applies to both degenerative and generative things in equal measure. What a person sows they reap and the human race is about to reap a bitter harvest unless it changes course because it has forgotten to plant the seeds of humility, awe, love, respect, compassion and reverence. These are the seeds of hope and the future for they have the pedigree of longevity.

BEWARE OF PUNCTUATION!

It is good sometimes to see the simple truth hidden within certain concepts that language can often marvellously offer. It could be asked as to which part of the human body is in control when humans set out to colonise things? The answer is the colon!

If a person doesn't activate the higher parts of themselves then the lower systems will get the opportunity to operate in realms that are not in their natural order or function to do.

Inside this colonising attitude human beings have crapped all over nature and the future possibility for those yet to come. The truth of this is easy to see in the mountains of rubbish modern cultures bury inside, on top of and above the planet.

This colonising attitude shows lack of respect for anything outside of itself and sees anything different as being in need of conquering and being put in its place. With this kind of attitude the cure is inevitably worse than the disease.

The human race has become constipated by its own self-importance. This has led to the dramatic side effects that can be seen in the world today. Such conquering attitudes leave a trail of misery and destruction in their wake. Kindness and compassion are not their way.

Perhaps the human race needs an enema to help unblock it! Much of recorded history has shown a lot of bad attitude from the human race, which has left a lot of crap lying around for someone or something else to clear up.

These are the lessons of history that humans need to learn. History is a great teacher for those who are wise. The vast bulk of it can teach a person how not to go on. Yet hidden within the chaos and madness are sequins of genius showing just how brilliant it can be when human beings shine in the way that their birthright subpoenas them to.

Each person is designed to shine in their own unique way and style.

The key to success is to see that there is nothing to fear, conquer or colonise. Everything a person meets is simply another part of themselves. The truth and embodiment of this principle is not a matter of academic learning, but an alignment and connection that a person can grow in themselves as they develop a knowledge of the Universe and how it works and their natural place within it.

With nothing to own, a person need never be on their own.

?

The appetite grows by eating.

Francois Rabelais

What the industrial economy calls "growth" is really a form of theft from nature and people.

Vandana Shiva

GROWTH

GROWTH IS SOMETHING THAT EVERY living thing does. Nothing is born large and then grows smaller as it matures. Everything that lives begins as something small and then grows during its life until it goes into decline and dies.

Growth is something natural and consistent for the survival of both an individual and any species and can be seen as a healthy process and sign of development and progress.

Growth also has another meaning with an unfortunate connotation. A growth is something that is unnatural and threatening to the life and order of the organism on which it grows. It is quite often cancerous and, if left untreated, it can kill its host.

This process of growth applies to all aspects of life, from the physical to the social to the political to the economic and so on.

In modern economic theory growth is mostly seen as the panacea for all our current problems. The view is that as long as the economy is growing faster than the problems that assail it then all will be well. Yet this process cannot be sustained in the long term because the economy exists within a greater fixed economy.

That system is the planetary ecosystem which has a fixed amount of energy and resources within it. We can go on developing technologies and ways and means for exploiting these resources in the short term, but ultimately this type of growth can only lead to the collapse of the economic system upon which is it based.

The reason for this is that all this growth is based on what can be called outer growth – expansion outwards. In cosmology this inflationary theory is based on the fact that the Universe seems to be expanding outwards from the point of Big Bang and condensing as it goes. As long as the Universe has something to expand into then all is well, but what would happen, if for any reason, it suddenly reached an end point? Would it then start to implode back in upon itself?

The same principle applies at every level of outward growth. This growth can continue as long as there are markets to expand into, but when the markets dry up then inevitable collapse occurs.

This would also appear to be true where the individual is concerned. Mostly the signs and trappings of growth in the modern world are measured by such things as personal wealth and fortune, with the world's richest person being the one with the most money or assets.

What kind of growth does all this outer wealth and richness really represent? Is it the healthy kind, or is it perhaps the cancerous kind?

Perhaps a way of viewing this is by looking at how this growth took place, because for something to grow it needs to be fed what it likes to eat. The growth of money and wealth is a particular animal that has very specific dietary requirements.

It has to be competitive, for to have a better chance to survive it needs to be able to better compete for resources than its adversaries. It needs better and more dominant access to both the resources it needs and also to the markets it wishes to use and supply.

This principle can be seen easily enough in modern cultures with the rise of multinational companies, who with their huge buying power, make it almost impossible for small producers to compete with them. They can sell their products cheaper because they can spread their profits over a much larger range of goods.

With a small percentage of the profit going back to the source, the owner of the business can and does become very wealthy indeed. This process continues whilst there are markets to expand into, and as it does so smaller businesses are subsumed into the larger one as its juggernaut-like growth continues.

Ultimately, like the growth of all empires in history, this outer growth process reaches an end stop point where, because the basis upon which it has grown is no longer sustainable, it collapses back in on itself. In short, it runs out of resources.

NOT ALL GROWTH IS OUTWARDS

What therefore of inner growth? Inner growth is infinite because it speaks about growing qualities in oneself rather than seeking to accumulate quantities of things.

Quantities are indeed truly limited, however qualities are not. Whilst the supplies of oil on the Earth, for example, are clearly finite and limited, the amount of compassion in the Universe appears not to be.

This suggests that a person can grow an infinite amount of compassion in themselves. The same could be seen to be true with regard to many other qualities such as warmth, love, hope, belief, kindness, generosity, care and many others.

What is more it seems that these are the very qualities that helped the Universe in its own growth process, and as such it would seem very wise for a person to grow these qualities in themselves. Such things are immortal - yachts, jets and money are not.

Mostly when people think about personal development they think about developing better skills in order to enable them to get what they want, which is mostly wealth, power and status. Again, these aspects are only temporal in their location and intermittent, at best, in their pleasure.

Real growth comes from within and emerges far more from giving than it does from receiving. This suggests that we ourselves should do the same by responding in similar vein to the gift of our existence.

It is therefore proposed to now look at the processes of natural and unnatural growth, and see how they may differ and what each may allow or not allow as the case may be according to their nature.

Natural Growth...

Works from inside to outside.
Proceeds from the unseen to the seen.
Moves from design coding to physical expression.

Is organic in its method.

Is part of the natural evolutionary process.

Does not pollute.

Unnatural Growth...

Always works from the outside first and doesn't go deeper.

Is forced in its methods.

Is not organic.

Works by over extension and thus causes stress.

Because of this it is prone to unhealthy mutation.

Pollutes and leaves unhealthy waste.

Is cancerous in the short, medium and long term.

Modern culture works by vast majority via unnatural growth.

This growth can, for a time, deceive the observer into thinking that it is true growth, for the initial yields may be good. This can be seen in modern farming methods where yields for chemical based farms are on average 20% greater than those of organic farms. The obvious deduction to be made from this is that modern farming methods are better than traditional ones.

However, over the long term chemical based farming methods undermine the soil and the environment as the chemicals affect all different parts of the ecosystem, from the soil to the plants and animals and rivers, plus they cause erosion and soil depletion.

Plus, despite what the anti-organic movement says, organic food is healthier for recent tests have shown that organic food contains twice as many antioxidants called flavonoids than non organic food does. Flavonoids help to prevent high blood pressure and thus reduce the likelihood of heart disease and strokes.

Plants produce flavonoids naturally as a defence mechanism and their production is triggered by nutrient deficiency. Feeding a plant with too many nutrients, such as inorganic nitrogen via the use of fertilisers, suppresses the development of flavonoids in the plant and therefore makes it less healthy to eat. It is probable therefore that the more fertilisers are used the less healthy the plants become over generations.

Because humans cannot wait to receive what they think they must have right now, forced growth methods are used without foreseeing the consequences that these actions might cause in later generations.

Steroids, for example, are pumped into chickens to give them larger breasts that look more succulent for the diner in the restaurant. It may look better because of its forced growth, but it is unhealthy because of what is in it and what that causes in the consumer.

As another example, years ago DDT was banned from being used for any kind of crop spraying because of its side effects. What was then discovered was that chrysanthemums displayed some of the positive properties that DDT had in helping to control some diseases such as malaria. It was therefore decided in Rwanda to turn large parts of the native forest over to growing chrysanthemums as a means of boosting the economy. The forests were largely cleared and the growing of chrysanthemums went well. However, a direct side effect of this was that it also undermined the ecology of the gorillas living in the area and almost caused their extinction.

The same principle applies in terms of forced growth where humans are concerned. This often happens when parents, for example, try and force their children into success or fame or into being some kind of genius. Mostly it ends in tears, for often the children are forced into this growth spurt before they are ready for it, emotionally or socially.

This also applies to children in terms of preciousness and fashion. Because of the bombardment children receive they are forced to grow up much quicker than even 20 years ago. The proof of this lies in the fact that the average age that girls now begin puberty is around 11½ years whereas 20 years ago it was 12½. Many girls can now have a baby at this age but by no means are they equipped to handle the experience emotionally. Yet the number of teenage pregnancies in the West is rising all the time.

There is also a proven link between forced growth and delinquent or socially unacceptable behaviour. The more unnatural things are forced upon people the more they will ultimately act in a detrimental way towards themselves and / or others.

This principle is now being discovered in children's education. If encouraged properly, children will build their own parameters and controls within which they are happy to act responsibly and learn what it is they need to know. If controls are imposed upon them in a dominant way they tend to rebel and react against them.

Another feature of unnatural growth is that it works by elimination of difference, rather than the process of natural growth which works by integration with the whole.

SUCCESS ISN'T GUARANTEED OR A BIRTHRIGHT

Natural evolution has caused the extinction of more than 99% of the species that have ever lived on Earth, sometimes through seismic and catastrophic events such as meteors striking the Earth or sudden and rapid climate change. However, the process of evolution to date, has always been organic in that these are all natural events.

Humans can and do directly affect this process due to their ability to shape and alter the ecosystems of the world. They are also causing countless extinctions at the same time.

This is severely threatening the biodiversity of the Earth's ecosystems. Humans therefore need to have a compassion and consideration for all life on the planet and not just their own selfish needs. They have the capacity for responsible stewardship but they do not have a mandate for wanton destruction. The latter is ultimately cancerous whilst the former gives rise to responsible and conscious evolution.

The human race's recent past has seen much unnatural growth. The future requires a reassessment of the kind of growth that humans want to see in the future. More of the same will ultimately mean less for everyone, unless the definition of more is rewritten to include both the terms *less* and *enough*.

What is it that you have had enough of, and what is it that you need less of?

*He who knows nothing is closer to the truth than he
whose mind is filled with falsehoods and errors.*

Thomas Jefferson

*When in that House M.P.s divide,
If they've a brain and cerebellum, too,
They've got to leave that brain outside,
And vote just as their leaders tell 'em to.
But then the prospect of a lot
Of dull M. P.s in close proximity,
All thinking for themselves, is what
No man can face with equanimity.*

Gilbert and Sullivan (Ioalanthe)

THINGS ARE NOT ALWAYS WHAT THEY SEEM

EVERYONE LOVES TO SEE A good magician do their act, whether it be card tricks, making things disappear, sawing someone in half or pulling a rabbit out of a hat. Not knowing how the magician does the trick adds to the mystery and wonder of it all. Yet the magician doesn't perform real magic, they simply use sleight of hand or diversion techniques to make the audience think that some magic has occurred. It is therefore an illusion, although to the observer it looks like something truly miraculous has occurred.

The reason they think that is because they do not have enough information about what has happened and so they believe what their eyes tell them to be the truth. The only person who really knows what is going on is the magician, for they have learnt the secrets of how to trick people into believing a different reality. A really good magician can fool people into believing what appears to be totally impossible because they are able to present things in such a way that people believe a different reality.

Perhaps politicians are therefore highly skilled magicians?

If they could somehow come up with a way of making each other disappear completely then that really would be magic!

Anyway, the point of this introduction is to highlight the fact that a good magician is a master of illusion. They do not really carve the assistant in half or cause someone to disappear or change their wand into flowers, it just appears that they do.

The illusion can always be explained but the magician is sworn to secrecy by the magician's code so the audience might never find out how the trick is performed. Unless a person can find out how the trick is done they can only either believe what they have seen or suspect that what they are actually seeing is not true, although they don't know what the actual truth is.

Truth is not always black or white and sometimes it can be white when all the evidence suggests that it must be black. Politicians, fundamentalists, evangelists, salesmen, newspapers, films and so on can present matters in a certain light and thereby persuade people to see reality through different coloured glasses.

There is the well known maxim that 'you can fool some of the people all of the time, all of the people some of the time, but that you can't fool all of the people all of the time.' There is no doubt some truth in this statement but the worrying fact is that all of the people can, at some point or other, be fooled for some of the time at least. The question is, for how long?

The way this is done is through the use of illusions, much in the way that a magician does, as described above. They can also be like a mirage, for whilst these images appear very real, they disappear as soon as the person approaches them. They come in all shapes and sizes and cause people to follow them in the erroneous belief that they offer the path ahead.

It is vital to pierce the veil of these illusions and seek the deeper truth that they might be hiding.

This chapter, therefore, is about two specific types of illusion, how they mislead people into not seeing what their situation actually is and how to move safely forward into the future.

THE ILLUSION OF CHOICE

One of the great illusions in the world today is that people think they have a real choice where the purpose and direction of their lives are concerned.

After all, a person can go to the supermarket and choose which brand of soap or washing powder they wish to use, what they eat, what to watch on television, what kind of car to drive, which school they send their children to, where they go on holiday, and so on.

But is this real choice or is it something else?

Consider the democratic political system, which works on the principle of one person one vote. This would seem to indicate that each person has an equal and powerful opportunity to exercise their right to choose which direction the political process takes, by voting for which candidate and party they wish to see in power.

Given that there are often very diverse candidates with wide-ranging manifestos this would seem to be a fair and equitable way for power to be divested to those candidates and parties.

The reality is something quite different, for the minor parties are never going to achieve power because they have too specialised or narrow a view to ever enable them to win enough votes to get elected. Conversely, those parties who contest the battle for power all tend to move towards the centralist or populist areas of the electorate because this is where the election is won or lost.

Political parties know that they are only fighting over a few percentage points in the middle and they therefore compete solely for these swing voters. They try and win these votes by giving those voters the choice that they hope will win their support. This appears to be a choice but in reality only offers a choice in respect of a few minor issues that might tip the balance between being elected or not.

This is illustrated by the fact that more and more in recent elections, in both the UK and the USA, the key issues always seem to come down to character attacks on the opponent rather than discussing key issues of importance for the society as a whole.

Think how much time during the last election was spent discussing key issues such as climate change, world energy consumption, global poverty and hunger, health care, Aids, debt relief, the unequal distribution of resources and so on. The parties know that these issues are a hot potato, and therefore agree not to debate these issues in depth because they are too controversial and because they are insoluble within the current political framework.

Because the politicians ignore them, the electorate is not being given a real choice as to what to vote for.

Also the political parties do not wish to alienate big business by addressing such issues, because if they do a tremendous amount of support and finance will be lost.

Choice should therefore be distinguished from selection. The reason this is important is that selection follows on from a choice already having been made by someone else. A person may think that they go into a clothes shop to choose something to wear. The choice of what they can select has already be made by other people who decide what this year's fashion is going to be and what styles and colours will be available. All the shopper can do is select from the ranges on offer or go to another shop where the same process occurs.

The trouble is that most shops offer similar ranges of products and styles so the choice isn't that wide. This same principle can be said to apply to all sorts of things, from education to medical care to news reporting to food and diet to housing, and to just about every aspect of human life.

It is possible to make choices beyond mere selection, but in order to do so a person needs to be able to see beyond the illusion of selection masquerading as choice.

THE ILLUSION OF DIFFERENCE

Alongside the illusion of choice people are trained to see others as being different. This is easily done, for different cultures have different languages, customs, religious practices, art, music, diet, education and much more.

These external differences seem to indicate that there are fundamental differences between people, and the number of wars that there have been throughout world history reinforces the point.

This simply illustrates that those who see difference in others are based on the outside of themselves. The reality is that we all share the same existence on this planet and we are all subject to the laws of nature, insofar as we cannot control those forces to any great degree.

Accordingly the illusion of difference is a luxury, and one the human race cannot afford to hold. Most of these differences come out of such things as greed, exploitation of resources and divergent fundamentalist beliefs. The concept of ownership, whether it be one of ownership over goods, land and resources or over the truth itself, is a fundamental misalignment, for who really owns a mountain, a river or the sky?

Biodiversity is one of the things that make this planet such a rich and wondrous place, but it is also essential in ensuring that the genetic mix of life is sufficiently broad to ensure that life can survive. However, the human race is threatening this fine balance due to its materialistic and exploitative way of living, and this undermines the very principles by which nature works.

Not only are humans challenging the biodiversity of other species, but also their own. This was evidenced when I climbed Kilimanjaro for going up the mountain I went on the Rongai route, which had very few people on it. Coming down we went on what is popularly known as the Coca Cola route – the reason being is that it the easiest route, with the most comfortable facilities, and yes, places to buy Coca Cola.

But perhaps an even greater loss is the cultural biodiversity that language offers the human story. Yet languages are being lost at a faster rate than birds, animals and plants with up to 10 of the world's approximate 6000 languages disappearing each year.

At least 20% of these languages are under threat compared to 18% of mammals, 8% of plants and 5% of birds. This is a tragedy of immeasurable cost, for when we lose a language, we lose a huge store of knowledge about so many things including art, science, religion, the environment, medicines to information about the unknown and the mundane. There is nothing more important than language to give insight into who and what we are.

When a language dies a piece of us all dies with it.

This ultimate expression of difference lies in the mindset that the human race is different to and superior to all other forms of organic life on the planet. This is an entrenched dogmatism that finds its way into all aspects of human life, from religious fundamentalism and creationist theories to science and the development of technologies, to obtain short term material gain. It extends to forcing nature to produce more short term yields with long term negative consequences to seeking to exploit other people or countries and their resources.

The poisoned chalice that the illusion of difference offers is that sharing is dangerous, for sharing leads to less being available.

The illusions of choice and difference are myths that need to be broken down and rebuilt into a new reality. The irony is that the human race now needs to make the right choices to make a difference where the future is concerned, otherwise we might as well select the best ways to make the most of our time left here on Earth before the future disappears.

Perhaps there is a place where real magic does exist and that miracles really do occur? Like the audience at the magician's show it all depends on where we look at things from.

Perhaps that is the way we need to think about the future?

Not from what is wrong, but from how magical it could be if things were full of wonder and amazing surprises.

When faced with impossible odds people often pull out from the depths of themselves the most miraculous range of talents and abilities that surprise even themselves.

If ever there was a time when we needed such magic to occur it has to be now.

What kind of practical magic would you want to see and perform where the future is concerned?

?

The love of money is the root of all evil.
The Bible

Fu bu guo san dai (wealth doesn't make
it past three generations).
Old Chinese Proverb

MAKE WEALTH HISTORY

THIS CHAPTER IS INSPIRED BY much of the recent debate concerning third world debt and the campaign to cancel the debts owed by Third World countries to the wealthier countries, the International Monetary Fund (the IMF), the World Bank and other institutions.

The problem of world debt is much deeper and more fundamental than anything the World Bank and IMF can sort out, for any proposed solutions at distance from the core causes of the problem can only be piecemeal and temporary. In fact, the terms and conditions institutions like these impose on the debtor countries are often extremely harsh and compound the problems.

The irony here is that the world's biggest economy is also the world's biggest debtor. The USA lends more money than any other but at the same time it owes far more money than any country it lends to. If net deficit was the measure of a country's wealth, the USA would be bottom of the league and thereby the poorest country on Earth!

However, due to the size of its economy, investors keep faith in it for they know they have to for if the economy of the USA collapsed then the whole world economy would too - and so it is kept afloat.

To illustrate this point, the budget deficit for the USA currently stands at the inconceivable sum of $8.2 trillion dollars. That is $8,200,000,000,000. To try and give some perspective to this figure here are some examples of what this kind of figure is worth:

It represents $1,500 for each and every person on Earth.

It constitutes 4 times the annual Gross Domestic Product of Great Britain.

28 Eiffel towers made out of solid gold could be made .

It is enough to solve the Palestinian crisis by re-housing every Palestinian and Israeli family in the West Bank in a $1,500,000 house.

Such a sum of money is not only vast beyond belief but is also obscene and a most telling example of a failing Western economic template. It also has an impact at individual level, for the USA also has the greatest level of personal debt per capita in the world with poverty levels rising all the time. 45 million people cannot afford health cover insurance, and indeed medical bills are the biggest cause of bankruptcy in the USA.

The total debt for the USA is 10 times that for the whole of the African sub continent. Yes, that is correct and reads as follows:

THE TOTAL DEBT OF THE USA IS 10 TIMES THAT FOR THE WHOLE OF THE AFRICAN SUB CONTINENT.

Plus, of all the countries in the Global North, i.e. above the equator, the USA has the higher percentage of its population living below the poverty line of any of those countries; a massive 12.7%. That's over 40 million people, or 1 in 8 people who definitely aren't living the American Dream.

These are incredible statistics that show that there is a real double standard when the West lectures and moralises to the Third World about debt and pontificates over whether it should cancel Third World indebtedness. Its own house is clearly in far worse order with the only difference being that the West can, for the moment at least, service its debt. But only just. When the tipping point is reached, and many experts expect this to be soon as dwindling foreign resources become scarcer and therefore more expensive, then a financial crisis of unforeseen gravity will inevitably occur.

In the UK there has been controversy about the funding that the political parties receive, particularly from individuals. There are allegations of 'sleaze', for many of the people who give or donate money to these parties often find themselves being awarded peerages. The political parties deny that there is any link between the two things but these rich donors are highly unlikely to give something for nothing because that is not how they made their millions.

The controversy has been further fuelled by the fact that some of the political parties have asked the people who have wanted to donate money (which of itself is perfectly legal) to change the status of the money given into a loan. The reason for this is that they do not have to declare loans in the same way that they have to declare donations. Plus, they would rather not have to show a possible link between donations and honours given out.

Further, all these political parties are deeply in debt because they spend far more than they receive. This clearly raises an issue of credibility, for how can any political party that spends far more than it earns claim any fitness to run the finances of the country? If it can't get its own house in order and balance its books then that is hardly a recommendation for running the country.

EVERYBODY OWES SOMETHING

Putting aside the debt of First World countries for the moment, it is time to take a view on Third World debt, how it works and what might be needed to address the issue.

Poorer countries are so indebted to the larger, more economically developed countries that they are kept on their knees in trying to get a better platform of stability and sustainability. They are given some aid but the repayment terms are usually so severe that they end up having to export resources and / or buy arms, which in turn worsens the situation. This process continues in an ever-increasing downward spiral whereby the country remains imprisoned by its position. This is how the politics of dependence works.

Much discussion takes place about the issue of world debt and how to deal with it with ideas ranging from cancelling it altogether to developing fair trade practices and so on.

The slogan for much of this effort has been *Make Poverty History*. It proposes not only dealing with the issue of crippling debt in relation to these poorer countries, but also different aid packages to help them get back on their feet. These efforts all fail to address a much deeper issue, which is: how did it arise in the first place?

Poverty is a symptom of something else and is not a cause in its own right. Humans have lived successfully by being able to harness enough from nature in order to survive and flourish as a species over countless centuries.

However if there are limited resources beyond which a society can sustain itself then supplies will have to be obtained from somewhere else. Wealthy countries therefore buy these resources very cheaply from poor countries and thus they maintain their own inflated standards of living and also keep the poor countries poor by not paying a true market value for the resources obtained.

Accordingly, the real problem facing the world is not actually one of poverty but rather one of excess wealth. There are enough resources to ensure that the world's population lives in relative comfort provided these resources are shared equitably and sustainably. But they aren't.

And just so it doesn't seem that this is simply a diatribe against the West, it is important to note that the greatest killer disease in sub-Saharan Africa is not Aids, but corruption. For reliable estimates suggest that possibly 25% of Africa's GDP is lost to corruption which has become totally endemic throughout the continent. With up to £75 billion being 'stolen' each year this means that millions of people die each year from the direct results of poverty being inflicted on the needy because money doesn't reach its intended goal. If money doesn't go direct into the hands of Western corporations then there are plenty of unscrupulous African political leaders with a tiered system below them to ensure that very little if any of the money gets to where it is most needed.

HOW'S YOUR MINDSET?

The mindset that exploits is not one that shares its secrets or benefits and it will invert the truth to suit its own view of reality. In such a way the issue becomes one of relief of poverty rather than one of confronting the obscenity of indulgent wealth and wanton wastage.

The governments of the world buy into this deception in a major way and reinforce the view that poverty is the real problem by feigning to make real efforts to help solve the poverty issue with aid packages or even talk of clearing the debt.

They only do this to quieten the clamour that arises in the world about such issues, but they know that even clearing the debt of possibly tens of billions of dollars is only a drop in the ocean of what the scale of the problem really is. They realise that giving aid itself doesn't address the fundamental causes of poverty and will in no way lessen the culture of dependency that the powerful nations have subjected the poorer nations to.

This control is further reinforced by conditions attached to any aid and the strict controls imposed as to what the money can be spent on. Often this means giving the money back to the West for things that are not really needed, with much of it spent on buying military hardware.

There is also often a condition attached that Western businesses should be allowed preferential access over local businesses to such things as using the country's mineral and natural resources. This means that the aid offered often makes the country receiving it far worse off than if they hadn't had the aid in the first place.

Not only are these countries not allowed to develop the technology and ways and means to harness their own resources, but also the Western governments make sure that they are not able to compete on a level playing field with these Western economies. The way that this is done is through the use of tariffs and subsidies.

Because they are so much richer than the Third World countries they have much more money available to them, and much of this money is used to provide subsidies to their own farmers, manufacturers and suppliers. This means that although it is costing the Western producers much more to produce their goods than the Third World producers, the Western producers are given subsidies sometimes to the order of 90% and beyond - so that their markets are protected and the Third World countries cannot compete with their prices.

Third World countries are not able to gain fair access to the markets of Western economies and thereby gain valuable foreign currency to enable investment to be made in their own infrastructure and growth. Thus the culture of dependency further propagates and proliferates.

This problem is further compounded by the terms of governance that are often imposed on these poorer countries in respect of any loan or aid packages. Frequently this ends up as being a case of the cure being worse than the disease because these conditions have such a negative impact. First World financiers see that economic governance of these third world countries is a primary cause of the problem and so they impose conditions as to how the money they are given is to be spent.

This means that they are allowed limited amounts of money to spend on things like education and health because they are not seen as being directly helping the economy to get back on its feet. Proper governance to them means developing business and exploiting any resources the country has so that it can pay back its foreign debt.

THE HINDERING HELPERS

Institutions like the IMF and World Bank are obsessed by the view that economic growth is the way out of poverty for these countries. They are perceived as being poor because of poor economic strategy, and that this is worsened by things like bad governance. This might be true, but it is not the primary cause of the problem and these institutions' policies only make matters worse.

The reason for this is that Western economic growth itself is based on unsustainable long-term policies. They rely on the exploitation of non renewable resources and seek to try to make some quick money whilst the resource is there and thereby create some short term local employment. They leave a trail of devastation, destruction, misery and a ravaged landscape after the resources have been exploited and waste, pollution and misery is all that is usually left behind.

These short sighted policies fail to consider that after these resources are gone the countries affected are left in a much worse state, because not only are they back where they started, but also their precious resources have gone as well. In the meantime they have also probably suffered a brain drain due to the governance requirements imposed upon them in that not enough money is available to encourage professional people to stay. Current statistics show that 70% of Africa's intellectuals live outside of the continent.

Conversely, they tend to have a population increase at the poor end of the population due to there being more money available in the short term whilst the resources are exploited and labour is required. Once the resources have gone there are no longer any jobs available as the positions offered were not long term sustainable ones. Therefore the suffering will be greater as the population reaches unsustainable long term levels.

The Western model is an example of what not to do where the future is concerned. The proof of this lies in the fact that if every country on Earth incurred economic growth to the degree that Western European countries have then it would need 3 Earths to cope with the demand for resources. If every country became like the USA then it would need 5 Earths.

Such economic growth would be a total disaster for the Earth and all the people on it. Economic growth as proposed by these institutions is therefore a disease and not a solution. All it will ensure is that in the long term there will be more people with less to share as everything descends to the lowest common denominator rather than rising to the highest. Any views that money and economic growth can sort the problems out are naïve and highly dangerous.

It may therefore in fact be best to leave these countries alone and let nature take its course. This may sound callous and uncaring, but in a way these countries have less distance to fall than the West before they hit rock bottom. The era of colonialism has left a clear and present scar on these countries, but their living standards aren't as artificially high as the West's and so the return to a balanced and sustainable way of life for these people is less problematic than it is going to be for the West when its own time of reckoning approaches.

These Third World countries would possibly, in the short term, suffer hardship whilst they adjusted back to a sustainable way of life. That is possibly inevitable anyway due to their population levels being so artificially high based on the promise of economic growth that they have been given. If they continue on with their current course of chasing the Holy Grail of economic growth then they will face an even harsher reality later on when economic growth is shown to be the fool's gold it really is.

If they were left alone from meddling Western exploiters and do-gooders then they might have a better chance of adjusting back to a sustainable way of life sooner. This statement is controversial, but what needs to be remembered is that these so called 'poor' countries often in fact have enough food to feed their own people. The main impediment is often not one of supply, but of cost as most of the starving simply cannot afford the food that is available. Also, much of the food the country does produce is exported to Western countries in order to obtain much needed foreign currency to service the loans from the West. So the food they need to feed their poor is exported to feed the places that loaned them the money and to repay the loans that those countries loaned them in the first place. Bit of a Gordian Knot really trying to sort that one out, isn't it!

Wealth is ***not*** the solution to poverty. Harmony with nature and the Earth is, and in this regard these so called victims could teach the West a thing or two because some of them still remember how to live this way (if they are allowed to). In the West this is now largely a forgotten memory and one that is in danger of becoming deleted from our genetic coding.

This is not suggesting that the poorer countries should simply be abandoned to their own devices to cope as best they can. It is however advocating that the approach to such matters needs to be rethought. Even in trying to help there is a danger of assuming that one knows how to solve the problem without truly knowing what the problem is or what caused it in the first place. This approach leads to further condescension and imposing of further governance and exploitation.

There is no such thing as a free lunch, especially where the starving world is concerned. They are damned if they do and damned if they don't, for whichever way they turn they will be exploited.

The net result of these blinkered policies is that the affected countries end up with a brain drain of people like nurses, doctors and teachers because the country has had to cut its budget for such professions and invest the money elsewhere. Further, the country's resources get exploited and the vast majority of the profits either go overseas to the First World countries that have licensing rights, or they go to the privileged few in the country itself where corruption remains rife.

Certainly the lot of the poor and needy at the bottom of the pile shows no real sign of improvement as a result of such campaigns. In fact it often becomes a lot worse because of such outside 'help' being offered. For Save the Children now regard the exploitation of children as young as 6 for sexual purposes by Aid agency helpers as being a serious and global problem. Is there any worse crime than this in the world or any problem that merits or justifies this kind of 'help'?

WHO HAS THE POT AND WHO HAS THE KETTLE?

It is a serious indictment of the state of the world that the world's richest man is worth something in the region of $US 70 billion. That's more than the total income of the world's 500 million poorest people for a year.

Perhaps, therefore, it can be seen that poverty isn't the real problem but rather that excessive wealth is.

How can the 'problem' of wealth be addressed in a meaningful and fair way? One thing to consider is that the making of wealth or profit of itself is not wrong, but rather the hoarding of it is. A way round this is to devise a system to encourage people to dispose of their wealth, or at least put it back into circulation to help others.

To do this it ought to be possible to devise a scheme whereby if people do not spend a certain amount of their disposable income then it is taken away from them and given to the poor and needy. There could also be a system whereby people earning above a certain level are taxed if they do not spend their money, and if they spend the money on certain worthy causes and projects then they could receive a rebate of a percentage of the money spent. If, however, they spend it on themselves or non charitable causes, there would be no rebate whatsoever and in fact they could be taxed some more to prevent them gaining any benefit from doing this.

A fair way they could derive benefit from having wealth would be to donate a minimum percentage of their income to charity, and the more they spend on these charitable causes the more they receive back at the end of the financial year as a rebate. Charitable causes could be operated in such a way that the more needy and truly charitable the cause then the greater the rebate to the person.

The same principle could also apply to the richer countries of the world. In this way a win win situation is created.

The problem of wealth can therefore be addressed by it being more widely and fairly distributed.

Such a system would take a lot to set up and administer, but it could be done and the benefits would be huge. Not only would it deal with the obscenity of extreme wealth, but it would give people the chance to apply and use their skills in a direct way to help others whilst at the same time incentivising them to do so. This not only helps the needy, but also creates a greater sense of inter-connectedness between all peoples as the problems of the world are dealt with by sharing them.

So do I think that such system could work? Not really! At least not without a change in attitude, and that attitude change is one of changing what we want. We want so much in this modern world and what we want is mostly temporal and temporary and these desires cannot make things fairer for all.

Money alone can't solve the problem of wealth! It needs a shift in mindset and attitude, especially in the West.

Until the West looks at its own attitudes and behaviours towards its poorer relations, then no meaningful and long lasting changes can be made. Money therefore isn't the answer, it's the problem! For it would only take 1% of GDP to effectively deal with the issue of world poverty.

The presence of world debt can only have happened because of the absence of something else. This means that the absence of those things therefore indicates that there is a world debt of them.

What are these deeper issues of debt facing humanity at the beginning of a new millennium?

Consider the following list of items for starters:

Communication
Connection
Decency
Fairness
Honesty
Honour
Humility
Integration
Integrity
Justice
Morality
Patience
Respect
Reverence
Sharing
Value
Humanity

If there were more of these things in the world there wouldn't be a need to sort out world debt - because there wouldn't be any.

The presence of something can only arise by the absence of something else.

Because there is a debt of these qualities in the world that leaves a space for other things to get in, and these can give rise to what humans see as world debt but are in fact simply symptoms of deeper misalignments. Such things as:

Arrogance
Blame
Capitalism
Communism
Consumerism
Duplicity
Greed
Hate
Imperialism
Irresponsibility
Materialism
Patronisation
Possession
Selfishness
Slavery
Wastefulness

The more human beings are based in attitudes that increase world debt the more the world's resources become depleted.

If they are based more in the positive attributes then not only is there no debt but there starts to be a surplus, because the source of where these qualities come from is itself infinite.

The way round dealing with the shortages in the world is to see and deal in what is bountiful beyond belief. These are the qualities mentioned above.

The strange thing is the more they are used, rather than diminishing, they in fact grow, for if something sees a return on its investment then it invests more. Everything likes to see a return on its investment. Why should the laws of Creation and the Universe be any different?

So, consider signing up to the Make Wealth History campaign today. You don't have to be a wealthy rock star to do so, but even if you are you can join too!

?

He who knows that enough is enough will always have enough.

Lao Tzu

Out of clutter, find simplicity;
From discord, find harmony;
In the middle of difficulty lies opportunity.

Albert Einstein

ENOUGH

THE WORD 'ENOUGH' HAS SEVERAL different meanings depending on the context within which it is used. For example, there is the meaning of something being sufficient for the immediate or long terms needs; or there is the meaning that says that something has reached a point of saturation and it's time to stop as in, "Enough already!"

This chapter seeks to address both of these meanings, for they complement each other when considering what is truly important where the future is concerned.

Often people pursue the more of something rather than simply seeking enough. The two mind states convey very different psychologies for the pursuit of more is based in materialism and can lead to obsessive and compulsive behaviour. When people pursue more they are often unable to stop themselves, even when they obtain the original thing they were seeking in the first place.

Once this has been attained a new target suddenly appears, and so the person engages in a cycle of seeking more and more more!

This can be seen quite clearly where the pursuit of money and material wealth is concerned. People driven by this goal often seek to make a certain amount of money so that they can live their dream, whatever that dream may be.

This requires a specific and very singular mindset, and once a person has engaged in this process it is very hard to stop for it literally becomes set or engraved in them. When this becomes printed it reaches the stage where it becomes like an automatic computer programme and it is very hard to override.

Accordingly, as a person goes past the point of having enough, suddenly they realise that the original target of enough is no longer sufficient and so they have to set new targets or goals to justify the continuing behavioural pattern.

This self-rationalisation process hides the truth that the pursuit of enough is no longer the real task - it has now become a pursuit of more. More is a drug because the more one gets the more one wants and the more one has to work to get it.

This pursuit of more is an impossible appetite to satiate. It is like trying to fill a bucket with water while there is a hole in the bottom of the bucket. The more things go in the top, the more they leak out the bottom and the more the person has to work to keep the bucket from running completely dry.

If they were to mend the hole in the bucket they would soon see the bucket fill up to the point where they have enough water.

So what does it actually mean to have enough?

This requires an assessment of what is truly important to the person. If this ongoing assessment process is pursued to any degree or depth it will soon be seen that there are not that many things that a person needs in order to have enough and most of those things are in fact quite simple.

A person needs food, light, shelter and warmth in order to survive. Yes, they may need the ways and means in order to get those things, but what is important to remember is that those ways and means are not goals in themselves.

The more a person seeks material things the more removed they are from themselves, and this applies at both individual and societal level. The pursuit of more leads to many of the problems that we have today, for when too many people want more then suddenly there is not enough to go around because not enough people simply want enough!

It is therefore a good exercise for a person to ask themselves what is enough. What is it that they actually need?

If this exercise is done regularly it leads to an increase in value for the simple things in life. It grounds the person in what is really important and causes them to run on a much more settled and slower internal speed rather than all the rushing around wanting the latest gadget or must have item.

ENOUGH ALREADY!

The other meaning of 'enough' is the one of: – "I've had enough of this. I am not prepared to put up with this any more. Make it stop, make it go away."

Most people face this kind of process at some point in their life, but it is rare for them to make the life changes that such challenges truly suggest.

To do so successfully a person needs to have a reason that is greater than themselves otherwise they will generally settle for something lesser.

At this point a person may find it useful to consider what it is that they have had enough of and what they wish to do about it. The temptation to try and sort it out in others is often an easy knee jerk reaction that isn't in fact helpful. The first place to resolve these issues is always in oneself.

Finally in this chapter there is this to consider: -

There is enough in the world for everyone to have what they actually need rather than perhaps what they want, for often there is a large gap between the two. What is necessary is for everyone to realise this fact and to share with others fairly and equitably. When this is done then, as if by magic, everyone will have more than enough to satisfy their needs.

And that's enough about enough!

Be the change you want to see in the world.

Mahatma Gandhi

Give a man a fish and you feed him for a day.
Teach him how to fish and you feed him for a lifetime.

Lao Tzu

Don't Blame Fast Foods For The World's Ills

THIS CHAPTER IS DEDICATED TO ***not*** blaming fast food chains for the current state of the world. Companies like McDonald's, KFC, Burger King, Taco Bell and others, have been blamed by some people for causing things such as deforestation to make way for farm land, contributing to global warming due to methane emissions from cattle, causing increasing levels of obesity and heart disease, and much more besides.

Even if this is true, it is it misses the point entirely.

Fast food chains only sell what people want to buy. The evidence for this is quite clear because firstly they sell an awful lot of fast food, and secondly they make a great deal of profit out of doing so.

They give the public what they want and not what they don't want. Not many companies make a profit out of selling people what they don't want, although many do make a profit out of selling people what they don't need and often selling them what is not good for them e.g. cigarettes.

In none of their outlets do fast food chains sell dog burgers. The reason for this is also quite clear. It is not that dog meat is in any way inferior to cattle meat (in fact in some Asian countries it is considered a delicacy). The reason they don't sell it is that Western people think of dogs as pets, and they wouldn't dream of eating 'man's best friend'. Accordingly, fast food chains wouldn't dream of selling it. It is therefore a perception issue rather than a moral one, for in India, where the cow is considered sacred, it is beef burgers that are off the menu.

When fast food became popular in the 1950's people knew a lot less about food than they do now; both the producers and the consumers. All they knew was that people loved the idea of fast food because it was quick and easy to get and relatively cheap to buy. Both parties were happy with the arrangement. It was only later that people started to become more aware of the process of food production and of the possible side effects caused by eating too much of these kinds of foods.

This has led to all sorts of things, from class actions about obesity to claims from smokers about not being aware that smoking could damage their health, and so on. However, these organisations are only supplying people what they want, and why shouldn't they do so?

It is often argued that these organisations should have a greater social conscience and should temper their ability to manipulate public taste through such things as advertising. Whilst there may be an element of truth to this, it again misses the key point. Responsibility for exercising choice rests ultimately with the consumer and not the producer. If a person is gullible and naïve they can't blame it on the producer. In today's world, with so much information available, no one can realistically claim ignorance as an excuse, whereas perhaps fifty years ago they may have been able to do so.

People can make informed decisions about their lives – if they want to. This is important because people often make choices about what they want *despite* the evidence and not *because* of it. Fifty years ago some brands of cigarettes were actually approved and recommended by doctors. Today such advertising is banned and cigarette manufacturers are forced to display logos on the packs saying things like "Smoking Kills".

Originally the cigarette manufacturers fought this requirement tooth and nail, but after a while they accepted it because they realised that what was printed on the packs didn't actually make any difference to whether a person smoked not. If a person wanted to smoke they were going to, regardless of the consequences.

The producer can't be blamed for a person's lack of will-power. Yes, they can be accused of exploiting this weakness via advertising and seeking to influence, and even manipulate, people's tastes, but it is not possible to exploit what doesn't exist.

This cycle of supply and demand is a self reinforcing one where producer and consumer each try and get the other to give them what they want. Often this pattern develops into one where the producer is in control by deciding to supply to the consumer what he wants to supply, and this means providing the cheapest product with the greatest mark-up possible.

All being well, the consumer will accept what the producer supplies and the more they buy it the more they want it. The producer knows that in reinforcing this relationship they need to convince the consumer that they are buying much more than just a simple product.

They are in fact buying a lifestyle and an image. That is what advertising is about, for none of it really tells the truth about the product. It flatters to deceive and, with most people being gullible, it works. If advertising didn't work suppliers wouldn't do it because it would be a waste of money. Clearly it isn't a waste of money because of the billions spent on it each year.

LIFESTYLE BURGER WITH FRIES

The problem is not with the producers (although they of course have their own ethical issues to deal with) but with the consumers, for they don't think they have a choice, or they exercise their choices poorly, or they let the producers decide what choices they should have.

The real power in making producers change doesn't lie in trying to make them change. That doesn't work. What does work is in exercising choice and using the power of yes and no. If enough people simply say no and refuse to endorse products that are of negative value to the health and well-being of the public then, ultimately, the producer will have to change the type of products that they supply. Otherwise they will simply go out of business.

People don't believe they have a choice or are lazy or apathetic. As a result they can't really complain if they are exploited. They have to decide what they want and then exercise the only real power that they have, which is individual choice. This is a most powerful tool and can apply not only to producers but also at governmental level.

Governments use fear as a main weapon in controlling people and how they think. This is quite a clumsy tool but it fools most of the people most of the time, causing people to respond in the way that the government wants them to. Otherwise why would people join the army unless the government persuades them that it is a good thing to do? How can it be a good thing to volunteer for something that increases a person's likelihood of being killed?

What if everyone simply refused to join all the armies of the world with immediate effect? Suddenly there wouldn't be any armies and therefore there wouldn't be any need to make any weapons, because there would be no one to use them!

Eventually governments would realise that their policies were not what the people wanted and that they would have to channel all their resources, efforts and money into worthwhile causes that people believed in and wanted to support.

This is where the real change of the future will begin – with individuals using the power of choice. It is here that the West can really offer leadership to the rest of the world, for in the West the consumer really does have much more choice than elsewhere. By exercising choice in a responsible way consumers can show their leaders and producers what it is they want and what they will and won't support.

This is already happening. For example, the Federal government in the USA is very hostile to anything to do with climate change as it thinks that any concessions on the issue will be harmful to the economy. It has therefore blocked any consensus on the Kyoto Agreement and many believed that that was the end of any chance of the USA cutting its CO_2 emissions.

Yet there is a growing trend for state legislatures to voluntarily embrace many of Kyoto's protocols because they see it makes economic and fiscal sense to do so. More importantly, these leaders also see that that is what most people actually want. They are simply giving expression to the wishes of the majority of the people, whereas the Federal government is actually doing something according to what they want.

The reason the government fears embracing such change is not because of the change itself but because of the precedent it would set.

People would suddenly get the idea that they can force their leaders to change policies that do not create a better future.

Well the truth is, they can.

They simply have to make choices rather than feeling that they are disempowered and helpless. They may not change anything through the official voting system, but ultimately that is not where the real power lies. It exists in taking personal responsibility for how one lives one's life and what one does.

EVENTUALLY YOU HAVE TO ORDER SOMETHING FROM THE MENU

It can only begin with oneself. For example, one person buying organic rather than processed food makes quite a big mark. Not only is it supporting the production of organic as opposed to processed foods, thereby making organic food more popular and ultimately cheaper to produce, it is also withdrawing support for highly processed foods, thereby making processed food that little bit less viable. This has to be a good thing as on average each person in the West consumes 7 kilograms of additives in their food every year. Plus, the more processed the food is, the harder it is to get rid of the additives out of the body so no wonder you've possibly been feeling a bit weird!

Being self-chosen also defies the government position, which often makes competition for consumer choice unfair as it gives massive support and subsidies to the processed food market and very little support to organic producers. This is a key reason why organic food costs more to buy, because subsidies received by the processed food farmers give them an unfair advantage over their organic competitors.

By being prepared to pay a bit more money for what is, in any event, a healthier and better product, a person is making many statements and not just one. It involves making an economic statement about fairness in the marketplace, a moral statement about the relationship with the Earth, a sustainability statement about the long-term use of the soil and how that should be managed, an energy statement about global warming and pollution due to chemical run off from the land into the rivers and the food chain, and so much more.

There is no point in blaming fast food chains for the state of the world. They are simply a representation of the state of the world and what it wants. The world needs to change its state rather than its institutions, and if this is done the institutions will change to follow suit. If they don't they will become extinct.

The balance of power in world affairs is shifting from the governmental and institutional realms back to the individual. The evidence in such matters can be seen in things like the recent Asian Tsunami where worldwide individual responses vastly surpassed and even shamed the response of the world governments. Governments are in fact scared of such responses and this is evidenced by the shameful behaviour of the Burmese military junta recently when it refused to allow foreign aid into the country following a cyclone that killed tens of thousands. The reason they did this was because they feared they might lose control of the country and so they would prefer many more people to die than let aid into the country.

This change in perception means that a person really can make a difference if they are prepared to simply give up a bit of their own comfortability and embrace a small amount of the process of change.

By being part of this process of change a person becomes part of the solution. By acting in accordance with their conscience they confirm the feeling of what it is they want. After all, which is easier – stopping fast food chains from selling their food or simply not buying it?

One person doing such things changes the power ratio to a tiny degree. Two million people doing this would make a big signal.

Imagine what it would be like if six billion did the same?

With this in mind if the human race can collectively tap into the same power source of expanded consciousness and awareness from the same mindset then amazing things can and will be achieved.

With this is mind, what conscious choice will you make to be part of that change?

?

The Future
Of The Past

So profound is our ignorance, and so high our presumption, that we marvel when we hear of the extinction of an organic being; and as we do not see the cause , we invoke cataclysms to desolate the world, or invent laws on the duration of the forms of life.

Charles Darwin (On the Origin of Species)

I am convinced that Natural Selection has been the main, but not exclusive means of modification.

Charles Darwin (On the Origin of Species)

QUANTUM EVOLUTION

BEFORE DARWIN CAME ALONG WITH his radical theory on evolution, life was simple. The Creationist theory of life held sway in that, as it says in Ecclesiastes, "There is nothing new under the Sun." God created the world and everything in it and the Biblical story of how the Earth and humans appeared was widely accepted. Humans were made as they are and they had not changed form since they were 'created'.

With Darwin came the understanding that humans evolved from previous life forms by a process of natural selection and adaptation. This is a neat theory that explains much, but it certainly doesn't explain all. Not by a long shot.

Darwin, unlike some of his modern followers, was an open and adaptable man and updated and evolved the book in later editions as new information and understanding came to light about his theory.

It is important to remember that Darwin postulated his theory before Mendel's work on inheritance and chromosomes in relation to dominant and recessive genes and long before the DNA code was discovered by Crick and Watson in the 1950's and the subsequent mapping of the human genome. This is significant because whilst Darwin noted and observed the process of adaptive changes made by species he wasn't aware of the genetic processes involved, although even today, as we shall see these processes are still in dispute.

This polarisation of views regarding evolutionary theory exists between the Neo Creationists, who deny in part or totality the

Darwin's theory, and the Neo Darwinists, who in turn deny the concept of Creationism (i.e. that there is a God who created the world and everything in it in literally seven days). It seems therefore that fundamentalism is not just restricted to religious conflicts over matters of faith, but that it extends to matters of science as well, and the murky waters where the rivers of these separate tributaries meet.

It is noteworthy that recent findings regarding the role of religious belief indicate that there are evolutionary advantages to believing in a higher deity of some kind. These advantages include the fact that people who believe tend to be healthier and live longer. This does not of course prove that any such deity does in fact exist, but it does show that it does appear to be a good move to believe that one does!

Even the Neo Darwinists would have to concede that this is correct, at least to a point. Where this goes awry is when it leads to extreme fundamentalism and dogmatism to the point where the person may kill others or even themselves in the name of serving their so called God. This is not a good move where evolutionary theory and natural selection is concerned for it tends to create evolutionary cul de sacs!

KNOWING WE DON'T KNOW

The one constant that seems to emerge from every new discovery made is that the more we learn the more we don't know. The more we realise that we truly don't know, the more open we might actually be open to more of the truth finding us rather than the other way around. If this is the case, then we open up more of our faculties to coming into play.

We are blessed with more than one type of faculty at our disposal and to base the discovery process on limited use of those faculties would seem to be folly of the highest order. For example, with the two sides of the brain the hemispheres are meant to work in a complementary way. However, most people however tend to develop dominance in one sphere or the other. Hence the oft run battle between science and art, faith and rationalism, masculine and feminine yin and yang in the search for truth.

Current research shows that the left hemisphere of the brain is to do with logic, literalness, assessment, rationality and sequencing. The right hemisphere tends to deal with things like context, emotional responses, intuition, instinct and synthesis. All these skills are needed by human beings, and with 100 billion brain cells at our disposal with over a quadrillion possible connections, it might be true to say that most people aren't using all the resources at their disposal! No wonder the school report often said 'could do better'!

With all our current knowledge about the brain and how it works it would be folly not to use as much of our cerebral faculties as we can to find out firstly where we are, and to then find our way forward into the future. That could be by either cool, clear, inarguable logic or by way of flashes of inspiration and genius or both. For at core are these things actually that different?

Latest research into the functions and workings of the brain tends to confirm that there are indeed masculine and feminine sides of the brain. Our brains are hard-wired to emphasise certain processes, with each person being a unique mixture of both influences.

These two brain influences are sometimes called the *S Brain* for the masculine side and *E Brain* for the feminine. The S stands for Synthesis and the E is for Empathy. It has been found that the masculine side of the brain is good at making technological advances whereas the feminine side is good at giving context to these technological advances.

What this suggests is that if we only have the former then we simply develop the technology to destroy ourselves, and it is not difficult to see that we are dangerously close to that point. Looking at it from the other point of view, if we rely simply on context and security all the time then we will arrest where we currently are and arrestation is its own form of guaranteed extinction.

Somehow we need a magic elixir of the two influences, and if we find it then not only do we have an orchestra, but we also have a concert with all parts of the brain working together towards better perception and nobler action.

BRAIN DOMINANCE

The course of human history suggests that the left side of the brain (masculine) has had more dominance and control more of the time. This may in fact be perfectly understandable if we use our feminine side of the brain for a moment and look to the context of why this may have been necessary. Before civilisation arose humans were in effect simply another animal and early developments of the brain were to do with evolving strategies for survival.

These were mainly physical requirements to do with obtaining food and repelling attacks from predators. With men being physically stronger it was only natural that they would develop these attributes to a greater degree than women. This has been confirmed by recent studies of the brain that show that the hypothalamus in the brain of men is linked to the areas of the brain to do with both sex and violence and that both are powered by the hormone testosterone. This is not the case with women's brains.

It has been found that male babies with more testosterone in the womb after birth tend to have less eye contact at one year old than other babies and that they also take longer to learn language and communication skills.

What seems to be the case is that this masculine brain dominance that enabled our early survival has been carried forward into modern societies when such conduct is not only no longer needed but also positively dangerous. Yet this masculine brain influence refuses to relinquish its territorial hold and sees other masculine dominated brains and even nature itself as being a threat.

Further research suggests that Autism is in fact a disease that is caused by a development of over male logic in its extreme form. This leads to obsessive behaviour, and in its most extreme, form Autistic Savants can often do things such as play a tune from total recall having just heard it once, or paint a 3D picture of a scene from memory having just seen it for a few seconds or do incredible mathematical equations in their head.

At the other end of the Spectrum, over dominance of the female aspects of the brain can lead to what can be called over empathetic behaviour. Here people can over identify with the feelings of other things to such a degree that they don't want to eat anything because it is another living thing, or think that the lives of people in soap operas are actually real, and so on.

Male dominated misalignments of the brain are much more common than the female ones. There is speculation as to why this is the case, but it is conjectured that because most modern societies are themselves male dominated then most illnesses of the brain will come as a result of the unnatural enforcement of the brain to operate predominantly on the left side rather than in a balanced way.

The question then arises as to what would be the right and left brain strategies that are needed not only for survival, but for our continuance and evolution?

It seems that both pathways of the brain will need to collaborate to cause / allow the next stage of human evolution. This applies equally at individual, societal and global level. Either it will all work together in an integrated way or it will fail.

It is not certain that the brain can understand itself, but perhaps it can understand what it is for and how it can best be put to use for now and into the future. Could it be that the human brain is hard wired to receive the future but that in order to do so it needs to have the right configurations and the right connections? It seems that genius is not about discovering something new, but rather allowing something that already exists to appear.

That is what this chapter about Quantum Evolution is all about.

IT'S ALL ABOUT THE GAPS

Darwin's theory of evolution doesn't, as some of his followers suggest, explain everything about the speed of evolution and the changes that have occurred. Many mathematical models have been constructed to try and calculate how long it would have taken life to appear on the planet, and to then evolve into the human form of today. The odds of this happening within the time scales involved are astronomical.

The most revealing aspects about Darwin's theory are not about the theory itself, but the gaps in it and the unexplained leaps that have taken place throughout the course of history. It has become clear to scientists that evolution is not just a plodding progression of many small changes over a long period of time leading to the differentiation of species.

What is important here is the fact that evolution does not proceed according to regular increments or according to predefined patterns of behaviour. It proceeds in leaps and bounds and is clearly subject to forces and powers that govern the process of change and adaptation.

What is meant by 'quantum' in this context is that the amount of evolution coming out of the system can't be explained by the amount of energy going into it. The progress made is disproportionate to what one expects according to rational projections of what is known.

Evolution has proceeded not in a linear progression but by surges, and the rate of this quantum change seems to be accelerating. The statistics for changes in the last 300 years, from population to economics to travel to use of the Earth's resources to food production and so on, provides evidence that the evolution currently occurring exists within a spiral of exponential change.

The amount of knowledge, information, technology, science, communication available today compared to 300 years ago is simply staggering. Then it would take weeks or months for news to travel across the globe. Now it is effectively instantaneous with satellites, cables, the internet, and so forth.

Globalisation is a reality not a dream.

Humans face a quantum leap where the next phase of human and planetary evolution is concerned. Yet the difference about this next quantum leap is that for the first time humans themselves are the major players and deciders in respect of what direction it will proceed. Previously the prime influence and driver in the changes to the planetary ecology have been external to human beings.

With the last big surge being at the time of the Industrial Revolution (as opposed to *evolution*) most of that new energy was used for economic and selfish purposes. The consequence of that process is that humans face many of the problems in the world today that they do. In effect humans elected to choose Unnatural Selection as the next step forward for since that time they have undertaken many processes to literally undermine their own prospects for success as a species.

Because humans have attempted to defy the laws of nature this has led to them being in a weaker position to respond to the natural progression of planetary and universal evolution.

On top of that humans are faced with another tidal surge of incoming energy from the Universe. Yet they appear not to be ready for it because of their compounded failure to respond truly and naturally to previous waves.

A CRAWL OR A LEAP?

This quantum leap is to do with not surging ever more outwards and away from ourselves, but inward to find the true pedigree of the human race's purpose. It is a leap of consciousness not conquest that is trying to happen, and many are finding themselves drawn to this light in ways that they themselves do not necessarily understand.

This is the way that quantum evolution works – by driving impulse and compulsion. This is the migration that is beginning to occur from the simple reality that things can and must change. When the Wildebeest cross the savannahs of Africa on their migratory journey there is no question of a decision being made, it is a subpoena from an unseen force that is far stronger than their ability to resist it.

There is much talk today in the world of entering a New Age of Enlightenment, the Age of Aquarius, a new 2,000 year Great Cycle, and so on. Whatever one may wish to call it, the fact is that many are feeling the early signs of such a signal. The influence of great events always cast their shadows before them. The jittery feelings humans may have about the future are therefore healthy, for they herald a sense of change and upgrade.

Fear may cause some to freeze, but faith and trust in the great unknown will persuade many to take the great leap needed. This trust was brilliantly illustrated in the third of the Indiana Jones films when, in search of the Holy Grail, Indy has to believe that there is a path across the great abyss in front of him. As he takes this leap of faith the previously invisible path appears beneath his feet.

This very much applies to the human race's own situation, for it cannot go back to what was for it is no longer there. It cannot go forward with the ways that got it here for they are no longer in season and perhaps never were. It has to go forward in a different way and needs to discover that way on the journey together.

The highest point of choice in this is to admit that there is no choice and instead to surrender to the living process of discovery.

The future offers sublime opportunities for one and all if humans can but rise out from their current story into the one currently being written with themselves as intended co-authors.

The fuel for this quantum leap lies in the fact that the real change that is onsetting is one of global consciousness and awareness. This calls for people to abandon parochialism and vested interest and see that the greater good lies in the greater cause.

Is it going to happen or is it a romantic New Age dream?

It is already happening; the question is can a person be part of it?

To which the answer is: yes, if they want to be.

Finally in this chapter it seems that evolution is not just something that an organism does, but it is a change driven subpoena because change is the only constant within the Universe. Evolution seems to have two types of inherent processes. These are: -

1.   The development of new systems to meet new challenges
2.   The shedding of old systems that no longer fit and prevent progression.

In this regard the reader is invited to consider for themselves just what are the new systems needed and the redundant old systems, both in relation to their own personal evolution and also in respect of our future as a species?

Having made conscious the need, who knows what may then be possible?

When things draw near or happen now, our
minds are useless. Without the words of others
we can know nothing of your human state.
Thus it follows that all our knowledge will perish at
the very moment the portals of the future close.

Dante's Inferno

Footfalls echo in the memory
Down the passage which we did not take
Towards the door we never opened.

T.S. Eliot

Life must be understood backwards;
but it must be lived forward.

Soren Kierkegaard

THE MEMORY OF
BEING HUMAN

THE TITLE OF THIS CHAPTER is inspired in part by recent research into whether or not water has a memory. This research is controversial to say the least, and often in such issues the agenda can become more about the person than the subject matter. It seems that scientists often have great difficulty maintaining their much vaunted objectivity when talking about other scientists!

The scientist in question was a Frenchman called Jacques Benveniste (who died in 2004). His early experiments suggested that water could 'remember' substances it had come into contact with, even if these other substances had been completely distilled out of the water. The water therefore seemed to have some kind of 'memory'. Whilst the early experiments were not conclusive it was an exciting idea worth pursuing - until politics got in the way.

What happened was that many mainstream scientists regarded Benveniste as running an agenda of trying to prove that homeopathy was a valid science. This in effect was what his experiments were alleging because his findings tended to support the homeopathic principle that lesser dilutions were more powerful in their effects than stronger ones. Benveniste himself, however, was at the time unaware of this homeopathic principle and was simply trying to understand how and why he had obtained the results he had.

His tentative conclusion was that water somehow had the ability to remember what it had come into contact with and that it could not only store the information, but it could also transfer that information onwards. This caused a furore at the time and Benveniste's scientific credentials were attacked. In effect, he was scientifically blacklisted.

However, he managed to continue his work for the rest of his life with some fascinating findings and insights into how water and other substances store information about the things they have come into contact with.

Whilst the hypothesis that water has a memory remains unproven the concept remains worthy of further exploration, especially if the principle is extended to the human condition.

The conjecture here is that whilst humans may have distilled out of their behaviour many higher qualities that constitute Being Human, nevertheless they have a memory of it somewhere in their DNA, psyche and collective unconscious. This can cause them to remember who and what they really are and behave in a more fitting way.

People today largely live in a culture of doing, acquiring, getting, controlling, owning, extending, consuming, building, improving, elaborating, perfecting, possessing, competing, securing, dividing and so on. The one word that is used to describe this process is apparently *progress*.

People feel they have to try to get ahead, and that if they are left behind then the maxim of 'the Devil takes the hindmost' applies. If they want to avoid this scenario then they have to be driven in a dog eat dog kind of way.

Inside of all this it seems that humans have forgotten something quite fundamental and important, that is: who and what they are, why they are here, what is their role, and what does it mean to be human?

In the absence of the thesis aspects of Being Human, the negative energy of such things as competition, greed, hate, cruelty, torture, selfishness, slavery, exploitation, oppression, subjugation and so on take precedence.

This process is brilliantly satirised in the film *Wall Street* by the character Gordon Gecko (played by Michael Douglas). In a speech to shareholders Gecko plays on their fear of missing out on making a large profit by addressing the issue head on. He states that greed is good, greed clarifies, and greed is what makes the wheels of business and the economy turn. This fact he says should be embraced and accepted for what it is, for it is the means by which the end is justified. He succeeds in winning the shareholders over, although in true Hollywood style he gets his come-uppance at the end of the film!

The point here is that all this doing and getting has caused humans to forget who and what they really are. Within the seeds of what many might regard as being evidence of the brilliant success of modern culture, the truth is that unless people remember who and what they are then those attitudes contain the seeds for a spectacular demise. History is full of examples of this rise and fall process, and the common symptom that always causes demise is that the culture in question always gets ahead of itself and thereby becomes unsustainable.

In other words, demand outstrips supply to such a degree that it becomes no longer viable and therefore collapses. The evidence that the human race is facing such a scenario now is overwhelming. Vested interest will try and hide and even deny the truth, but when the tide is coming in there is nothing anyone can say or do to prevent that fact as King Canute ably demonstrated to his sycophantic followers. It is therefore best to admit to the reality of the situation and to then respond as needed.

History repeats itself for those who do not learn its lessons.

This is not saying that the present is without merit and that the past is all romantic and nice and people should pine for living in caves and communing with nature. Rather it is saying that over time, to different degrees, the human race has lost its way.

To look at it another way, if people do take heed and change direction and channel all this doing energy in a more creative way then the future has amazing possibilities.

This memory of Being Human is not something that was there once and gradually got lost until it disappeared completely. It is always there somewhere, with its influence strong at certain times and places and weaker in others. Today it has mostly weakened but is something that the human race needs to make much more conscious in order to help find the way forward into the future safely and carefully.

There are two types of memory - episodic and semantic - and it seems that both have been somewhat faulty in their recall of our history.

Episodic memory is to do with recalling what has happened and could be associated with the left side of the brain. It remembers the events that have happened. One would think that this literal memory would be fairly accurate, but that is not the case for no two people have the same recollection of what may have happened. As things get passed down the generations these 'facts' can become elaborated upon, enhanced, deleted or ignored altogether to suit the view of whichever party is looking at those facts.

Semantic memory is to do with giving meaning to the events themselves. It gives them context and significance and interprets them according to the values of those who are looking at them. This means that all events are open to interpretation and 'spin' because bias is a much harder thing to avoid than most people may care to admit.

The true use of both of these types of memory together can lead to an incredible breakthrough in relation to the truth of the human journey so far, the situation we find ourselves to be in today and the future as it is currently unknown but soon to be known.

Perhaps these two aspects of the memory can tell us if we ask the right questions, for example:

What is the truth of our situation?

What is the significance of being human beings and what is that calling for?

For if we don't remember our pedigree how can we come from it in making key decisions about the future?

?

All the world's a stage,
And all the men and women merely players:
They have their exits and their entrances;
And one man in his time plays many parts,

William Shakespeare

Famous men have the whole Earth as their memorial.

Pericles

EPIGENETICS

IN RECENT YEARS THERE HAS been much research into genetic and evolutionary theory, especially in relation to human DNA and what characteristics people inherit and how.

The genetic code of DNA is made up of the letters ACGT, and the various gene patterns and combinations of these letters cover everything from eye colour to height to genetic disorders and inherited diseases. Until recently it was thought that DNA was a fixed physical structure and what a person inherited physically was what they got - end of story.

Before the human genome project it was thought that humans had approximately 100,000 genes. Scientists are now of the view that there are far fewer genes and that the number is more likely to be in the order of only 30,000. This has prompted surprise and has caused scientists to wonder how, if there are fewer genes, all the information that is inherited can be passed on?

This is where the study of Epigenetics applies, for what is being referred to here is the study of *heritable* changes in gene function that occur without a change in the sequence of nuclear DNA. This includes the study of how environmental factors affecting a parent can result in changes in the way they are expressed in the offspring.

What is meant is that it seems that the genetic coding of humans remembers what has happened to it and this information can be passed on to subsequent generations, even though the physical structure of the DNA itself does not appear to have been changed in any way whatsoever. This 'memory' can be passed on and the effects made manifest in future generations, even though these generations themselves have no direct experience of the environmental factors that triggered the symptoms in the earlier generation that experienced it.

This process has scientists both baffled and intrigued for it seems to defy all previous ideas of genetic inheritance. This suggests that not only is there a *seen* aspect of inheritance, which scientists now have a much better understanding of since the genetic sequencing made possible by the human genome project, but there also seems to be an *unseen* part to inheritance.

This links closely to the previous chapter where it seems that water has a memory of what happened to it even though the cause of that memory has been removed from the water's physical processes.

It also extends the whole research into the relationship between nature and nurture beyond simply what happens to individuals in their own life and into the genetic world as well, in that it may be possible for nurture aspects to be inherited as well as nature ones.

REMEMBERING THINGS BEYOND ONESELF

If true, this is a radical breakthrough in understanding for it suggests that things like attitudes and beliefs can be inherited as much as the colour of one's hair. This then poses questions for human beings as to which attitudes are dominant and which are recessive as well as which ones are useful and which ones are not?

Unlike the physically inherited sequences, it seems that humans can choose, at least to a degree, which attitudes they wish to be dominant and which ones they wish to be recessive. This may be unconscious, but nevertheless the evidence seems to support this hypothesis.

As human beings have evolved and become more modern, their attitudes have changed and mutated. In particular, the attitude human beings have to nature and how they relate to it. The dominant attitude that has appeared has become one of controlling or overcoming nature rather than working with nature in an organic and symbiotic way. The gene that perceives humans as being a part of nature and having to work sympathetically with nature and all other forms of life within it seems to have become recessive and is in danger of becoming extinct.

Like water, even if this attitude is diluted out of the human genetic it can still be remembered and therefore reactivated. This is what is happening as more and more people begin to wake up to the reality of what kind of legacy they wish to leave for future generations in terms of our relationship with the planet.

Epigenetics suggests that not only is it important to consider what kind of physical environment is left for future generations, but also what kind of internal moral and spiritual environment is left as well. It seems that the internal one is far more important and powerful than the external one, for the external one is simply an outplay of the internal one.

What is also interesting is that it seems the most powerful time of 'printing' for the next generation of these unseen genetic influences is different for boys and girls. In girls it is when they are in the womb, and for boys it is when they are just entering puberty. The key point here is that for both it is when their sexual reproductive abilities are put in place – for girls their eggs appear in the womb although they can't be fertilised until after puberty onsets, and for boys it is when they enter puberty and begin production of sperm.

This suggests that these ages are very important, for both genders and the societies that they live in need to consider what kind of impressions their children should receive at these times. It is now well established that babies in the womb receive and process many signals from outside and are printed by them.

In boys their teenage years are pivotal and rites of passage ceremonies in many cultures mark the transition from boyhood to manhood. At this age boys need to become aware of their increasing power but also the need for responsible use of that power at personal, social and planetary level. If these forces are not harnessed in a purposeful way at this time then they can run out of control later on during their adult years.

These times should be an opportunity for the child to be printed with positive impressions of who and what they are, the value others have for them, the role they can play within the world and the challenges and opportunities that lie ahead of them.

If attitudes, and indeed feelings, can be inherited then the elders of society need to take responsibility in how they print and code their children as far as values are concerned. Mostly this goes on anyway, it is just that what has become dominant in terms of what is important has become misaligned in many cultures.

What needs to emerge is the sense of awe, wonder and responsibility that people feel about being alive and the part that they can play in making changes for the better for the future.

CHAINS AND SEQUENCES

This means changing human genetic structure through choice by what people think, feel and do. This is quite an extraordinary concept for it lifts evolution out of simply being natural selection, according to the physical environment that people find themselves in, to a higher level where people can naturally select what attitudes and qualities they wish their descendants to inherit.

If this is right and these qualities and attributes become increasingly dominant, they will naturally become ever more powerful and influential as the next generations appear. This then makes evolution both conscious and voluntary.

Accordingly, a person can change the future simply by how they think about it. This concept is not an entirely new one for many cultures have had something similar within their processes and decision making. For example, when faced with important decisions some American Indian tribes ask themselves how the decisions they are about to make will affect not just themselves but, more importantly, those who will be living in 7 generations' time.

This is something that the current generation could usefully adopt when facing some of the crucial decisions that need to be made. This can only help to shift the balance of the genetic footprint from being an external one of a worsening legacy to an internal one of rebalance and realignment to what is really important.

Epigenetics says that humans can engage in the process of evolution in a much more constructive and purposeful way than perhaps they thought possible. Whilst they may not see the full fruits of these changes in their own lifetime, nevertheless the unseen powers and forces that they initiate now can change the tide of human history for the better.

Originally Epigenetics was regarded as being strictly a biological process, but now it is extended to include the relationship of an organism with its environment as well as its heredity. Therefore, in thinking about the future, this suggests that we could usefully ask ourselves: -

1.   Just what do we see our heredity to be? Is it just all down
      to Darwinian natural selection and DNA or is it something
      more?
2.   What do we see our environment to be? Is it just the land,
      the sea and the sky, or do we take into account the moral,
      ethical and spiritual landscape as well?

How we answer these questions will define how we think of ourselves and will decide what kind of road map we will lay down where the future is concerned. To avoid them will mean we will go into the unknown with no map at all.

Perhaps now is the time for the human race to become the first species on the Planet to escape the law of Natural Selection by consciously dropping the 'S' and thereby elevating into their next level. Natural Election suggests the freedom to be what one elects and not be subject to the carnal only dominance of what has been.

WHAT'S YOUR BAG MAN?

Way back in the 50's and 60's the phrase, "What's your bag, man?" was a real catch cry amongst the cool and the hip. Perhaps in the spirit of this chapter the question could be updated to ask: "What's *in* your Bag, man?"

In a world of politicians who are all concerned with their legacy, perhaps we can consider the word BAG in a specific way to consider the legacy issues we ALL face?

As humans we all carry the weight of human history in our individual and collective DNA. So BAG could be seen in this context to mean, by acronym:

Baggage
And
Genius

The baggage is the unfortunate things we have done as a species that have jeopardised our future. We all carry a connection to, and a responsibility for, that part of ourselves, whether we like it or not. We can't claim; "But, I wasn't there," because the fact of the matter is that part of us *was* there.

Denial is part of the baggage. Acceptance of personal and collective responsibility is part of the redemption.

We can therefore let go of some of that baggage by deciding that those unfortunate aspects of what we have become shall no longer be a living part of our DNA.

If we can rise to this challenge and jettison enough of the baggage that we have all been lumbered with, then all we are left with is the genius of the human story - and what a story! Human history, and therefore our DNA, is full of sequins of brilliance and shining examples of what works, what makes life better, and what the future needs.

We carry this formula for success in our genetic coding as an unseen, latent potency that awaits recognition and activation. We therefore need to take individual and collective responsibility for this genius aspect of ourselves just as much as we do for the baggage side.

A person might, when confronted with the weight of this responsibility, cry: "Who me, a genius? I don't think so."

The counter to this argument is easy to find, for within each person's DNA is clear evidence of genius. After all, everyone's ancestors have, despite all the odds, survived and flourished over countless thousands of years to produce – you! They were all clearly geniuses of one kind or another because countless others didn't survive.

We all have, as Epigenetics suggests, an unseen part of ourselves that can, if activated, offer the future a better option rather than a lesser one. Finding this part of ourselves and living it ought to be a new dictionary definition of genius.

With this in mind, what is *your* story?

And in particular, what is the plot of this story and what is the main character like?

A Liar ought to have a good memory.

Quintillian

He who knows himself is enlightened.

Lao Tzu

TOTAL RECALL

THIS CHAPTER BORROWS ITS TITLE from the Arnold Schwarzenegger film of the same name. In brief, it is the story of a man in the future who has his mind stolen without his knowledge and then his quest to find out who he really is and how he can get his identity back again.

The analogy to the human situation of today is clear to see. The human race has had its true identity stolen and, just like the character in the film, they have been happily living a ghost life thinking that it is their actual life.

Yet, just like the character in the film, the human race still carries vestiges of memory that knows who and what they really are.

Similarly, each person has within their memory banks feelings, knowings and recall of every single thing that has ever happened to them in their life. Luckily, they are mostly kept in storage awaiting retrieval, for the person would not be able to handle the flood of impressions caused by remembering every single event that ever happened all at the same time.

These memories await recall as needed, although sometimes they simply pop up for no apparent reason. It's a bit like a computer where sometimes a button is pushed on the keyboard and it causes something that has been stored in the memory of the computer to come back up on the screen. It may be something that has been stored for years while the person who put it in there has completely forgotten about it in their conscious memory.

This is why sometimes people suddenly recall something that happened to them when they were 5 or 6 years old.

The understanding of this process lies in the fact that events themselves cannot be destroyed and the print of them is lodged both in the person and in what Jung called the 'collective unconscious'. The print of these events can be superimposed over or relegated out from conscious experience, but they cannot be destroyed and therefore can be reactivated. This is why people can return to places of extreme emotion or feeling in their lives and the mere fact of being there again can reactivate the same feelings that the person may have felt many years earlier.

Could this principle also apply to the human race as a species and continue across generations? In other words, is it possible for the memory of certain things to be passed on to the next generation, even though that next generation may themselves have had no direct experience of the 'memory' being passed on?

This may well be the case, for the instinct of humans seems able to pass things on down the generations. For example, there seems to have evolved in humans an in born fear of snakes and spiders. This is because many of them are highly poisonous and humans somehow have within their psyche a deeply engraved alarm where such creatures are concerned. This is not a learned response but an instinctive one.

This concept is now well accepted in genetics, although scientists are not yet sure how it gets passed on. This genetic passing on of instinctive responses also applies to many other animals.

If this principle of passing on such rudimentary, but vital for survival, information is via the instinct and some genetic mutation, could it also apply at a higher level as well?

Is there something locked up within human beings that could tell them the reason for their existence and cause them to modify their behaviour accordingly? Could this lie deep within the memory banks of each and every person, waiting to be reawakened?

A CODED MEMORY

In the spirit of *Total Recall* could the very reason and premise of existence have existed in the very moment of Creation - and if so did

Creation put it there? At times different individuals and groups seem to have got close to this reason and purpose during the human race's evolving journey of consciousness.

Humans can choose to remember who and what they are or they can forget. What they choose has consequences in terms of their behaviour. The trace of world history is mostly evidence of the fact that humans have largely forgotten their true pedigree, for how else can war, disease, famine, greed, slavery, torture and cruelty be explained?

However, they can just as easily choose to remember, for although it may now be mostly subliminal and unconscious, it is nevertheless the most primal of feelings that humans can have. It exists not just in their carnal level of existence, but in the more evolved yet ethereal higher parts of themselves – their soul and spirit.

Each human cell has within it the Total Recall of how, where and why it was created and it knows what purpose it has to serve inside a greater purpose. A liver cell knows through cell differentiation just what it has to do as part of the liver function, but its primary higher purpose is to help keep the person alive and well.

Perhaps the same principle applies to humans as being cells within a higher intelligence? Unless they can remember why they exist they will become disconnected and, by analogy, cancerous.

If, on the other hand, they begin to remember their true function they can have total recall of their true, natural identity and restore themselves to a life of meaning and promise rather than adopting a false persona based on misguided choices.

If humans remember who and what they are and where they have come from then perhaps they might also remember the future?

If any question why we died;
Tell them because our fathers lied.

Rudyard Kipling

We are what we believe we are.

C S Lewis

Rescue From
Abandonment

BECAUSE OF THE WAY AND style of modern living human beings
have adopted, the human body has largely been forced to abandon or
let fall into atrophy many of its natural primary systems. Not only has
the use of such systems - such as smell, hearing, taste, sight and touch
- become weakened, but many others as well operate at much lower
levels of performance than they are capable of.

Part of the reason for this is that many of the things humans have
to deal with today are extremely toxic and damaging to these natural
systems. Post Industrial Revolution city living doesn't require these
systems to work in the same way as living in natural environments does.

City living is a very recent development, where human beings are
concerned, with the oldest known examples of city type living probably
dating back no more than 15,000 years, and more likely to be in the
order of 10,000 years. This time lapse is tiny in terms of the life of the
planet, or indeed the appearance of the human model in its current
form. Therefore humans have not yet fully adapted to such living
circumstances, and perhaps never truly will.

Some adaptation to this way of life has however occurred, for city life
doesn't require certain senses to work in the same way as they do in natural
ecologies; indeed some of them are shut down by this process of urban living.

Not only does this relate to what was called the primary senses
mentioned above, but also higher systems such as intuition, instinct,

clairvoyance, telepathy, knowing, dowsing, healing and so on. Modern humans have often abandoned many of these higher systems to such a degree that they no longer even believe that they have them. And if you don't believe you have them then you won't!

As a result of this disbelief they often test these higher faculties in laboratories to see whether they exist or not. This is rather bizarre considering the fact that these higher systems evolved in natural ecologies and not artificial ones like those that exist in a laboratory. Unless some new discovery has been made recently, there aren't chemical formulas for empathy, compassion and love.

INDUCTION OF NEW SYSTEMS

The trace of this can be seen throughout the course of history, and here some examples will endeavour to illustrate the point.

Prior to the 14th century artists couldn't really paint in perspective, so the paintings they drew reflected life as they saw it but were subject to their ability to convey the images they saw onto canvas. Suddenly with the development of the ability to draw in perspective a new dimension of art was literally revealed.

When Captain Cook visited the Polynesian Islands for the first time he moored his large boat off the coast and rowed ashore to meet the natives. The islanders considered Cook and his men to be Gods as they thought they had rowed to the island out of thin air. The reason for this was that the islanders couldn't see the main ship. Because they had no pattern in their brains to enable them to form such a picture their brains refused to 'see' the boat. Even when Cook landed and pointed to the easily discernible boat just off the shore, still the natives could not see it. It was only when they were taken out to touch the boat that their brains allowed them to see it.

When Lawrence of Arabia wanted to celebrate a victory he had portraits painted of the important sheiks that had assisted him in the battle. He then gave them the portraits as presents. Because they had never seen paintings before the sheiks had no reference for blobs of paint actually representing portraits and therefore to them it was just paint on paper. They could see no form within the painting even though the pictures were very clear likenesses of them. Even when someone pointed out the various features within the painting they still could not see them.

This suggests that throughout human history new systems of intelligence and cognisance have appeared and evolved and these give permission for things to be seen in a different way to how they were previously seen. An example is the long held perception that because the Earth seemed to be relatively stable it was assumed that everything else must move in relation to the Earth; therefore the Earth must be at the centre of the Solar System.

This then became an article of faith and even a point of religious dogma. It was not until sufficient evidence and empirical proof was obtained that the Earth revolved around the Sun that the existing theory could be changed.

Much of the reason for this abandonment and atrophying of human faculty acumen comes down to the fact that ever increasingly humans place reliance for assessing truth on things outside of themselves. Machines do more and more of what human beings used to do for themselves. The more this happens the more the previously used human faculty becomes redundant due to lack of usage. As the saying goes, "If you don't use it you lose it."

Before long machines will be falling in love with other machines on behalf of their owners! In a way this already happens, with such things as computer dating agencies and the like, where supposed perfect matches are found by computer profile and analysis.

Human beings have begun to dangerously evolve away from using their natural systems and increasingly rely on unnatural ones instead. At this rate human beings will build a total dependency upon such machines and things external to themselves. They already have all the systems they need because nature gave them to them. These primary systems are ultimately much more reliable than the secondary external ones for they have evolved over millions of years.

These systems need to be rescued and put back into service for they are an integral part of the navigation system needed if human beings are to safely and bravely find their way into the future.

As a curio, is it merely coincidence that *rescue* anagrams to *secure* and if not why not?

?

Change is the law of life. And those who look only to
the past or present are certain to miss the future.

John F Kennedy

Live your life as though your every act
were to become a universal law.

Immanuel Kant

PROJECTION

THIS CHAPTER HAS SOMETHING OF a Jekyll and Hyde nature about it, for it contains both fortunate and unfortunate aspects at the same time.

The unfortunate aspects stem from the realms of Psychology and what is called the Projection Complex. In this a person projects onto others the blame for the situation they end up in. This applies to parents, teachers, siblings, friends, family, employers, the government or anyone else who influences the person's situation.

In this the responsibility lies with everyone else except the person themselves, for to admit that they may be responsible for their situation is too big a pill to swallow.

This complex is based in the ego and stems from feelings of inadequacy and the need to rationalise these feelings by externalising the causes of the situation a person finds themselves to be in.

It may be that others have indeed made the person's life difficult, but in the rationalisation process this is carried to an extreme position whereby the person claims that they are the innocent victim of the state of affairs. Mostly this is not true and the person is a free agent to change their situation, should they wish to do so, but they choose not to. They would rather blame others and this serves the double purpose of also masking their own feelings of shortfall or inadequacy.

In extreme cases this can cause pathological behaviour in the person and even paranoia.

This was the case with Adolf Hitler. He developed a pathological and obsessive relationship with his mother and this in turn developed into a full-blown Oedipus complex. This was further powered by the fact that he had an overbearing and bullying father. Hitler tried to suppress or hide this complex but in trying to do so he only made it worse. Hitler was notorious for his violent mood swings, and his rages were extremely explosive and his sado-masochistic tendencies have been well documented.

These violent mood swings caused Hitler to alternate between self-loathing on the one hand and megalomania with a sense of messianic destiny on the other.

The self-loathing side of this projection complex carries a sense of never quite being good enough. In such circumstances a person then seeks to blame others for these feelings.

Usually this relates to others in a person's immediate circle, such as family and peers, but in Hitler's case this involved world power politics so this complex escalated to monumental proportions in the Final Solution where over 6 million Jews were killed.

It is not being claimed that Hitler's projection complex was the only cause of this policy, but it certainly was a part of it. A projection complex involves a person not feeling clean about themselves and this in turn can develop into Obsessive Compulsive Disorder (OCD) where in extreme cases a person feels so unclean they have to wash their hands literally hundreds of times a day.

In Hitler's case he looked around for reasons as to why he felt dirty, for he himself was not of pure Aryan stock but of mixed and mostly lowly stock. In searching for a scapegoat he blamed the Jews for diluting and polluting the purity of the Aryan line.

It is astounding to think that much of the tragedy and infamy of the Second World War might result largely from a single individual's Oedipus and Projection complexes, but there is much evidence to indicate that this is true.

The case of Hitler is an extreme example, yet many people do something similar albeit smaller way. Nevertheless the damage caused to self and to others can be substantial.

WE ARE AS WE ARE

The main cause of this syndrome is that a person is usually in some form of denial that they have turned out the way they have because of certain decisions they have made. Yes, they may have had unfortunate experiences that have fashioned and printed them in certain ways, but as an adult they can either be a victim of those experiences (which leads to the Projection Complex) or they can use those experiences as a lever into forming a better self.

Failure to take responsibility for one's attitude and behaviour leads to the classic symptoms of blame, bitterness, self-loathing and hatred. These are not qualities that can in any way help a person build any kind of true picture of who and what they really are. All they can see is what is wrong with them, and as they are not prepared to accept responsibility for this they need to project blame onto others. The more they do this the worse the feelings get and the more they need to project the blame onto others. This eventually leads to some kind of explosion.

The way out of this downward spiral is to look at other meanings of the word 'projection'. These include 'a plan or forecast', and also 'momentum'. Both aspects are crucial in finding a pathway into the future.

First it means choosing to project a different kind of energy that counters any negative feelings that may appear to be justified, but are in a deeper sense not useful or constructive. Nelson Mandela was once asked if in his 27 years as a prisoner in South Africa he ever hated the guards that oppressed him. He replied that he did not hate them because if he did so then that would prove they had won. His refusal to blame and hate them shows that he took responsibility not only for his actions, but also for his state of mind and what he would and wouldn't project on to other people as a result of that situation.

He realised that his conduct and actions in response to the Apartheid regime carried certain consequences if he was caught, so he accepted those consequences with humanity and dignity without becoming bitter or judgmental upon others about it.

This is a shining example of how to avoid developing a projection complex; by taking ownership of one's life and deciding what kind of person one wants to be rather than being formed into something lesser. Great people don't avoid or deny the bad things that happen in their lives; they harness them to forge themselves into something better. The fuel in this process is the reason *why* the person would take these things on in themselves and form something better from it.

LIFE AS A PROJECT

The next aspect of projection is the conscious decision to choose to project generative and constructive things towards other people. Anything lesser is conditional and is based in a form of negative projection and powered by fear.

To project good things about others again requires willpower. It also leaves the person free to be themselves for they are not dependant upon what others think about them in how they behave. They choose to be warm, kind and generous because they want to, not because they think they should or that they will get some kind of benefit out of it.

In this the keyword is *genuineness*.

This speaks of personal work done on self, acceptance of how things are and deciding to generate better things than what one may have personally suffered.

A recent example of this occurred when a young Palestinian boy was killed in the crossfire between opposing forces. After his death his parents asked for his organs to be donated to other people who needed transplants. In fact some of his organs went to Palestinians and some to Israelis. When asked why they allowed their son's organs to go to Israelis when it was an Israeli bullet that had killed their son they replied that they simply wanted their son to be remembered as someone who had helped save the lives of others, regardless of their colour, creed or religion.

Such actions dwarf the platitudes spoken by politicians and transcend the problems the human race suffers, elevating the human condition to a higher plane.

This is the art of conscious projection.

This in turn links to the other meaning of 'projection', which is to do with movement.

Movement is two things in one: every movement involves movement *towards* something and movement *away* from something else. This is an obvious yet extremely profound truth, and makes conscious choice about what one projects from self onto others vitally important.

What one projects towards others (or self) moves them and it either moves them closer towards themselves or further away. Usually when unfortunate things are caused to self by others then the tendency is to adopt the 'an eye for an eye' stance, but this only ends up with everyone becoming blind.

To respond at the same or lower level is in fact a sign of lesser development and can only power a person's projection complex in a compounding way.

Ultimately the best way to avoid getting hit by these 'bombs' is to be somewhere other than where they go off, for in that case they can't hurt the person.

This is not a projection *complex*.

It is rather a projection *simple*.

It is the outer complexity of living life today that causes people to fail to see the true simplicity of how they can consciously be an agent for good things in the world, for others and for self.

The maxim of 'do unto others as you would have them do unto you' is one that encapsulates this principle exactly.

The evidence suggests that, despite its simplicity, most people do not enact it, for the world is full of difference. Because of this fact mostly people do unto others in seeking to get an advantage.

Ultimately this is self-defeating for a person because doing unto others is ultimately doing unto self, for what goes around comes around. If they are projecting gain over another then they are coming from the lesser of themselves and that investment will in turn be returned with interest, i.e. a greater self-diminishment.

Mostly people don't realise that this is how the principle of 'do unto others as you would have them do unto you' works in reverse. They would rather interpret the saying as being, 'do unto others so that you can gain an advantage over them.' This causes them to think that in order to get what they want they somehow have to win over the other person.

This leads to a selective morality where the principle of 'do unto others as you would have them do unto you' is something that *everyone else* should sign up to, but somehow the person are an exception. This is because they are more important than all the others.

A world full of such exceptions is an unexceptional place.

No Need To Be A Threat

When the principle of do unto others as you would have them do unto you is truly and fully applied then the world and its people are truly emancipated, for if everyone does unto others as they would have them do unto them then many of the world's problems would literally evaporate.

This is in itself a projection but not one that is unknown to the human race; it is simply one that has largely become forgotten in the civilisation era of the human story. In this period of incredible technological advancement somehow the projections and priorities changed from being integrated and compassionate social groups to disparate and divided ones.

This, coupled with the exponential growth in the human population since the Industrial Revolution, and especially in the last 100 years, means that the perception is that there isn't enough to go round. This projection is true as long as people see others as a threat and hoard and withhold from others whilst expecting the others to share what they have.

It is not a lack of resources that threatens the human race's future the most, but rather selfishness. The culture of 'me first, me last and any more me again' is one that places the long-term future of our species in serious peril. The only projection that can come out of any such attitude is that sooner rather than later resources will run out, and the more they look like running out the more will have to be invested in protecting one's so-called rights to these resources, i.e. military action.

If people project to share and develop the resources and know-how they have, then the irony is that there's is plenty to go round. As a starter, with the USA spending about $400 billion per year on its military budget, think what could be achieved if this and the other military budgets were applied in a constructive and positive way rather than in a negative and destructive way. Quite a lot!

The additional irony is that such military budgets are called *Defence* spending. It is *Attack* spending, no matter how politicians try and justify it in terms of the threat posed by other hostile states or terrorist organisations. For if everyone is defending then who the heck is doing all the attacking? As Ghandi said: 'You can't shake hands with a clenched fist.'

It is accepted that some of these so called 'others' do sometimes pose a genuine threat due to their own projection complexes and that the world, as a result of this, is often an unsafe place. The solution however doesn't lie in the long-term escalation of the means of warfare, but rather in understanding the reasons for these fears and developing ways of working around them.

Perhaps the next model of evolution that may apply to human beings is evolution by co-operation, not evolution by random mutation as some Neo Darwinists would have us believe?

This is not a foreign concept, for most successful species work by this method in some shape or form otherwise they would become extinct. Nature is full of examples of inter-species co-operation or symbiosis - where the relationship benefits both parties.

Modern societies seem to eschew or are suspicious of this process. That is the wrong projection. The correct and most successful projection would seem to be to share what you have before it runs out!

What, therefore would be the first thing you would want to share to ensure that you don't lose it?

THE FUTURE OF THE UNIVERSE

Space: The continual becoming: invisible fountain
from which all rhythms flow and to which
they must pass. Beyond time or infinity.

Frank Lloyd Wright

For me, it is far better to grasp the Universe as it really is than
to persist in delusion, however satisfying and reassuring.

Carl Sagan

SPACE – THE FINAL FRONTIER

WITH THANKS TO GENE RODDENBERRY and the *Star Trek* crew, this chapter takes its title from the catch-phrase from the series. *Star Trek* bases itself on the premise of exploring Outer Space and to "boldly go where no man has gone before." This is exactly what the human race as a species has begun to do in relatively recent times.

It is only just over 100 years since mankind witnessed the first powered flight of the Wright brothers at Kittyhawk. My home country, New Zealand, does however claim that a certain Richard Pearse may have flown before them - but that is another story!

Since that time the progression has been truly phenomenal. As a separate and identifiable species, humans have existed in their current recognisable form for perhaps 3 million years. For all of that time, except for the last 100 years, they have been totally earthbound and grounded by the laws of gravity.

Yet in the last 100 years humans have been able to design machines that are powerful enough to overcome the forces of nature and to escape the Earth's atmosphere. They are even able to land some of their number on Earth's nearest celestial neighbour - the Moon.

All of this has happened in the last 0.000333% of the time that human beings have existed in their current and recognisable form.

The pace at which this expanding of horizons has grown is simply breathtaking. Few people actually believed President John F Kennedy when he said in the early 1960's that there would be a person on the

Moon before the end of that decade, yet he was proved right when Apollo 11 landed on the Moon in July 1969.

The space programmes of the world continue apace with countless billions being spent on all sorts of missions allegedly to help us understand the Universe and how it works, whether there are other forms of life in the Universe, whether there are other planets that could prove habitable for human life and many other scientific experiments supposedly for the greater good.

The question in response to all of this has to be: *why?*

Perhaps there is something that we are missing here on Earth? Answers on a postcard please as to what that might actually be! The evidence suggests that nothing is actually missing, for all that we need is already here. It seems that everywhere else in the Universe, nearby at least, does not have what is essential in order for us to live so why all the hype and expense about it?

Whilst the quest goes on into *outer* Space, little is spoken about the possible journey into *inner* Space; for what might be hidden there for humans to find. After all, that is what human beings are fundamentally made up of – space.

Although people think and feel that they are very physical, the truth is that they are not. It is simply the electro-magnetic forces that make it seem that way, for they are made up of atoms that have physical properties due to their arrangements and interactions. To illustrate this in analogous terms, if a proton of Hydrogen was seen to be the size of a tennis ball placed in London then its electron would be in New York - nearly 3000 miles away!

Consider then how many atoms go to make up one human being. It is billions upon billions.

In real terms, the amount of actual physical matter in each and every person is less than the head of a pin. This seems impossible to believe because a human being feels so tangible and solid, yet that is simply the miraculous operation of all the forces and powers of nature that keep the space between the vast spaces in a stable holding pattern.

The inter-relationships between these forces are much more advanced and complex than any space craft engineering. What else could account for cell differentiation, specific organ function, hormone regulation and so much more when well over 99% of a human being is simply 'empty' space?

Clearly, the space within people is not empty it is simply mostly unexplored. The reason is that humans base the vast majority of their life experience in exploring the more physical aspects of things whereas the truth is that, in raw terms, they are made up mostly of forces, impulses, signals, waves, vibrations and impressions. None of those spaces within people are empty; they are highly charged and full of latent energy.

A RELATIVE JOURNEY

A far more important journey to undertake in relative terms than the one into Outer Space is therefore the one into Inner Space.

What unknown marvels and wonders lie hidden waiting to be discovered?

What talents, skills and abilities await people if they have a natural awe, wonder, belief and reverence for the design they have been given?

Perhaps people might see that they lack for nothing and need not look outside of themselves for solutions to problems which they have created by being on the outside of themselves in the first place.

What lies hidden within this last great unexplored continent? Perhaps everything that human beings need to push the right buttons that Mother Nature has given us. It does seem that nature has given humans a whole extra set of buttons in their evolutionary journey compared to other flora and fauna life. Unfortunately we have been playing around with some of those buttons in a rather reckless and wanton way and this has led us into the situation we now find ourselves to be in.

It seems that the pushing of the wrong buttons coincides with an evolutionary drive for the model and species to refine and develop. With the button of 'choice' – the most powerful one that humans have – has come the ability to divert from the true course of upgrade and spiritual evolution.

The first thing to do when pushing the wrong button is to stop pushing it! There is no point in pushing the button harder to try and get it to work differently. The button does what the button does, and if that button is not generative then it is best to desist from using it and find one that works better.

The evidence suggests that it can be done. There is no other way to explain the genius that has graced the human journey. It must be that Mozart simply found the music genius button in himself and found out how to push it in order to make such marvellous music. Michelangelo claimed that when carving a great statue all he was doing was removing the bits that weren't the sculpture. The great saviours and masters of human history found the way to push the button of true religious feeling and then tried to pass this feeling on to others.

In thinking about the future and the great discoveries yet to be made, one of the most exciting and telling researches yet to be done is the one inwards to find out who and what we really are and what we can and need to be.

It is doubtful that we will find any answers to the meaning of life on Pluto, especially since poor old Pluto has recently been demoted from its status as a planet to that of being just a large bit of rock. It will be interesting to see how Pluto reacts to this once the bad news reaches it!

Meanwhile, perhaps take a look inside and see if you can find somewhere within the space you call you, your own piece of good news about the future.

Once you find it, how will you announce it?

The difference between genius and human stupidity is that genius is probably finite.

Albert Einstein

Men go abroad to wonder at the heights of mountains, at the huge waves of the sea, at the long courses of the rivers, at the vast compass of the ocean, at the circular motions of the stars, and they pass by themselves without wondering.

Saint Augustine

IS THE UNIVERSE AN INTELLIGENT PLACE?

IT IS EASY FOR HUMANS to presume that the Universe isn't an intelligent place, because mostly it is full of space and space doesn't seem to be intelligent. It just seems to be ..... space, and that space seems mostly to be filled up with things that don't appear to be alive, let alone intelligent – things such as stars, planets, meteors, comets and lots of big gaps!

Humans tend to think intelligence exists primarily in human form alongside other lesser types of intelligence or pseudo intelligence in the various forms of life that exist on this planet. Accordingly, they don't see the Universe to be intelligent in and of itself. Yet the Universe appears to be a very intelligent system. It works incredibly well and very precisely. The question is: is the Universe intelligently designed to work the way it does or is it simply because of the way that it works that it appears to be intelligent?

Consider the fact that the Earth spins on its axis at 1000 miles per hour and that it orbits around the Sun at around 66,000 miles per hour. This is incredible engineering, for all the time that it does this it doesn't make any noise! The actual spinning and orbiting make no perceivable noise whatsoever despite the size of the Earth and the speeds involved. The engineering behind that is quite extraordinary because even the best engineered man made objects, if they have movement of any kind, do make some kind of noise.

Further, despite the orbiting and the spinning a person can pick up a cigarette lighter and place it on a table, and providing there are no earthquakes or sudden gusts of wind, they can come back a year later and it will still be there.

All this suggests that there may be some kind of intelligence at play behind the design of the system and how it operates. It can't be proven yet, but it can't be disproved either.

If the Earth were 10 miles closer to the Sun, or 10 miles further away, then life as humans know it on this planet couldn't exist. That is only 10 miles out of 93 million! The balances and the finesses involved in this are truly amazing. Some might say that the reason life exists is due to a very fortunate series of coincidences, often called the Goldilocks Effect. But why do those coincidences exist? Plus the question remains: why are we able to have awe about all this and what is awe for?

Then there are the forces of gravity. If there were 1 % less or 1% more gravity throughout the Universe then it would collapse. The forces that hold the Universe together are extremely exact and precise.

Humans are fortunate to live in a Universe that works by such forensic and detailed principles. They are lucky because they wouldn't exist if that were not the case. The distances over which this engineering works are billions upon billions of light years. It is quite beyond the human ability to conceive how big the Universe is and how fantastic it is and yet the margins of error that allow it to work in the way it does are minute.

In thinking about the possible intelligence of the Universe there is perhaps a final consideration to bear in mind.

The greatest evidence we have of any intelligence within the Universe is the human being. Human beings have the ability to reason, to think, to perceive, to understand, to develop, to grow, to learn, to be moved by things. There are a huge range of responses that they are able to give expression to that are far in advance of most other life forms that exist on the planet.

What is also important in thinking about this is that intelligence grows and evolves. If it didn't it wouldn't be intelligence! The evidence for this is that from birth to death intelligence and wisdom are properties that are grown and developed through people's lives, out from the experiences they have within it.

This is something that can continue throughout the life of the person because it seems as though the Universe is growing in its intelligence and refinement on its own evolutionary journey. Then perhaps on the other side of this life, they may join the Universe in a kind of different dimension of intelligence according to the richness and level of intelligence that they have managed to gather during their life here on Earth?

The Universe certainly appears to be an intelligent place. If so, there must be things that humans can learn from the way it works.

Therefore, each person can make it a more intelligent place by the way they add things up about their life and what they do to make this planet a better place for all.

These kinds of considerations have enriched many cultures of the past and can most definitely enrich all our futures together.

So what lesson has the Universe got in mind for you today?

Before God we are all equally wise - and equally foolish.

Albert Einstein

It is in fact a part of the function of education to help us escape — not from our own time, for we are bound by that — but from the intellectual and emotional limitations of our own time.

T. S. Eliot

ARE THERE OTHER FORMS OF LIFE IN THE UNIVERSE?

THE ISSUE OF OTHER FORMS of intelligent life within the Universe is something that has preoccupied human beings for many thousands of years. Of all forms of organic life on the planet, it is only humans who have the ability to even contemplate such issues and the range of theories about it is vast, from little green men on Mars to God in all his / her / its various incarnations and everything in between.

Yet what is meant by life?

As a starter position, it is known that all life is energy and that energy itself cannot be created or destroyed; it can only change its form. Assume therefore for a moment that the Big Bang theory (yet to be absolutely proven) is correct and that the Universe began when something exploded from an incredibly dense almost nothing into the expanding universe we have today.

This suggests that everything that is in the Universe today was existent in terms of its energy at the moment of Big Bang. (This widely accepted view is known as the Steady State Theory.) All that has happened since then is that that energy has changed and modified its form in billions of different ways over the billions of years since the Big Bang occurred.

This further suggests that each person was not only present at the Big Bang but that they were part of it! They may not remember it (obviously!), but they were there in some shape or form, for all forms of life have evolved out from that event. This planet and all life on it originates from that event and is an amalgam of different parts of the Universe, finding a period of order amongst the chaos before it evolves again into a different form of energy and continues its journey through the Universe.

What this says is that before a person was here they were another kind of energy and that now they simply have a semi-stable and temporary form. However, their component parts must have come from all corners of the Universe, if they track the journey of their trace elements back far enough. This makes compiling the family tree a bit more difficult than perhaps previously thought!

This therefore suggests that people themselves are an alien life form living on this planet whilst they are 'living' within the blue-print of what currently constitutes the human form.

There is perhaps an even bigger part to this mystery. No one has ever been able to capture in a bottle the vital spark that animates all life, yet mysteriously disappears at the moment of death when the carnal body simply stops working. The carnal bit goes back to the Earth to be broken back down again over time, but the fizzy, vital, electric bit simply seems to disappear. This it cannot do, for energy cannot be destroyed. It has to go somewhere, and therein lies a mystery within a riddle within an enigma within a puzzle!

Finally, if humans are constituted of different parts of the Universe, could it be that some of those parts have come from the future? If so, this would suggest that we have within us actual knowledge of what the future is like and what will be needed.

This in turn adds a whole new dimension to the saying 'know thyself', for rather than trying to remedy the mistakes of the past we ought to be listening to the intelligence that the future has to offer and which is coded within our very design.

So what intelligence might *you* have brought from the future?

Home is where the heart is.

Old Proverb

Land of Heart's Desire, Where beauty
has no ebb, decay no flood,
But joy is wisdom, time an endless song.

William Butler Yeats

CHOOSING WHERE
TO LIVE IN A WORLD
OF NON LOCALITY

AT FIRST GLANCE OUR WORLD seems ordered and very well defined. Night follows day, spring follows winter and time moves in a linear direction from the past to present to future. However, things are not always what they seem to be, especially when one starts to penetrate the world of the obvious and look into the world of the sub-atomic and causal realms where the rules of the game appear to somehow change.

For example, for many years it was believed that in the sub-atomic realms the atom was made up of particles such as protons, neutrons and electrons. This gave rise to the Particle Theory of physics. Then it was discovered that the electron was less physical in its presence than previously thought and that it acted more like a wave around the denser core of the atom. This in turn gave rise to the Wave Theory of sub-atomic physics.

Then later still it was discovered that electrons could act like either a particle or a wave and that they could even act as both at the same time! Further, it was believed that how they acted depended upon whether they were being observed or not! This led to the realisation that there is no such thing as absolute objectivity as whether they like it or not, the observer is part of the experiment they are conducting.

Their influence may be minimal, but nevertheless it is always a factor. After all, they designed the experiment in the first place!

This both intrigued and confused physicists for the more they looked into the micro worlds the stranger things became. Instead of finding certainty about the nature of force and energy it became more enigmatic and defied all their attempts to classify and define how the Universe works.

The quantum world became stranger and stranger with many theories emerging to try and clothe and cloak the mysteries of what was being discovered. Much, if not most, of this research work remains theoretical in the sense that it has not been able to be tested experimentally and, as every scientist knows, unless and until a theory has been empirically tested then it remains just that - a theory.

When these theories are put to stringent and rigorous scientific testing then they are often found to be incorrect, or at least need modifying to include new findings, e.g. when the Earth was found not to be at the centre of the Solar System.

Dark And Light Energy

Another relatively recent theory revolves around the fact that it has been discovered that since Big Bang the rate of expansion of the Universe has increased rather than decreased. This defies all logic, because after an explosion of energy there is always a slow down of velocity, much like what happens when a person throws a ball and it slows from the moment it is thrown until it comes to rest.

Yet all the scientific measurements confirmed that indeed the Universe is expanding at an ever increasing rate. This, not surprisingly, completely baffled scientists who then began to look round for a theory to try and explain this anomaly.

In effect, there is too much energy and matter in the Universe to account for the *actual* physical matter and observable energy of the Universe, and therefore some of this matter and energy and matter must be 'missing'.

Scientists then came up with the idea that there must be 'dark matter and 'dark energy' hidden within the Universe in order to explain the fact that the Universe is continuing to expand at an ever increasing rate rather than a decreasing one. According to their calculations, the observable and currently measurable Universe we occupy accounts for only 4% of the matter and energy needed to explain how the Universe works, and therefore the remaining 96% must be made up of this dark matter and dark energy.

Despite most theoretical physicists accepting the principle of dark matter and dark energy there is absolutely no evidence or proof for their existence. No dark matter or dark energy has ever been found and nor have any experiments proved their existence. Therefore it remains, for the time being at least, simply a theory.

Theories are important for they help create a circumstance where conjectures and hypotheses about reality can be postulated, tested, challenged and adapted as new evidence comes to light.

Sometimes, like other disciplines, physicists have trouble letting go of their theories or get prickly when challenged to produce evidence to support them. Often they produce rather long mathematical equations to show that the model they have constructed makes logical sense. But just because something looks beautiful and seems to make sense doesn't mean that it is right as the early makers of Earth centric orreries found out!

The main point, however, is not whether the theories are in themselves right or wrong, but rather whether they cause us to think differently about the nature of our reality.

In this regard it is interesting to look at the concept of non-locality, which has developed out of the most recent discoveries in particle physics. This suggests that rather than being a particle or a wave, an electron is neither and both at the same time. It is everywhere and nowhere because it is non-local or not fixed. The only time it becomes fixed is when the observer looks at it and fixes it as either being a wave or a particle.

It can therefore be in more than one place at the same time. This means that the principles of physics do not apply in the previously thought rigid way that they were supposed to as things can travel faster than the speed of light because they are not travelling somewhere else, but rather to another part of themselves.

The theory is that everything in the Universe has at least the potential to have this non-local aspect and therefore has the ability to not only travel faster than the speed of light, but also to connect to every other part of the Universe.

This is provided it is able to act in a non-local way.

There is no actual empirical proof of this theory yet but the theory is very exciting and the repercussions, if true, could be incredible. It could mean for example, that you are from here and somewhere else at the same time.

LOCAL, GLOBAL OR UNIVERSAL?

The principle of non-locality is a vital consideration in thinking about the future, for much of the cause of the problems for the human race has been local thinking and local action. The more local the thinking has been then the more entrenched the problems have become. This is further compounded by the fact that local thinking tends to be fixing in its nature, and the more fixed something is the harder it is for it to change its position. One of the most amazing features of non-locality is the ability of elements to change their position immediately because they are not subject to the usual laws of gravity and resistance.

But which came first, the escape from the normal laws of physics or the principle of non-locality? In one sense it doesn't matter, but it would seem that the principle of non-locality comes first.

This suggests that the human race needs to review its situation from a non-local place, for it is only from such a place that integrated solutions can be found. Further, if the world situation can be looked at from a non-local place then it also suggests that better and different positions can be taken almost instantaneously.

In such a state the quantum reality of the world's situation could easily change from the perceived problems and shortages to opportunities in abundance. Despite the stated agenda mostly appearing to be the former, the deeper reality is that the latter is truly the case if people can escape local thinking.

This certainly can't be done from the current state of local thinking and vested interest. What is therefore needed is to view reality in a different way.

The principle of non-locality suggests that there is no such thing as oneself and everything else for everything in the Universe is interconnected and inter-related. Further, everything that is done affects everything else, much like the 'butterfly effect' spoken of earlier.

If this was perceived to be the case then people would see that it is not possible to act solely in a local way and that all actions affect the whole state of the Universe. The problem here is that people can only see the immediate and short term results of their actions. If they get immediate and personal benefit then, as far as they are concerned, they are winning.

This is true whilst people remain selfish, ego based and local. The mindset needs to change from ME to WE, with WE being the non-local reality of the entire Universe.

If this principle of non-locality can be grasped then it will increasingly transcend down into the key decisions facing the human race and the actions it needs to take. The way forward cannot be based firstly in making such decisions in isolation.

We need to change our reality.

This could be easily achieved if we change our awareness.

After all, we all came from stardust and one day we will all return to stardust.

This makes the whole Universe our home and this suggests that we should treat it and everything in it with respect and care, for who knows which part of it might be our next home? This further suggests that we should try, wherever possible, to keep it neat, tidy and pleasant for who would want to live in a dump if they had a choice?

The irony is that the more local and parochial a person is the lonelier they become. To be a friend to the whole Universe means a person is not only more consciously a living part of its reality, but also more in tune with their own reality.

If this were so, people would see that local thinking is an anathema to life itself.

Ultimately, the 6,700,000,000 humans here on this planet share the non-local reality that we all float through space on a tiny blue ball that travels around the Sun at 66,000 miles per hour. The tolerances that support life on it are so fragile we'd be insane to upset those balances with local and selfish thinking.

It is not exigency that will cause humans to move from local to non-local thinking. It is rather a sense of connectedness and integration within which the key ingredients are awe and wonder and a reverence for the beauty of it all.

In such states lies the quantum reality of the true situation facing humanity and the keys to finding the way forward together.

Want to try and help save the planet? Then why not try and help save the Universe instead? Trying to save the planet is far too local a view and anyway the best way to get rid of a 'problem' is to get a bigger one instead! By doing so you might at the same time help the scientists find the missing bits of the Universe. They are right that bits are 'missing', but it's not dark energy and dark matter that's missing, it's light energy and light matter. The best place to find some of this elusive energy and matter is inside you where something very clever put it for safe storage.

And here's the proof that you have an unlimited supply in you. Smile and see what happens in you and around you.

THE FUTURE OF LIGHT, TIME AND OTHER STUFF

And God said "Let there be light." And there was light.

The Bible - Genesis

All the darkness in the world cannot put
out the light of a single candle.

Anonymous

LIGHT AND DARK

IF, AS THE BIBLE SAYS, 'in the beginning there was the Word,' then what were the first words spoken by Creation? Apparently they were "fiat lux" – let there be light. (It is not certain whether it was Latin or some other language that Creation used!)

Whatever the case, it must have been a cosmic event beyond parallel, for out from the void, light was somehow created.

Yet where did Creation get its light source from? It must have been from inside itself for the laws of physics state that it is not possible to get something from nothing.

This is a clue as to how human behaviour can activate the higher levels of what is curiously called en*light*enment. For why is it that some people have developed spiritually throughout the course of history more than others?

Often the view is that these people have connected to God or something higher than temporal existence, and perhaps this is true. Yet could they have in fact connected to the light source that is already *inside* them but hidden? The suggestion here is that it is not possible to connect to something that a person hasn't got a bit of already.

It has been discovered that the Pineal Gland is responsive to light and secretes (a curious word that is very close to the word *secret*) hormones in response to different influences. The previously held view was that the pineal gland actually did very little and probably had no continuing usefulness in terms of human evolutionary progression. It now appears that the absolute reverse may be true and that the pineal gland and its activation may be pivotal in terms of what may be the next step in human evolution.

It is said that the Buddha sat under a Bo tree and became enlightened. It has been discovered that the Bo tree secretes Serotonin, which is now known to help in the activation of the pineal gland. An extraordinary coincidence, or did the Buddha know exactly what he was doing and why? Whatever the case, it might be worth getting the leaders of the G8 to sit under a Bo tree for their next meeting just in case it works!

If nothing else, if they sit there, and in a moment of blinding insight, realise that mostly they are middle aged men who are not needy and that they in fact do not in any way represent the demographic diversity of the human condition then this would suggest that the Bo tree effect really does work!

UPSIDE DOWN AND INSIDE OUT

There seems to be an inverse law to do with light and dark, for inside the human body it is dark - at least physically. Perhaps there is something else inside that can light up when humans connect to something powerful?

The most powerful source of light in the Solar System, in physical terms, is the Sun. Yet is there anything on this planet that might match it? Could it be the human spirit in its most incandescent forms? After all, on a 'heat per area basis" one human being generates more heat than the same area of the Sun. Who is to say that the same principle doesn't apply to light?

If the very first action of Creation was to create light, did it perhaps do so to see if any light came back so that it could experience itself? In the same way that we draw inference and meaning for our own lives from the relationships we have with other people perhaps Creation operates in a similar way in experiencing itself? It certainly couldn't see what was going on in the farthest vestiges of the Universe if there wasn't any light!

Physical light is one of the denser levels of light through which force and energy is transmitted around the Universe. What if there were other levels of light, far finer and more powerful, that humans do not even have the instruments to measure? Could the light of the spirit be such a light? How far out into Creation might that be transmitted and thereby visible to something that has the eyes to see? Could such light travel faster than the speed of light itself?

This may appear to be fanciful but then so was the idea of the existence of infra red and ultra violet light before they were discovered, because they were outside the visible spectrum until instruments were invented to prove their existence.

The light of the spirit is definitely a subject worthy of further investigation. It does perhaps shed some light on the expression: 'Being switched on.'

What, therefore, is the key to being switched on?

It is suggested that the word 'inspiration' is a good place to start from as it contains the word *spirit* within it. In fact, *inspiration* anagrams to — *an ion spirit* which could be seen to mean, a charged spirit.

This suggests that it pays to be inspired about the future rather than being full of doom and gloom, for gloom cannot be seen by anything, nor can it be seen out from.

It also suggests that there is a charge in living and being human.

So what is that charge and what does it call for?

You can't blame gravity for falling in love.

Albert Einstein

You have power over your mind - not outside events.
Realize this, and you will find strength.

Marcus Aurelius

To Overcome Gravity
You Need Light

ONE OF THE MOST AMAZING discoveries made by Albert Einstein during his remarkable life was that light bends as it travels through space. He predicted this would be confirmed when experiments were carried out to test his theory.

A few years later when there was a transit of Venus the observations made proved that Einstein's prediction was indeed correct. The reason why light bends is that as it travels through space it is moving through a three dimensional media that is full of objects such as stars and planets that all exercise a gravitational pull on each other and every other thing in their proximity.

If light were to travel through a pure vacuum that had no gravitational forces present, it would travel in a straight line. However, space is not a vacuum and there are ever present forces that affect bodies travelling through it. As Einstein predicted, the nearer an object passes by another space body and the greater the mass of that body then the greater the gravitational force of that body the more the object will be bent from travelling in a straight line through space.

An example of this effect occurs where the Sun exercises such a powerful gravitational pull on all the planets of the Solar System that it manages to keep them all in orbit around it despite the substantial speeds that all the planets travel at. The reason the Sun can do this is that its mass is so much greater than the all the rest of the planets combined (the Sun represents well over 99% of the entire mass of the entire Solar System).

This is quite amazing, for on the one hand the forces that keep the planets in orbit are not too weak to let the planets fly off into outer space, and on the other hand not too strong to cause them to crash into the Sun itself. It also bends the movement of objects, including light more than any other body in the Solar System.

The things that exercise the most gravitational force, therefore, are the things with the greatest mass. Black holes have the most mass of anything known in the Universe with the gravitational force they exert being so great that even light itself cannot escape from them.

The principles of how gravity works are relevant in thinking about the world situation and the future. In current times mostly people worry about the gravity of the situation facing the human race unless something is done to change things. Yet the more grave people think the situation is the more things remain the same, for gravity keeps things in place.

Whilst people think things are grave they can be easily controlled, for they mass together and think that nothing can be done to escape the orbit that they find themselves in. The more they think like this, the more the gravity of the situation has a hold on them and the more the light inside them disappears into a black hole.

Einstein showed that gravity affects light and this insight has opened up new fields of research about the nature of time and space into what is often now called the 'space time continuum'. Time and space are no longer seen as absolutes but rather as relative properties. They are integrally linked and affect each other in ways that our conscious minds have difficulty grasping.

One of the things that Einstein didn't consider was how light might affect gravity, and also whether gravity itself is always a constant property or whether it too might be relative, or that there might be situations where its effects could be lessened or even negated. What would happen to light if this could be done? For example, in the absence of gravity could light possibly travel even faster than the speed of light?

As stated previously, scientists have postulated that 96% of the Universe is 'missing' because the Universe is accelerating in its expansion rather than slowing down. They have therefore come up with the idea that the extra 96% beyond the known mass or matter of the Universe must be made up of dark matter and dark energy.

Not all scientists agree with this hypothesis, and some even argue that the anomalies in the figures could be explained by the fact that gravity may have variable effects throughout the Universe.

If somehow the human race could escape the gravity of its situation what might happen?

Gravity appears to bend light and slow it down and can even cause it to disappear into black holes. If the human race could connect to the light of their situation then perhaps the reverse effect of what gravity does to light could happen, i.e. could a great deal of light in the world cause the effects of gravity to be ameliorated? Or, if it were possible to lessen the effects of gravity, would that increase the speed of light?

This may sound like science fiction but it might be possible given the research being done into things like antigravity and antimatter devices. Certainly the theory holds true that if gravity could be lessened then light should be able to travel faster.

It would be wise therefore to focus on the light of the situation rather than the dark. This doesn't mean to make light of the situation but it certainly does mean to allow light into the situation.

So is there more gravity or more light in the Universe?

Logic indicates there must be more light than gravity because if there was more gravity than light then the Universe would be just full of black holes from which no light could ever escape, and this would make the Universe a very dark place indeed.

As we can see lots of light in the Universe, this suggests that light is the pre-eminent force in the Universe and therefore it would seem to be a good ally in seeking where to place one's allegiances about the future. The one thing that the Universe seems to be doing as it expands at an ever increasing rate is spreading light throughout itself.

We would therefore be wise to do the same to ourselves and each other.

Time is a sort of river of passing events, and strong is its current; no sooner is a thing brought to sight than it is swept by and another takes its place.

Marcus Aurelius

To see a World in a Grain of Sand,
And a Heaven in a Wild Flower,
Hold Infinity in the palm of your hand,
And Eternity in an hour.

William Blake

Once we accept our limits, we go beyond them.

Albert Einstein

TIME

WHAT AN AMAZING, ESOTERIC THING time is! For what actually is it, in fact, unto itself? Humans may have clocks and calendars by which they measure seconds, hours, days, months, years, centuries and so on, but is that what time is or could there be more to it than that?

If the first measurement of time that is known of is in seconds or parts thereof, is there somewhere where time is measured in firsts? Perhaps there is a clue hiding in the fact that *time* is *emit* backwards, or is it that *emit* is *time* backwards?

Einstein showed that time is not as linear as humans might think, and the principle that governs this is that nothing in the Universe is static or fixed – including time itself.

This was such a radical idea. It suggested that the laws of physics needed to be reviewed, for much existing theory was based on establishing fixed constants (such as light) from which empirical measurements could supposedly be taken. This was no longer absolutely the case.

Everyone knows the expression: 'time flies when you are having fun', and it also seems to drag when people are bored or fed up. People also have experiences of time seeming to go into slow motion when they are involved in something like an accident. It has been discovered that in a sense time does slow down in such circumstances for the body produces chemicals to prepare the person for the shock and possible injury to follow. A side effect of this is that it puts the person's awareness into slow motion. It is amazing that the body is to be able to do this and also prepare for the possible injury to follow by dulling the sensitivity and producing symptoms of shock to help the person cope with the trauma.

Further, the apparent properties of time seem to change when humans age. When people are young the days seem to fly by and the years seem to take longer in coming around. As people get older this process seems to reverse with the days being fuller and longer and yet the years seeming to whiz by. Although the clock might say that there are 60 minutes in every hour, the truth appears somewhat stranger. No two hours are the same and no two people have the identical experience within them.

Perhaps this brings a new understanding and perception to the concept of flexi time? Time is not as rigid as the human system of measurement would suggest. In a Universe where nothing is truly constant, except the process of change, it follows that time must, will and does indeed itself change with time!

Consider how many adjustments have been made to the calendar over the centuries to try and make up for 'lost time'. Indeed there were riots in the Middle Ages when, in order to update the calendar, 10 days were deleted. The question is what would people have done with those missing days?

The other kind of missing days could be all the lost tomorrows – especially those tomorrows that people put everything off until. This is one way in which humans are tricked into not fulfilling their potential, for tomorrow never comes. The more something is put off the harder it is to do. This is because of the fact that everything grows - and this includes inertia.

There is the expression that if a person wants to get anything done then give it to a busy man (or woman). The busy person does not have to overcome the inertia that the bored or lazy person does. They already have momentum, and this is paramount in getting things done.

Time for the busy person is a very different commodity than it is for the lazy person, for the latter is bored and looks for ways to occupy the time whereas the busy person looks for ways to win more time. Secondly, a person operating at greater efficiency is more likely to be able to take on board another task amongst existing ones than a person who is trying to go from inertia to action.

A person only gets the time they earn and the quality of that time differs from person to person. The quality people get out of life depends upon the quality they put into it. In the 'instant everything' world of today the things that hold the most value are those that have had time spent over them rather than assembly line production processes. Yet the human race is largely adopting assembly line attitudes to things like education, work, health and living in general. This is done mainly to *save* time.

Yet how is it possible to actually save time?

It is well known and accepted that there are ways of doing jobs that mean less time is spent doing them. However, that doesn't actually save time, it simply means that the job in hand takes less time, which in turn means there is then an opportunity to do other things.

Perhaps time, therefore, isn't as linear as it is mostly thought to be. It is often said that the past cannot be changed, but is that strictly true? In the new paradigm of the space/time continuum, perhaps things from the past can be changed and altered in ways that human structured thinking might not in the first instance allow? Could things latent from the past be activated, furthered or evolved whilst the negative effects of past events are ameliorated and safely relegated by having their influence lessened?

This reassessment of the nature of time continues and it is fascinating. For example, a recent trend in Hollywood film making is to not follow a blockbuster with a sequel but with what is called a prequel. This concept was unheard of until a few years ago. Where did the perception to do this kind of thing come from? Why did it appear? What is it trying to tell human beings?

Could it be that the Universe releases certain perceptions at certain points in time to allow humans to see themselves in a different light and change and evolve accordingly?

Did Copernicus discover the fact that the planets revolved around the Sun? Or was that information released to him by something trying to make a point to the human race saying that it was not the centre of the Universe and that perhaps it might care to rethink its position in the affairs of Creation? A person can only see: -

1. What they have trained their eyes to see; and
2. What they are permitted to see.

Tony Kearney

THERE'S NO TIME TO WASTE

Human arrogance causes us to believe that we discover everything new that is revealed. But reality may be more prosaic in that information is released at specific times for reasons humans may not be fully aware of at the point. After all, it took millions of years for the human model to discover the use and control of fire, and even longer to discover the wheel. Yet there were only 66 years between the first powered flight and landing on the Moon.

The human race's understandings of evolution and time are changing at an ever increasing rate. Scientists are now considering seriously the concept of parallel universes adjacent to this one and suggesting that it might be possible for the same set of events to reveal a different outcome in each one. A few years ago the very same scientists would regard such an idea as being Science Fiction or New Age psychobabble! If what they suggest is possible then perhaps time itself is much more fluid than previously thought, so not only can the future be changed but also the past.

For example, whilst the physical events of the past might not be able to be changed, perhaps it is nevertheless possible to change the influence of those events as they pertain to the present and the future. This could apply at both individual and global level. Whilst for an individual it is not possible to change the physical fact of something having happened to them, at say age 10, the continuing influence of that event can be changed, altered, relegated, super-imposed upon, refined, magnified or whatever.

A possible example of this was during the Truth and Reconciliation process in South Africa after the ending of the Apartheid regime. By facing and dealing with the issues of the apartheid years many of the potent legacy issues of that dark regime could be relegated. In this way the affected parties could move forward and face the future with a more open and cohesive approach.

It is said that time heals all wounds, and perhaps this is true. Things like guilt and shame cannot exist in isolation. They have to become attached to something that has happened to the person or group to which these influences relate.

It is possible, therefore, to alter these influences by consciously seeking to be remedial upon them. For example, whilst the occurrence of war cannot be altered, the pain and suffering inflicted by it can be lessened by learning the lessons from it and changing the behavioural patterns that led to its happening in the first place. However, if lessons aren't learnt then history tends to repeat itself and the wounds of such events are never given the opportunity to heal properly. This is like repeatedly picking the scar off the top of a wound so that it never gets a chance to heal properly.

Relegation is one method where the influence of the past can be altered. Another is superimposure. As cultures over the centuries tend to physically build over the top of previous ones, so this can be done in respect of influences by placing new ones on top of old persuasions.

This also applies at individual level, for everyone has events and occurrences in their lives that shape or scar them in many ways and continue to influence them unless they are able to safely relegate or superimpose over them. The converse also applies where good things that have happened are concerned, for these events need to be promoted and amplified wherever possible.

The physical moment of events is like a capsule within which there are multi-vitamins that can be released and activated at different times. The mistake that is often made is one of perception. Having experienced an event in the past people can tend to think that that is the end of it.

Time is more like a matrix than a straight line. How the past influences today and tomorrow depends on the choices people make according to what they deem to be important and give credence to.

There are set pathways or possibilities down which a person can travel and what these are depends upon what went before. There is a balance between the known and the unknown and for humans there is always the sense of the future being the unknown. What kind of unknown awaits depends upon previous decisions that have been made in respect of the past unknown and the choices that are made in the present about the current unknown.

For the future itself there may even be a sense of it seeing humans as being just as unknown to it as the future is unknown to us.

It is not possible to choose what doesn't yet exist, but it is possible to create the circumstances for it to appear.

Choice appears to be the key word within this, but not in the way that humans may often think.

An old limerick might help give further insight into this: -

> *There once was a man who said damn.*
> *It appears to me now that I am.*
> *Just a being that moves that moves*
> *In predestinate grooves*
> *In fact not a bus but a tram.*

Predestination may exist in terms of there being an established set of railway lines down which there is permission to travel. In that sense the future could be fixed, but what is not fixed is which of the routes humans individually and collectively choose to take.

THE CHOICE OF TIME AND THE TIME OF CHOICE

Perhaps it is like a restaurant menu with multiple choices for starters, main course, dessert and wine. In this analogy it seems that humans have a very large menu indeed to choose from in this lifetime and beyond. With this perspective it may be possible to change the influence of time.

Time could be likened to the sea and the events that passing through it are like ships sailing across its surface. As the ships sail through the sea they cut into the future and leave things in their wake.

The influences from the past, present and future of time are all happening continuously and at once rather than one after the other. The passengers on that ship perceive time in a certain way according to their experience and the direction the ship is steered in.

To see this feature of time it is necessary to be able to view time in a lateral rather than literal sense, and also see that time has not only more than one level, but also more than one dimension to it.

It may be possible that time can travel in more than one direction at the same time. This is similar to continental plates meeting and colliding and folding in and over each other according to mass, density, and speed. The speed of these changes depends on the size of the paradigm, for in relative terms at one end of the spectrum there is no such thing as instant change and at the other there is no such a thing as forever.

The measurement of time depends on the accuracy of the measuring device and the context within which it is measured, for there is no such thing as a constant to measure 'pure' time by.

Each person is therefore, in some shape or form, timeless.

Death is nothing more than a shape shifting way to pass from one set of experiences into another set. So too is birth.

The human eye can detect a match being lit from 10 miles away in total darkness. What is to say that the Universe cannot detect human illumination across billions of light years and respond to it?

Finally, in this brief research into the nature of time, there is the expression 'spending time'.

This is an odd expression yet perhaps it gives a clue as to how to think about our current situation. Human beings have spent too much time doing things that are not useful to the future, and that kind of time has nearly run out.

However, there is another kind of time that they can tap into to do with what is timeless, and this extends beyond matters of local concern. If humans can remember what this kind of time is to do with then there is time to make the changes that are necessary in order to ensure that they have time to share a better kind of future.

This requires us to see that not only is time relative but so are we all and everything that we see.

So with this in mind, what do you now think of your new, extended family?

?

We can conceive that electricity itself is to be understood as not an accident, but an essence of matter.

Lord Kelvin

Ninety-nine percent of who you are is invisible and untouchable.

R. Buckminster Fuller

THE FORCES OF LIFE

HUMAN PERCEPTION OF LIFE IS like looking through a keyhole into another room. Humans can only see and hear a tiny fraction of the visible and audible spectrums and most of what exists is therefore beyond their conscious awareness. That doesn't mean to say that what they are not conscious of doesn't exist, for we know that many of these things affect us in many ways.

All life is a network of complex electromagnetic waves and forces interacting in highly sophisticated ways with some kind of order at play. Could this order be intelligent?

Where does one draw the line where deciding what intelligence is? For example, most people would say that an atom is not intelligent. Yet ultimately humans are made up entirely of atoms, so if atoms are not intelligent where do human beings derive their intelligence? If the construction and process of an atom isn't intelligent then intelligence can only be perceived as something that lives outside the physical make-up of any organism.

This leads to another – 'which came first: the chicken or the egg' type conundrum as to whether life is composed of complex electromagnetic forces or if complex electromagnetic forces compose life? Few scientists would say that gravity is life, yet it affects every single life form on this planet without exception.

Some may stretch to calling gravity a life force but stop short of calling it life itself. Yet it, like themselves, is made up of the forces of electricity and magnetism and is subject to the same laws of physics.

Gravity might therefore legitimately be conceived as being an expression of life, but again this is dependant upon the definition of and concept used to, describe life.

Experiments have shown that all living forms of life respond to electromagnetic radiations, rhythms, vibrations, frequencies, oscillations, pulses and so on. After all, the first thing to do to check if a person is alive or dead is to see whether or not there is any sign of a pulse or electromagnetic activity in the brain or heart.

Curiously, the latest theories of Big Bang suggest that there wasn't just one Big Bang but rather a series in the form of pulses. This would suggest that there could be more than a little truth in the maxim of the ancients of: 'as above, so below.' It also seems to counter the Creationists view of life in the Universe in that God apparently made Creation all found and perfect. Further, there is nothing to suggest that this pulse like movement of the Universe is not continuing today.

THE INFLUENCE OF THE UNSEEN

It has been clearly researched and documented that Solar Flares, for example, clearly affect behavioural patterns on Earth. More suicides, outbreaks of violence and crime and depression occur immediately after these flares happen.

By logical extension this could lead to finding some vindication for some of the more prudent claims made by Astrology. Not the absurd claims in newspapers all round the world every day, but some of the more sensible ones, such as the fact that research has shown that more people get admitted into mental institutions at full moon than at any other time of the month. This is where the word 'lunatic' comes from - originally meaning 'under the influence of the moon.'

It has also been discovered that this background radiation or pulse of electromagnetic force, as it appears on Earth in both its natural and unnatural forms, affects all life in some way or other. For example, it is now becoming accepted that the unnatural use of electricity and magnetism has a detrimental effect on the human system causing things like birth defects, leukaemia, cancer and many other illnesses.

The human design runs on very fine electromagnetic forces whereas the ones used to run cities and their electrical supplies are comparatively very coarse. This is illustrated by the fact that if a car is driven past these electricity pylons with the radio on the reception on the radio is distorted by the coarse electrical signals coming off the pylons. If it is doing that to the radio it must also have a substantial affect on human beings who come into contact with it.

This has been, and continues to be, denied by the main antagonists to this idea – electrical companies, the military and the government because of the costs involved if they were to admit it to be true.

Despite the politics, enough research has been carried out to establish that life responds to all sorts of electromagnetic forces and influences and all illnesses must therefore trace their origin back to an electromagnetic cause.

Countless billions each year are channelled into finding a cure for cancer, and some success in treating it has occurred. However, this hides the deeper reality, which is that the percentage of people suffering cancer has quadrupled since the Second World War, as has the number of types of cancer.

Therefore more research should be carried out into finding out what is causing it and then into altering the behavioural pattern that gives rise to it at both individual and societal level. Most, if not all cancers are caused by some kind of unnatural electromagnetic influence, be it radiation, pollution, chemicals in food, an attitude in the person or countless other forces that end up as a physical condition. By treating the symptom it can only be possible to do a patch-up job. Treating the whole is what is needed, for in doing so a person can cut themselves off from the source of the harmful electromagnetic force, whatever it may be, that is causing the condition in the first place. Otherwise it is likely to return again.

Pure 'scientific' treatment of things such as cancer does not generally sustain unless it is accompanied by some kind of lifestyle change as well – in effect a re-education programme. Mainstream science dismisses such techniques because they are regarded as being quack New Age remedies. But what if they work? The evidence suggests that many of them do.

There is also the great God money to take into account in considering all these issues, for money drives so much in the world and the reasons why things are and aren't done. Consider, for example, the ramifications if it was accepted that overhead power lines are dangerous to human health and as a result of this finding it became necessary to sheath such power lines and place them underground? The cost would be astronomical and of course it could set a precedent that people who claim that their illnesses were caused by such power lines.

Or what would happen if it was universally accepted that in the long term whilst organic farming does initially lead to lower yields than chemical based farming (which it does), nevertheless it is much better for the land itself and the environment (which it is)? Also that it increases bio-diversity and is more sustainable, and even more economical, in the longer term than chemical based farming (again, all of which is true).

What would happen if it was accepted that a dramatic way to reduce cancer would be to reduce chemicals and additives in food?

The truth is that the world economy might well collapse if any of the above, or many other scenarios, were accepted and embraced. This is because the world economy has become dependant on these industries, which is a kind of cancer in itself.

A QUESTION OF BALANCE

This is not meant as an attack on all science and all modern medical treatments of disease. Some of the work done in these areas has been truly wondrous and has brought a lot of help and relief to many of the world's needy. What is being said is that research is needed into the cause realms and from there bold and honest decisions need to be taken on how to go forward into the future.

Otherwise the level of problems left to future generations may be such that today's children's children might not have the resistance to fight the unnatural forces they are forced to deal with.

Much of the unnatural electromagnetic background radiation from such things as power plants, noise, smog, electricity, microwaves, mobile telephones, computers, chemicals and so on undermines people's immune systems and therefore weakens them against attack from bacteria and viruses. This problem is further exacerbated by the fact that many of these bacteria and viruses have themselves developed an increased immunity against the drugs that have been used to try and control them in the first place.

This has contributed to the rise of the Superbug, for it is known that the smaller something is the quicker and more adaptable to change it is. This is proving to be the case as the so called war with the bugs enters a new phase. The things humans do to cause the weakening of their own defence systems often cause a strengthening of the bug's systems as they mutate, evolve and change to meet these new challenges faster than humans can evolve their defence systems to fight them.

Antibiotics had a brilliantly effective start in fighting disease a little over 50 years ago. Now there are very few that remain effective because each time one is used the natural human defence system is weakened against future attack.

The proof of this is not difficult to find for every year in the United States 50,000 people who are admitted to hospital die of an illness they contracted *inside* the hospital and not from what they were suffering from when they were admitted. In Britain the statistics are no better.

THE IMMUNE SYSTEM

Everything is governed and runs by electromagnetism. The immune system itself is ultimately an electromagnetic process that operates by recognising and responding to invading alien electromagnetic signals and then tries to eliminate them.

This system has evolved over millions of years but doesn't have a 'profile' on unnatural electromagnetic radiations that people introduce into their bodies by various methods. The body tries to produce a response, as best it can, to deal with the problem but often the person does not see the symptoms until it is too late.

The converse is also true for good electromagnetic signals introduce a healthy and generative frequency that improves the workings of the immune system.

As an example, being in love has been shown to bolster the immune system because the resonance of good feelings creates beneficial effects throughout the body. This is also why such things as meditation are especially good for western people because they mostly run at overly fast and unnatural speeds.

It has been found that this background electromagnetic radiation works by what is called the 'tuning fork principle'. As everything vibrates it causes a resonant response in what it comes in to contact with for good or for ill.

THE RHYTHM OF LIFE

All life works by and responds to rhythms and cycles, from the electron circling the proton of an atom to the spiralling of galaxies as they float through the Universe over countless aeons of time. All of this is governed by electricity and magnetism in one form or another.

Electricity and magnetism may be defined in simple, easy to understand terms as follows.

Electricity = the flow of energy
Magnetism = the field of energy thereby created

Everything in the Universe has both aspects applicable to one degree or another. Even a solid lump of granite is not really solid; it is just that its current form gives it the relative state of being much more solid than water. If subjected to enough heat and pressure (which is simply a different form of electricity and magnetism), the granite will change its state from solid to liquid and then even to gas.

This is reversing the process of how it actually formed in the first place, for if the Big Bang theory of how the Universe was formed is correct then what happened was that something very small and very solid blew up. What has been happening since is a congealing, evolving and expanding process of the inherent forces of electricity and magnetism.

Everything, therefore, has a 'life force' both within and around it.

Healers know this to be true, for in the use of crystals for healing purposes it is known, either directly or by trial and error that certain crystals have certain properties that have been 'captured' over the millions of years that it has taken them to form. The flow of electricity through them and the magnetic fields around them induces certain properties that can be beneficial to some conditions. The same principle applies to such things as herbalism, Tai Chi, meditation, Feng Shui, colour healing and acupuncture for they all work on the principle that the flow of electricity and magnetism (energy) affect things that they come into contact with.

It has been discovered that the wearing of certain magnets on particular parts of the body has a powerful remedial and curative effect. Nobody, as yet, really knows why it works. All that is known is that it does work, particularly for things like stress, backache and the like. By using the magnets it somehow changes the energy flow from a blocked or wrongful process to one that is more natural and this allows the beneficial side effects.

Conventional medicine regards some of these 'practices' with suspicion and often ridicules them, but they themselves operate the same system in a different form. The pill-based culture of western medicine works by introducing different resonances into the body which then have specific effects on the body and its processes via a pill. Both systems, therefore, can and should learn from each other.

A person doesn't have to be Einstein to know that sitting next to a waterfall is good for getting rid of a headache.

The flow of water drawing off static and positive ions is simply a scientific explanation for what people have known for thousands of years: that it simply works. The scientific understanding of how it works is useful because its application can then be used more widely and intelligently.

The human factor cannot be ignored in all this, although science often thinks it can be. The placebo effect shows that if a person thinks that they have taken something to make them get better then quite often they will get better, even though the pill they have taken is neutral in its effect. This applies not only to the person taking the remedy but also to the person administering the treatment, for research has shown that when the doctor or healer thinks positively about the treatment they are administering this can also have a significant influence on its effectiveness.

When scientists measure crystals in a laboratory for so called therapeutic effects and don't find them, what they fail to realise is that often the effects can only be 'activated' according to the electromagnetic powers of the person using it. This is a kind of 'Open Sesame' effect. Two people can try and use the same tools for healing but one may have a success and the other not. This is due to the healer's development, or literally *charisma*.

Things like crystals, herbs, chants, ceremonies, medicines, mother kissing it better, are all media through which an electrical charge can flow. Its success depends on the skill and connection of the healer and also the belief of the recipient. It's as though the healer / doctor / shaman represents the positive cell of an electrical circuit and the patient represents the negative or receptive cell. The media through which the healing takes place (pill / chant / crystal, etc) is like the earth of the cell that completes the circuit. It is curious that the third part of the circuit is called 'earth' for that is what makes the circuit 'safe'.

LEARNING FROM WHAT WORKS

Modern science and medicine often dismisses these 'alternative' systems as primitive and unproven but, as stated earlier, they themselves actually use them. For example, bedside manner is considered to be a vital part of the healing and recovery process in hospitals. If it was purely just a physical process then surely robots would be better doctors as they carry no risk of infection. Humans instinctively know that healing is a holistic process and yet they often appear to be suspicious of what they don't fully comprehend.

These principles seem to be readily accepted in other aspects of daily life. For example, nearly a quarter of the world's population believe that chanting a few words over some bread and wine together with some hand movements and ringing of bells changes the state of bread and wine into the body and blood of a man who died 2000 years ago. If this is true then there must be some massive change of state in the substances involved, for physically they do not change to any measurable degree.

The same affect applies to the principle of Holy Water in that it is alleged that water blessed in certain ways can carry certain healing properties, e.g. at Lourdes.

What has been discovered is that water does hold a charge and varies according to where it is taken from and what it has come into contact with. Water isn't just water. It seems to have a 'memory' of what it has come into contact with, even when the substance that it has come into contact with is distilled out from it.

The crystalline quality of water is affected not only by the atmosphere, pollution and chemicals, but also by music, light and what is said to it!

This may sound extraordinary but is simply a logical extension of some of the principles expressed in this chapter.

Energy pulsates, throbs, vibrates, moves and flows throughout every particle of space, for there is no such thing as pure space or gaps, there are only differentiations in how much force and/or matter there exists in any given 'space'. Look up at the stars at night and whilst there appears to be 'space' between the person and the star they are looking at, in reality there isn't. All the way from the person to the star there is light from the star in every part of that journey, and indeed heat. It simply gets stronger and more pronounced nearer to the source.

If everything moves then in order to move it has to move something else. For example, if a person pushes their hand out in front of them they may think that they are simply pushing their hand into empty space, but this is a misconception. They have to push back the whole Universe to be able to move their hand out in front of them. The reason they can do so is simply that the resistance is less than the energy they have produced in pushing their hand forward. Or, putting it another way, the flow of electricity in the system is greater than the weak magnetic field around the person and therefore they are able to 'puncture' it with their movement.

The converse is also true for if the movement is weak then the magnetic field is such that the object will stay in a state of rest until such time as intervening stronger force comes along to make it move. Therefore, although gravity is a relatively weak force in itself, it can quite easily influence small objects and control their movements.

This helps explain why people are easily influenced and controlled. Because they think they are a small object in the greater scheme of things, they therefore think they cannot influence world events, or perhaps even their own lives. Because of this thought pattern they are mostly subject to the control of the greater mass and conformity of the governments and institutions of the world who often use the 'gravity' of the situation and the fear that this instils as a way of influencing people's thinking and behaviour.

CAUSE AND EFFECT

The movement of bodies is a crucial area of research into the worlds of cause and effect in studying electricity and magnetism. Not always does size matter the most in these worlds. It is movement of the right kind that causes the most effect. For example, a tiny bit of snow rolling down a slope can suddenly turn into a giant avalanche because it gathers energy unto itself as it moves. This is also a principle of understanding in homeopathic medicine where the principle of 'less is more' is applied. All great world movements and changes begin with an idea. How big is that? Is there a machine that can measure the size of an idea?

This snowballing effect is well known for Roman armies were always told to break formal marching step as they crossed bridges. Whilst the resonance of their marching in step was known to cause them to be able to march for longer distances, it was also known to cause bridges to collapse if they kept up the rhythm as they crossed them.

This principle is now well known amongst physicists and is often called the Tacoma Bridge Effect after the famous incident where the Tacoma Bridge was destroyed. What happened was that the speed and direction of the wind was such that it caused the materials in the bridge to become destabilised and weakened, i.e. the electromagnetic forces between the various parts of concrete and steel were undermined by a simple gust of wind playing the right note.

The Japanese have a saying that "the battle is won or lost in the first look in the eye." It was even said that some Samurai warriors could actually kill their opponents simply by shouting, for the frequency and pitch of their shout could shatter the opponent's nervous system.

Many cultures seem to have developed some kind of exorcism practices in order to purge a person of demons or things that possess them. One thing that these technologies all have in common is that they introduce a frequency or rhythm that is designed to break up the holding pattern of the thing that is in possession of the person.

Whilst harmful or unnatural electromagnetic wave patterns or resonances can damage human systems, there must be others that carry beneficial effects and indeed break up everything from cancers to tumours. This is what symptom based 'cures' also try to do by using radiation and chemotherapy treatments to attack the growth.

Other more natural treatments also work on the same principle but do not have the unwanted side effects of these treatments. These are things that should be researched further for Mother Nature has a curious way of providing the remedy needed if only people can find the right place to look.

The subject matter of this chapter is vast. It permeates throughout every single particle of the Universe and Creation from black holes to planets, stars and galaxies as they journey through time and space. These seen and unseen forces affect each and every aspect of life and are the cornerstones upon which life can and does exist. Without them the Universe has no shape.

Humans do not own or ultimately control these powers, forces and influences. They can, however, choose to work with them or against them according to what their priorities and values are. This suggests that a greater understanding and appreciation of not only how the Universe works but why it works the way it does is needed together with a healthy respect for its possible intelligence and purposes, if the path into the future is to be safely found.

Perhaps the future then is simply a case of mind over matter? If we have the right mind state about the future then nothing will be the matter and nothing will be able to stand in the future's way.

As W B Yeats said, "There can be neither cause nor effect when all things are co-eternal."

So, with this in mind, may the force be with you! The question is, which one?

?

The robbed that smiles, steals something from the thief.

William Shakespeare (Othello)

No one has ever become poor by giving.

Anne Frank

SMILE: YOU'RE HAVING YOUR PHOTON TAKEN!

HOW MANY TIMES A DAY in how many different languages around the world is a person asked to smile to have their photo taken? There must be countless millions of photographs taken each day with people endeavouring to capture magical and special moments, from births to marriages to special occasions with family and friends and much more.

All these photos are seeking to preserve for posterity important moments that carry value and meaning. This is why people want to be at their best in the photos. They want their memories to be happy, which possibly helps explain why people don't tend to take photos of unhappy times - because who wants to go back and relive difficult and stressful times all over again when they were painful enough the first time round? People want to call over to themselves the good times and special occasions when they shared warmth, value and love with those they care about.

Hence the urge to smile when having one's picture taken to the point that often people are encouraged to say 'cheese' or something similar because it makes it look as though they are smiling. Saying cheese, however, often artificially forces the lips into an unnatural apparent smile that isn't natural, but at least it gets people in the mood!

Smiling is a unique and truly human action. It sends many messages to the people being smiled at and even to the person who is doing the smiling. To the people being smiled at it says that the person doing the smiling regards them as a friend and not a threat and that they can feel safe and at ease.

It also has a profound affect on the smiler because genuine smiles release chemicals such as endorphins into the bloodstream which have a beneficial and healing affect on the body. The more a person smiles the healthier they will be, and studies have confirmed that happy people are healthier and live longer.

People want to look back at their past and retrieve from those experiences good feelings that bolster them or cheer them up later in life when they look at the photos again. This must suggest that there is more within a photo than just a physical record of an event that happened at some point in the past.

Many might argue that it is nothing more than a simple record of a past event and that seeing that record again activates the memory in the brain of the person looking at the photo. This in turn connects the person to feelings they recall from when the photo was taken and they also add new and additional feelings to the experience.

Could there be more to it than that?

Recent research into consciousness challenges many long established views about the nature of reality and perception. Much of this work focuses on wave frequencies and how information is stored and transmitted, both internally and externally.

The main method whereby this information is accessed and transmitted is through light and research seems to indicate that this is done not only externally but also internally. This is a radical concept for it challenges the assumption that it is simply dark inside us and therefore how can light be a means of transmitting information around the body? The traditional view has long been that the information has been stored and communicated simply and solely through the nerve network or neurones, synapses and dendrites.

Whilst it is true that they play an important and significant role it appears that they are in fact more of a messenger system rather than the message itself and there is a more quantum truth about how this information is received and processed.

What this suggests is that human beings truly are creatures of the light; in fact that is what we are in fact made up of and how we communicate.

When a photo is taken it records a moment of light on a piece of paper and this light can literally switch on a person's own lights when they look at that photo, possibly many years later. Could it be that something actually comes off the photo that triggers a response in the person looking at it? Something certainly seems to happen when the person looks at it for it always causes a greater response with a person who relates directly to the photo than to a person who doesn't. This helps explain why people get bored looking at other people's wedding and holiday photos because they have no triggering wave power in them for that particular event.

What is this secret storage and transmission place of energy?

PHOTONS AND ENERGY

Latest research suggests that the primary and most powerful source of energy storage and transmission is photons, for photons are the smallest particles of light that we currently know about. They seem to exist far more widely than previously thought and, because they are made of light, they can travel at the speed of light. This could help explain why certain information can be transmitted as fast as it is and also how quickly it is processed.

There may also be some deeper truth in the Bible story in Genesis where the very first line talks of in the beginning there being light. If light is the most efficient and effective way of storing and transferring information, then perhaps the Universe in the moment of Big Bang coded the whole of the void into which it began to expand with genetic information about its intelligence and intention?

There does appear to be some scientific back-up to support this. With photons being the smallest possible unit for carrying light, it suggests that this is the common denominator that not only all organic life shares, but the whole Universe shares too. We exchange photons with each other and our surroundings all the time.

It is as though we are in a total state of flux but do not realise it to any deep or meaningful degree and therefore tend to function in a mostly inefficient way.

It therefore seems that greater consciousness of the quantum reality of our situation is needed.

Because if this is obtained then more people can release more of their photon energy from within - and who knows what that would allow and cause?

Thinking must be a form of light for all energy seems to trace its source back to light in some shape or form.

How a person thinks about the future is vital, therefore, for either their thinking releases photons or it doesn't. If the thinking is centred about what is wrong, or purely about themselves and their own personal needs, then it seems that this is an inefficient and ineffective use of the light stored within them.

If a person chooses to think about the future in terms of possibilities and how things can be so much better than they are now, then they can become an agent for the light.

It is sometimes hard to think about the future in a positive way when one considers the daily reports of global problems of climate change, famine, floods, war, disease, over population, pollution to ever decreasing resources and so on. This only adds to the darkness and cannot ultimately bring more light into the world. Attempted solutions based in stopping what isn't right can only ever prevent there being more darkness. It cannot of itself bring more light.

The way to bring more light to the situation is to release more light from within. That is what makes us tick and keeps us alive. It is also what we ourselves gift back to the world when we are in the best of ourselves through such things as joy, happiness and love.

This is why people want to smile when they have their photo taken. They want to be seen to be releasing the best of themselves into the picture so that it is stored for future use. It seems that this might be literally true for each time a person looks at something they physically change its reality. This is because they fire photons at it through their eyes and bombard the object they are looking at, thereby releasing some of the photons stored in the object they are looking at. This explains why people like to look at old photos because they are literally releasing good energy from those stored photon memories. It may also help explain why, sometimes a person can have a strange feeling and turn around to find that another person is looking at them. They can literally feel it from the photons the person 'fires' at them.

A person can therefore decide what kind of photons they release from their eyes when they look at anything they turn their attention to. If they look at things through the eyes of what is wrong then they will tend to *see* more of what is wrong and thereby *release* more of what is wrong. This then will lead to them making unenlightened decisions about the future.

If they look at things through the eyes of what works best then their positive photons will connect with the positive photons of what hasn't yet been released from the potential of the situation. This creates the opportunity for the release of potential energy - which given the number of photons involved is a very large amount indeed - and it can create a chain reaction.

HAVING THE EYES TO SEE

The reality of this situation is well known, for everyone has had the experience where two people look at any given situation and one person sees only the negative side of it and the other person sees only the opportunities. This is a matter of perception and focus and is often today translated as a person being someone who either sees a glass as being half full or half empty.

If the human race is about to have its photo taken for the future how would it want to appear in the photo? And if the future is looking to invest its light and hope then what is it going to be looking for?

Surely it will be looking for something that is the same as itself, for the principle of resonance is to do with how energy is best transferred and translated around the Universe. In short, like goes to like and like causes like.

The challenge, therefore, seems to be to rise above the clear and obvious problems the world faces if it doesn't change its ways. It wasn't the darkness that caused the problems to appear, but the absence or withholding of light.

Each person can be a real and powerful agent of change where the future is concerned, not by what they do as a first principle, but by who and what they are. When a photo is being taken in the dark a flash of light has to be used to enable the picture to come out. The darkness isn't cancelled out, but rather a flash of light is released to superimpose over the darkness.

This is where the remedy lies where the future is concerned.

All a person has to do is smile whilst they are having their photon taken!

But, be careful! Recent research in Japan has shown that the forced smiles people are made to wear when dealing with clients and customers causes muscle strain. It can even cause stress and depression, which is the exact opposite of what a genuine smile causes. So make sure your smile is genuine, because the Universe doesn't need stress or depression!

As Groucho Marx once famously said; "Genuineness is the key to success in life – and if you can fake that you've really got it made!"

It's a really funny line, but not quite true!

So go with the first part of the quote and delete the rest and see what happens.

?

Peace begins with a smile.

Mother Teresa

Two things fill the mind with ever new and increasing wonder and awe; the starry heaven above and the moral law within.

Immanuel Kant

LIGHTS, CAMERA, ACTION
SMILE: YOU'RE ON
CANDID CAMERA

THIS CHAPTER TITLE COMPRISES TWO elements of the visual media. The first relates to the well-known phrase in filming a scene for a film or perhaps a television show; the second comes from the famous TV show called *Candid Camera*. In this people were put in situations that they weren't aware of and were secretly filmed to see what their reactions would be.

The phrase, "lights, camera, action" in the context of this book might also apply to the situation of the human race here on Earth.

The first thing that came to the Earth was light and with its arrival the stage - like that of a film set - was ready. The light brought with it the sequences and codings for all life that might ever stir on the Earth. It gave definition and substance to what would otherwise simply be another inert rock floating through time and space like every other inhospitable satellite.

Could it be, therefore, that the human race itself is on camera and being watched? It is certainly something that has preoccupied the human race for as long as recorded history and beyond - the question as to whether or not we are alone in the Universe. This quest has manifested in everything from belief systems about the existence of

God to religion to whether there might be other forms of intelligent life elsewhere in the Universe and so on.

Whatever the case, there is within the human psyche and consciousness a wonder about whether or not we are alone on our tiny blue sequin that floats on the vast ocean of the Universe.

There is, as yet, no actual proof as to whether or not we are alone. The chances, however, are reasonably good that somewhere else in the Universe other forms of intelligent life may have evolved, and indeed some of them may be far more advanced than our own. Some say that they wouldn't have to be that advanced to be ahead of our own, given the way that we behave on our tiny island home!

This sense of being watched or on camera is something that the human race alone, of all the species on Earth, possesses. It is a strange, and in many ways inexplicable, feeling that haunts our existence.

Like actors on a stage they might not be able to see the audience due to the stage lights, but they know that they are out there and that they are watching them (the actors) perform. They can sometimes know how the audience is responding, but often they can only get senses of how it is going.

What they do know is that for the audience to enjoy the show the material needs to be well written and well acted. This helps the audience relate to the subject matter and hopefully learn something from it.

Therefore the human race could be seen to be on CCTV in that the Universe might be watching to see how the human race is acting. Obviously, this cannot be proved but it might be a useful way for humans to think about their behaviour. Because they think that if no one is watching they can get away with behaving badly.

Once the lights and cameras are in place then the action can begin. The question for the human race actors in this play is: what is the subject matter and who are the players? Is it a thriller or a romantic comedy, a historical tragedy or a futuristic science fiction blockbuster? Does it have a happy ending or does it end in desolation and despair? Who are the heroes and who are the villains, and who wins through in the end?

The difference in this film is that the action is real and not make believe and the actions of the players affect the future.

As Shakespeare so eminently put it in *As You Like It*:

All the world's a stage,
And all the men and women merely players:
They have their exits and their entrances;
And one man in his time plays many parts,
His acts being seven ages. At first the infant,
Mewling and puking in the nurse's arms.
And then the whining school-boy, with his satchel
And shining morning face, creeping like snail
Unwillingly to school. And then the lover,
Sighing like furnace, with a woeful ballad
Made to his mistress' eyebrow. Then a soldier,
Full of strange oaths and bearded like the pard,
Jealous in honour, sudden and quick in quarrel,
Seeking the bubble reputation
Even in the cannon's mouth. And then the justice,
In fair round belly with good capon lined,
With eyes severe and beard of formal cut,
Full of wise saws and modern instances;
And so he plays his part. The sixth age shifts
Into the lean and slipper'd pantaloon,
With spectacles on nose and pouch on side,
His youthful hose, well saved, a world too wide
For his shrunk shank; and his big manly voice,
Turning again toward childish treble, pipes
And whistles in his sound. Last scene of all,
That ends this strange eventful history,
Is second childishness and mere oblivion,
Sans teeth, sans eyes, sans taste, sans everything.

With such a view of life there can be a tendency to think: what is the point? If the world is a stage and the human race is on camera then there is a great deal of point indeed.

Like everything in film-making, there is a director who can cut the scene if he doesn't like the way it has been acted and ask for it to be done again. If that doesn't work then the whole scene can be cut from the film and the actors replaced if they can't get it right.

Perhaps it would be wise to regard ourselves as undertaking a screen test before the real shooting of the film begins? In a screen test the director looks at many different actors to see which ones might be suitable for the various parts within the film.

The actors, on the other hand, really want the part as it will hopefully help build their career.

With this in mind, lights, camera and action is not a bad way to think about the future.

As regards the *Candid Camera* reference, the key thing was that people were caught on camera but off guard in unusual circumstances to see how they would react.

The key lay in the fact that everybody reacts to such surprises in a unique and totally idiosyncratic way. Some are completely flummoxed, some fly into a rage, whilst others panic or even weep.

The one thing that happens to them all at the end is that the producer (Allen Funt, in my day) comes out and puts his arm around the person and says:-

"Smile, you're on Candid Camera."

It is at this point that the reality of the situation hits the person and they can then place the events that have happened to them in a greater context.

With this scenario in mind, what would happen if the human race found out that it had been on Universal Candid Camera and all its actions and reactions had been recorded? What would our reaction be to that fact and what is the greater context that we would seek to place that fact into?

?

In all chaos there is a cosmos, in all disorder a secret order.

Carl Jung

But what is happiness except the simple harmony
between a man and the life he leads?

Albert Camus

COHERENCE AND INTERFERENCE: I'M SORRY, COULD YOU SAY THAT AGAIN?

ONE OF THE BASIC LAWS of physics is that of entropy, which says that over time things reach an increasing state of disorder as they break down and decay from their existing forms. This does however beg the question: where does all the order keep coming from before it becomes prey to the law of entropy? For otherwise by now we should be left with absolutely no order whatsoever.

If things were simply just breaking down all the time then no order could exist and neither could evolution happen because there would be no stable forms out from which new and emergent life forms could appear. This suggests that entropy is only a part of the story and that it is a necessary part of the refinement and evolving process of life itself. There appears to be a method, or even intelligence, in the way that forms and order are built up and then broken down and then reconstituted into yet another form.

This proposes that there is a constant state of flux between energy and matter rather than there being simply a case of one or the other prevailing at any given time. They are, in fact, different expressions of the same thing and can therefore move freely from one state to the other in a logical and coherent way.

Scientists do not really understand why order exists in the Universe for there are no simple reasons to explain its existence. There is no rational explanation for how and why a fertilised egg knows how to split and differentiate so that it eventually develops into a human being. Whilst the codings for certain specific characteristics may exist within the DNA structure, the process of cell differentiation and specialisation still remains largely a mystery.

Latest theories in this area are focusing on the idea of coherence and that there might be some form of unseen, quantum intelligence that exists within and between living things that gives them their form and their ability to communicate.

Coherence literally means that things are on the same wavelength, and the more things are on the same wavelength the greater the power between them. If two things demonstrate coherence then their wave patterns show an advanced and amplified pattern far beyond that of just adding the two together. If the two wave patterns show discordant coherence (interference) then their patterns tend to cancel each other out.

The idea of coherence in nature excites scientists for it seems to show that there is inherent order and intelligence within the design of things and that there are definite benefits for the life forms involved. This applies both within an individual organism and in groups as well. The greater the degree of coherence that exists, the healthier the individual and group will be.

Coherence is also to do with understanding or things being intelligible. If things aren't coherent then, at the risk of stating the obvious, they are incoherent. Incoherence is a state of disorder and therefore inefficient, ineffective and possibly dangerous.

It is easy to misunderstand what something else might be saying if there is incoherence between the parties. For example, when the Spanish discovered Mexico they asked some of the local Indian tribes what the peninsula they had landed on was called. When the Indians replied by saying *"Yucatan!"* which means, "I don't understand you!" the Spanish assumed that that was the name of the peninsula, and that remains its name today.

Coherence is the primary state that the Universe seems to exist in rather than entropy, for coherence allows for the flow and communication of information.

Entropy is simply a process of breakdown to allow greater coherence to appear. It is almost as though this process goes on to help more and better order to appear. Only when entropy appears as an end in itself does coherence lessen and complete breakdown occur.

This can be seen at individual level where it has been discovered that a lot, if not most, illness is caused by lack of coherence within the body. Obvious examples of this are when a person eats something that is poisonous or not good for them or they smoke, overeat, or drink too much alcohol or take drugs.

These substances destabilise the natural state of coherence within the body and prevent it from working at optimum. As another example, it can only be destabilising to a child's level of coherence when it is estimated that by the age of 18 the average American child will have seen approximately 18,000 murders on TV. This can only introduce incoherence into their faculties.

THE UNIVERSE DOESN'T SPEAK GIBBERISH

It is not merely physical substances that cause either coherence or incoherence. How people think affects their coherence and well-being. Tests show that people who have an optimistic outlook on life tend to be healthier and live longer, as do people who believe in God.

Coherence is difficult to achieve for people today because they are constantly being bombarded with all sorts of different signals and messages that they have to absorb, assimilate, translate and process. This is made worse by the fact that many of these messages are incoherent to the natural state of order that the human design is meant to operate under. Many of the messages received are about breakdown, difficulty and what is wrong in the world. In short, messages of entropy.

This creates a state of increasing entropy and incoherence to the point where people come to believe that the principle of entropy is the predominant state in the world and the Universe. It is little wonder that when people try to communicate they have difficulty understanding each other because they don't even understand themselves.

The main cause of this entropy is interference, which occurs when there are too many signals being received for the intended signal to be heard clearly. This leads to confusion for the message cannot be heard clearly and may well be misunderstood.

If the lines of communication are clear and uninterrupted then a person is able to listen to what is going on, both inside and outside. This is why it is so important for people to have quiet time where they can stop all the noise and simply listen to what their systems might be trying to tell them. When a person does manage to get into these states they can then think about things in a different way and make better decisions about the future.

At the next world conference on global warming and climate change perhaps the world leaders should do a meditation before beginning the conference, for this could help quieten the noisy agendas that they all have and help put them on the same wavelength.

To many this may seem like a ridiculous idea, but it can't be much worse than what happens at the moment with all sorts of different needs and demands being bandied around like there is no tomorrow. There might not be if that way of going on continues for much longer!

Most scientists doubt whether higher human faculties, such as clairvoyance and telepathy, actually exist and claim that laboratory experiments are, at best, inconclusive. What they do not realise is that the design of the experiment itself is either coherent or incoherent to these higher human systems.

Therefore, in seeking to make the experiment objective they, in fact, influence the chance of it being successful by often creating an incoherent atmosphere. Those scientists who have pursued these studies further and to a deeper level have found that a warm and non-challenging environment helps these higher systems work better without necessarily compromising the objectivity of the test itself.

SETTING THE ECOLOGY FOR BETTER UNDERSTANDING

This suggests that in order for coherence to work better there has to be an atmosphere of warmth and trust. Again, the world leaders could take a leaf out of this book and meet in less formal circumstances and perhaps bring their spouses and children. Their decisions are primarily going to affect their children's future, so perhaps if their children were actually present they might think about things differently.

Children have much better natural coherence than adults, for whilst young they are not so prone to pick up on the interference and noise of the everyday world. This is something they develop as they get older.

Therefore, there could be a United Nations Conference for children on world issues and the adults should be made to attend, listen and implement the keynote decisions of the children at the conference. Not all of them might work, but it is highly likely that their proposals will bring better results than the highly politicised and vested interest decisions the adults often come to.

It is rather unlikely that children would come up with ideas such as genetic engineering and cloning because in a coherent state such ideas would not even be possible to conceive. It is only the incoherent state of the world and the mess that it has got itself into that causes adults to look for desperate solutions to problems.

Whilst scientists might say that activities such as genetic engineering and GM foods can be safely policed and controlled, they do not have any idea as to how such activities affect the inherent order and coherence of the organisms they are dealing with. They are, as a result, creating a state of entropy and disorder.

They may think that they can control the genetic splicing and mixing, but changing the electromagnetic field causes not only physical changes but, far more importantly, it rearranges its coherence and therefore causes it to transmit and receive different signals. This establishes an incoherent wave pattern and the more this pattern is reinforced the more powerful it becomes.

The arguments against things like genetic engineering and cloning are often presented as moral and even religious arguments, and these clearly have validity. Equally powerful, however, is the argument that science itself would make against such activities. It is one thing to cross-breed animals and plants at physical level to try and obtain optimum breeds, but to seek to do so at cellular and sub-atomic level is fraught with dangers.

Children tend to have a natural affinity with the practical and are highly unlikely to make such rash and dangerous decisions as some of their elders.

The UN has, in fact, already had such children's conferences but the major problem with them is that they have no mandate for any kind of influence on the real decision making process in the world. Lots of talk is made about how important and valuable they are but they are not given credence in the corridors of power. The same could be said of UN women's conferences, for they too are likely to come up with sensible and rational decisions about the future because they are less prone to incoherence than men are.

However, what is really needed is for men, women and children to all find a common wavelength where the future is concerned. This is not hard to find because it already exists within the human design and within all living things and the Earth itself.

Everything in the Universe moves to one degree or another. Even rocks, mountains and continents move over time and the Earth itself moves through time and space as it orbits the Sun whilst at the same time spinning on its axis.

Everything moves, not only of its own account, but also in relation to everything else and has its own particular resonance, vibration and wave pattern. When it meets anything else there is mixing of wave patterns which can either cause enhancement, disorder or they can cancel each other out.

In the world today the patterns that people live under destabilise the natural coherent wave patterns that are inherent within their design. The biggest contributor to this destabilising of the natural inner order within is stress.

Stress, in all its many forms causes an undermining of natural coherence and causes things to behave in an uncharacteristic manner. This happens not only to human beings but to all forms of life when they are put into stressful and unnatural circumstances. For example, animals in zoos often start to behave in uncharacteristic ways and sometimes harm themselves when stressed.

Human beings aren't that different, for not only do they put animals in zoos so they can look at them, but they also build their own zoos for themselves. These are called *cities*. City living is one of the biggest causes of stress with the pace, pressure and demands of modern life being very punishing upon the internal order of the person. With all the noise, pollution and cramped and overcrowded living conditions it is little wonder that people struggle to find meaning or coherence in their lives as they are assailed from all sides with impressions, signals and frequencies that shake them from head to foot.

Without any kind of stable inner core in place these frequencies start to undermine the person's coherence at every level and changes them into something that is no longer themselves. In other words, they develop a new wave pattern of incoherence that they now identify as being themselves. They might, for example, start to think of themselves as being a doctor, lawyer, teacher, housewife, factory worker or whatever, because that is, in fact, what they have become.

Not only that but they also then start to develop ceremonies or customs that reinforce this pattern of behaviour making it even harder to escape its influence.

The problems emerge when different groups of different wave patterns meet and have different and conflicting interests. This literally leads to a disturbance as each group sees the other group's wave pattern as a threat. Mostly people aren't consciously aware of what is happening and simply react according to their existing established wave pattern.

Because they are removed from whom and what they really are, they can only assume that they have the right wave pattern and the other wave pattern must therefore be wrong. Yet the reality is that if people were not so removed from themselves they would never see another human being or group as a threat and nor would they themselves be one.

The first thing they would see when they looked at another person would be a friend because the first realisation would be that the other person was a fellow human being and not a stranger.

This is what children do when they meet another child for they, in a way, see another part of themselves. They do not even notice things such as skin colour because it is not yet in their wave pattern to do so. Sometimes they notice strange and alien wave patterns about the adults they meet, which is why they sometimes appear to cry for no apparent reason.

There is a lot to learn about coherence and the future from children. We should take the time to listen to them and seek their counsel whilst sharing the benefits of what we know has worked for the good of all so far. This can only be a formula for success.

It's not the answers we have for children that is the key to the future, but the questions we have for them. What, therefore would be your first question to a class of 9 year olds?

?

THE FUTURE OF MEN AND WOMEN

Let not men then, in the pride of power, use the same arguments that tyrannic kings and venal ministers have used, and fallaciously assert that women ought to be subjected because she has always been so.

Mary Wollstonecraft

The source of all life and knowledge is in man and woman, and the source of all living is in the interchange and the meeting and mingling of these two: man-life and woman-life, man-knowledge and woman-knowledge, man-being and woman-being.

D H Lawrence

THE FUTURE OF MEN
AND WOMEN

IF YOU ARE A MAN reading this chapter there may be reasons to be afraid; to be very afraid!

For the latest news is that men might become redundant as recent scientific research has postulated that the Y chromosome that men carry is gradually becoming weaker in its genetic influence. Therefore in a few hundred thousand years it might not be needed at all – and therefore neither will men. Women will be able to clone and engineer children to their desired taste and so the need for men to father children will have disappeared.

This threat of redundancy is compounded by recent books regarding the alleged conspiracy by men to suppress the sacred feminine influence throughout history so that they could stay in power and control.

Men's long held and long assumed position of pre-eminence appears to be under threat.

Whether or not any of this is true misses the point entirely. Whether Jesus married Mary Magdalene and moved to France to start a family is not really relevant to the people of today, unless a person builds their life on articles of faith as dogmas to be followed at all costs.

Many people do indeed do this and use it as justification for oppressing others because their articles of faith not only allow them to do so, but demand it. Tradition is therefore an easy way to justify oppressive and outdated behaviour patterns.

The way to behave now cannot be found in the past, it can only be found now. The past can give guidance but the way forward lies in the now. It must be that the strongest suit the human race has in its hand is that there are two genders that have endured all of world history and have survived to this point together.

The fact of two genders, two expressions, two styles, two natures, two frequencies, two divinities, two rhythms within the one species, must be able to tell us a great deal about how to think about the challenges facing the human race now and into the future. For each person spends their life being one or other of these two expressions.

The human race could therefore be likened to an electric cell, with the genders representing the positive and negative cells, whereby connected electricity can flow through it.

They need to work according to their true nature in order to enable the natural flow of electricity to occur. There is no use in either cell trying to be like the other because two negatives won't allow the electricity to flow and neither will two positives. This goes some of the way towards explaining why ideas such as equal rights for the genders is actually a flawed concept. In such a situation the question arises as to where those rights are derived and from which perspective people are deemed to be equal?

If it is seeking to grant women the same rights as men then that is a misaligned premise, for trying to place women at the same level as men is condescending and patronising to women.

It has been said that human rights are what masters give their slaves; freedom is what God gives a person. Therefore, until the genders are able to treat each other with freedom, respect and value then the necessary breakthrough in gender relations will remain an unfulfilled dream.

Whilst an upgrade of rights is desirable if it leads to an improvement of the situation of women in the world, there are higher levels of mutuality to reach for by men and women together. Otherwise the richness of the exchange between the genders gets blurred in some kind of political correctness.

This process of departure from naturalness between the genders has been a long and aggregating process. This displacement also occurs more predominantly in advanced cultures where the so-called battle of the sexes and the alienation and misunderstanding is the greatest.

The expectancy in the West to be in a nuclear family as a self-contained unit creates pressure on the relationships within it. There must be something in the fact that simply by changing the order of the first two letters of *nuclear* the word *unclear* is revealed.

With all the bombardment young people receive about relationships, love and sex they end up confused and pressured into being what they think they should be for everyone else except themselves. It is little wonder, therefore, that the world of gender relations seems both unclear and nuclear to many people.

What leads many away from the natural truth of themselves is propaganda. Because of this the true relationship between the genders gets easily lost in role playing rather than the natural dignity, quality and mutual enhancement that ought to be the case.

THE TREND OF RELATIONSHIPS

As far as recorded history goes, in the last 10,000 years men have been dominant where the ordering and structuring of the vast majority of cultures and societies has been concerned.

It is men who have mostly been the leaders, determined the policies, gone to war, fought over territory and subjected women to various forms of suppression. Even in the West, only 100 years ago a woman's property automatically became her husband's upon marriage, he was entitled by law to beat her if she refused to have sex, and women in most countries did not have the vote.

Most cultures have developed their own forms of suppression of women over the centuries. This includes the practice of suttee in India, female genital mutilation, forcing women to cover up by wearing the hajib and burdah, and much more from education and job discrimination to viewing women as sex objects and forcing them into prostitution and worse.

Yet all the legislation about equal rights or the rise of feminism will not lead to real and fundamental change where the relationship between men and women is concerned. What is needed is a change in the attitude that the genders have about each other and how they might work better together in mutuality and partnership.

History reveals much where the partnership between the genders is concerned. After all, history is almost *HIS STORY*. So where is *HER STORY*? It has been sanitised, edited and censored by men.

Fear has caused men to betray their true and inner nature and rely more and more on the physical, by imposing themselves on the world and women as well. Their outer strength has, in fact, become their greatest weakness.

Men mostly think that they can find themselves within the possession and use of power, but that is a departure from the truth. Real power can only be found in surrendering to how one was meant to be. It cannot be natural to be a bully, a tyrant, hot and aggressive, threatening and loud.

Yet these are the techniques that many men have adopted to gain power rather than being as they would naturally be.

GOD IS A MAN – OFFICIAL!

The next avenue to pursue in this gender research is a big one, in fact the biggest of all - God! For the image that most cultures and religions in the world carry about God is that *HE* is a *MAN*. Expressions like 'God in *HIS* mercy' are used and this reinforces the myth that not only is god in human form, but that *HE* is a man.

The image of God is one of a wise, sage-like, elderly gentleman who looks a bit like Socrates, or some other wise man from Athens, who sits on a cloud 'up there' in heaven pulling all the strings about what goes on down here.

This view is reinforced through most religious teachings given to the young such as the fact that it took God six days to create the Universe and that on the seventh day *HE* rested. Yet how could God create the Universe unless God itself contained the duality of both the masculine and feminine principles? Was the feminine expression an afterthought by God to give the man something to play with? As ludicrous as this sounds and is, this is the story or history as it has mostly been passed down through the ages.

The story of Adam and Eve illustrates this view. Adam (curiously enough Adam = A dam) got lonely/bored and so God (the man) felt sorry for Adam and decided to help him. When Adam was asleep God took one of his ribs and from that rib he made Eve. Later this experiment went badly wrong for Eve tempted Adam away from the truth by offering him forbidden fruit from the tree of life. Poor Adam was clearly the victim here, for that is how the story is portrayed.

The truth is that it is the feminine principle that gives birth first. The Universe itself works primarily by this principle for it is continuously giving birth. This reality is confronting to men's egos for it suggests that the higher part of their journey lies in acquiescence and service to this principle rather than in seeking power and control over it.

It is noteworthy that it has been rare for women to start wars through the ages. Nor have they been the main promoters in developing nuclear weapons, exploiting the planet's resources, abusing human rights and developing systems of torture. They are not champions of polluting the finely tuned atmosphere of the planet, nor are they the main protagonists where violence and crime are concerned.

These pursuits are alien to the feminine principle and this shows two things: firstly that women are more likely to find these negative practices abhorrent or unacceptable; nor do they generally condone or practise them.

Secondly it says that the legacy that men have created indicates that they are not in touch with that feminine principle to any great degree. This enables them to perpetrate some of these horrors for they have managed to suppress this higher part of themselves or block it out from their decision making processes.

Somehow, deep within the psyche and consciousness of humanity, the seed has been planted and grown that women are somehow lesser than men and need to be kept in their place. This view extends into such stories as Mary and her alleged immaculate conception.

An ordinary woman was deemed not to be good enough to house the divine presence of God so she had to be impregnated by God direct. This concept of Immaculate Conception was not something that the early Church itself advocated, but it came to be adopted later in Church history as the role of women became more and more marginalised.

Could it therefore be another part of the male myth to keep the status quo maintained?

Consider the article of faith for so many people in the world today – the Bible. It is often said that the Bible we have today is the authorised version of God's word in its two forms: the Old and New Testaments – or by anagram, the Old and New *Statements*. Only 500 years ago it was an offence punishable by death to own a copy of the Bible. Indeed, William Tyndale was burned at the stake for translating the Bible into English.

In the 4th century AD there was an emergency meeting of the Church clergy as there were already many different versions of the Bible in circulation with often wildly conflicting interpretations. A Council was held to decide what should be in the Bible and what should not. This Council was attended by men only as women priests have never been allowed in the Catholic Church. A standard Latin version was agreed and the bits that have been left out are now called the Apocrypha, which means hidden. The 14 books omitted from the official version contain much feminine influence that would counterbalance the over-masculine influence that remains within the authorised version.

It is therefore not surprising that the most common prayer in the Christian Church begins "Our Father who art in heaven....", but where is the 'Our Mother'?

This mother aspect is something that the earliest and most primitive forms of art pay tribute to or worship; the Earth Goddess and the ripeness offered by the female form. Men were confronted by the more natural affinity that women have to the rhythms and cycles of the Earth and thereby sought to gain some kind of parity through other means. Perhaps this is where civilisation began, for what was it the civilisation of?

It is fascinating that a woman's menstrual cycle is similar to that of the moon.

This suggests that menstruation is much more than simply a physical process of ovulation and discharge that a woman goes through once a month in order to keep her available to become impregnated by a man. It has long been known and understood in esoteric circles that this process is part of the woman's deep and occult connection to the Earth and the forces and rhythms of nature. Yet most of this understanding has long become lost or hidden during the course of history.

Also consider for a moment the major religious saviours and prophets throughout history. Why is it that they are, by vast majority, men? Part of this comes from the fact that most of the cultures that gave rise to them are mainly male dominated. Therefore not only is man made in the image of God but, more accurately, Man makes God in the image of himself.

Perhaps there is another feature in this. The conjecture here is that the appearance of these saviours or masters as men is to balance out or compensate for some extreme behaviour more commonly propagated by men. It is rare for women to torture, pillage, murder, rape, destroy, carry out genocide and so on. Women over the course of history have tended to stay truer to the line of natural behaviour due to their design and gender function, i.e. the giving birth to life and the nourishing of it. Men can more easily forget this line and stray from it, for not only have many of the great saviours been men, but so have most of the great dictators, conquerors, suppressors and imperial controllers and enslavers of other lives.

This is not natural to men, and they might give pause to reflect that it is far better to be steady and constant in how they behave individually and collectively. Erratic behaviour undermines the true line of evolutionary growth.

This is not meant to be some kind of men bashing for women must, for their part, have allowed the men to take this control. For this to have occurred, both genders must have departed from their natural and connected mutual purpose.

Nor is women trying to compete equally in a 'man's world' any kind of true equality. It is simply competition. Cavemen still exist today and they still go "Ug" to each other, although today they are not threatening each other with a club, they are using weapons of mass destruction or corporate business logos and make killings on the stock market as well as the battlefield.

One of the Achilles heels that men have is that when they feel insecure they tend to compete. No amount of encounter group sessions can remedy this situation for the only thing that can unite men is a common purpose. There must therefore be something in the way of being a Gentle Man that is little understood and seldom demonstrated by men, particularly those who wield the power.

In a true man the natural balance is to be gentle on the outside and firm on the inside. Compare this to how men in the world are forced to go on, forever striving, competing, winning, pushing back space, earning money, seeking promotion, getting ahead, and so on. They are caused to be ever thrusting, pitching, acquiring, and so often end up on the outside of themselves.

To compensate for this outward pressure and stress they often go loose and soft on the inside and end up developing a need to be dominated when they are away from their outward control persona. This explains in part why men who get to positions of high power sometimes develop perverse sexual habits; they have lost themselves in their outer life so they also become not themselves in their inner life. They therefore lose themselves twice.

The same also applies to women in an adjacent way. A lady is meant to be firm on the outside and gentle on the inside. She will know what she will not have or allow because that which she cherishes and nurtures will accept nothing less.

The over-riding principle is one of life-giving and life-affirming and she will resist anything that will lessen or diminish that stance. By seeing herself, (or allowing others to see her) as lesser, is a diminishment of her natural process and function.

THE CEREMONY OF GENDER

This knowledge has been well known to primitive cultures where women and men developed behaviours in order to regulate their processes together. As an example of this, in many of these cultures it is the men's role to hunt for food, forage, fish, find new territory, and so on. In doing these kinds of activities mostly away from the regulated atmosphere of the village or tribe (the standard of which is held and maintained by the women) the men might become hot and aggressive.

Therefore elaborate ceremonies were developed to 'welcome the men folk home.' These ceremonies were in fact a regulating process whereby the men were conditioned and cleaned up from their pursuits in order that they did not bring back certain hot natures into the village.

As the understanding of how and why these processes are important gets lost, the potency of them diminishes. The more this happens the less the need for them is perceived. They become either quaint traditions or abandoned and lost altogether or worst of all, become no longer politically correct.

This relationship between the genders in its higher forms could be characterised by the imagery of the lady carrying the standard below which things will not be allowed to go and the gentleman being the champion of principle that will be upheld. What a magnificent coupling that can be. What comfort and encouragement that can offer, each to the other. What teamwork it can lead to. How inspiring it can be, one to the other.

In a man the power lies in what he says 'no' to as a first principle, and for the woman it lies firstly in what she says 'yes' to. This is not based in terms of positive or negative, good or bad, so much as what is governing the decision making process. The key word in this is that of power, for this is perhaps the most misunderstood and misapplied word in human history.

Power has come to mean power or control over someone or something else, and in its lower aspects this is exactly what happens. This leads to the subjugation of another rather than using that power to liberate and set free. In its higher, natural aspects power means an ability or capacity to do something. In physics power means work done per unit of time.

The power of everything lies in what people say 'yes' and 'no' to. The more powerful their 'yes' and 'no' systems are, the more another aspect of power is activated. This is to do with the rate at which electrical energy is fed into or taken out from a device or system, i.e. the person.

'Yes' and 'no' are not different, for inside every 'no' there is a 'yes' and inside every 'yes' there lives a 'no'. As stated earlier, the approach for the genders is natured slightly differently but complementary.

All this does not mean suddenly adopting behaviours because that is how one thinks one should behave. What it means is to embark on the journey of being true to one's gender as part of the natural expression of a life. One doesn't find this in magazines or via film or pop stars lives or in cosmetics or fashion. One finds it inside oneself, for it is not something to be learned as such. Rather it is something to be unlocked from the pedigree and promise of what one already is coupled with the brilliance of what one could yet be.

PYRAMIDS AND CIRCLES

One of the ways that this departure is characterised is through the development of hierarchies or class systems. Men in particular fall prone to this for they are more analytical and logical in their approach to things and therefore tend to classify things in a more structured way. Women, on the other hand, tend to be better at inclusivity and power sharing. The best form of decision making process would be to involve both natures equally wherever possible because both methods give the other context and perspective.

The key words in this whole relationship between the genders are communication and dialogue and it is vital that these are formed around a purpose. Without a purpose things can only be personal and ego based, which is why so many relationships go badly wrong. The premise of any relationship can and must set the agenda for its ways and means, what is important and the protocols that will be applied.

It is rare to find genuine dialogue and communication going on in the world. Mostly what happens within any communication is that people communicate through a series of monologues or speeches. One person does their speech and then stops and then the other person does theirs, and so it goes on. The reason this happens is that people don't know how to listen properly. A person listens *at* what another person says rather than listening *to* what is being said and what is behind the words.

It seems to be significant that the word *listen* anagrams to *silent* for there seems to be no more important factor in listening than for a person to quieten their own internal noise in order to receive what another person is saying. Men are prone to pitch, rather than yaw and wait for things whereas for women the weakness can often be one of passivity; of quiet acceptance and resignation to the way things might be.

Women do not need equality or liberation from suppression and oppression. What they really need from men is recognition. If men truly recognised women for what they represent then there would be no need for equality or liberation because it would already be there. The way that men can better appreciate these qualities in women is to better recognise the deeper qualities in themselves.

The question is: what are these qualities and how do men and women recognise and express them?

He is half of a blessed man. Left to be finished by such as she;
and she a fair divided excellence, whose
fullness of perfection lies in him.

William Shakespeare

Understanding is a two-way street.

Eleanor Roosevelt

MEN AND WOMEN AND THE EVOLUTION OF SENTIMENT

THE STUDY OF EVOLUTION IS today generally approached from the standpoint of it being a biological process of natural selection that has no intelligence as a driving force within it. Even the mention of the words 'intelligent design' can almost make the Neo Darwinists of this world have a fit of apoplexy. To them the concept of intelligent design has no place within empirical biology for it is simply a dressed up version of Creationism which holds that God literally created the Earth and everything in six days and that on the seventh day he rested.

The problem facing the Neo Darwinists and the Creationists is that both only have a part of the picture, and seemingly a rather dogmatic and inflexible part at that.

It is quite clear that the Creationist view of the Universe being created in seven days is not a sustainable one given the fossil and archaeological records that are now available about life and the history of the Earth. The Biblical view of how the Universe began should be looked at as being a theory that was based on the information and intelligence available to people at the time.

New evidence has since come to light to show that most of that theory should now be discarded. The parts of the theory that haven't yet been disproved should remain as conjecture awaiting further evidence to either prove or disprove it. For example: the question of whether God was or wasn't involved in the process of creating the Universe.

Whether there is or isn't some form of higher intelligence within Creation still remains unknown and may remain unknowable. The irony is that, for atheists and true believers alike, the existence or not of any higher deity remains an article of faith for both.

The Neo Darwinists would assert that all can be explained through the principle of natural selection whereby the organisms that are best adapted to suit the needs of their environment are the ones that are most likely to survive and prosper at the expense of those less well adapted. This idea is both profoundly simple and logical and the evidence to support this theory is great and compelling.

The fact of this process working doesn't, however, get rid of the Creationists and intelligent design advocates as quickly as the reductionists would like, for the Darwinian model does not explain why things mutate and adapt. What is the ghost in the machine that causes the organism to change in order to survive?

Biologists may assert that in the sea of random genetic change it is simply the case that those that change in the most beneficial way survive. This is a bold assertion for they cannot prove that there isn't some kind of intelligence within organisms that makes them able to adapt and respond to the changes in their environment any more than Creationists can prove that God did it. Some organisms even seem to be able to anticipate change before it happens by having certain adaptive systems in place before the external changes occur.

In the cold, analytical world of Neo Darwinism life and evolution is simply a game of chance and odds. Either a species makes an adaptive change or it doesn't. If it does it survives, if it doesn't it becomes extinct. Perhaps this is correct but perhaps on the other hand it isn't.

Or possibly, like the theory of Creationism, it may need to adapt its original thesis?

The main problem here is that theorists do not like changing their theories. This in itself is not beneficial, for theological inflexibility (either Creationist or Darwinian) suggests that at some point in the future there may be none of either left on the planet!

Whatever the truth of the human story as to how and why we got to be here, the arguments as to whether it was Creationist or Darwinian or both or neither are, in the final analysis, academic. The fact is that we do exist and the question is whether we can exist in the future and, if so, what adaptive changes are and will be needed to do so?

Despite what the biologists might say, the evidence suggests that adaptive change is not merely biological. Believing in some higher deity causes a person to have a healthier immune system and live longer than someone who doesn't. This must be depressing for Neo Darwinists, for not only are they likely to die out in the future, they will also get less time to enjoy their life here!

Just because belief in some kind of higher deity is a beneficial adaptive change it doesn't, of course, prove that such a deity exists. Conversely, Darwinists can't legitimately or even reasonably claim that such a deity doesn't exist. All that can be said is that such belief is a beneficial adaptive change that can have positive consequences.

This adaptive behaviour to do with belief has itself mutated over the centuries since it first appeared thousands of years ago in different directions. The ones that develop fundamentalism, dogma and intolerance tend to lead to war, murder and suppression and as such are not beneficial changes.

On the other hand a belief in a benign, higher deity and a practical application of what that higher deity may want humans do – which is to love each other and do good deeds – appears to be a positive adaptation.

This suggests that human relationships would do well to be placed on this footing in order to facilitate positive genetic and spiritual change where the future is concerned. It is not the biological changes that have got the human race into the perilous state they find themselves in, but changes in attitudes and values. These have evolved generally in a negative direction and need to be corrected.

It is arrogant and dangerous to criticise or mock ancient peoples for their paradigms of the world as they were simply interpreting reality and translating it through their particular filters at that time. The evidence suggests that the filters that modern humans have are much more dangerous than those of ancient peoples, for the ones of today can lead to much more damage.

WARP ISN'T HEALTHY

As misaligned views get developed and passed on they become ever more warped and out of date regarding the truth of the situation. This then leads to increased dogmatism, fundamentalism and inflexibility.

This principle applies in all areas of knowledge but in particular, in respect of the content of this chapter, it applies to gender relations. At some point in history men decided that they were superior to women and that they would therefore adapt their societies to reflect that fact and reinforce it through the customs, religions and social practices of their societies.

Current theories suggest that this process effectively began around the same time as modern civilizations – around 8-10,000 years ago. City living led to shortages in food and therefore men developed a patriarchal and patrilineal system of government to ensure that their position was better protected than that of the women.

It is not coincidental that the beginning of men asserting their power over women occurs at the same time that humans start to make a significant and damaging impact on the Earth. It is also around this time that humans began to be able to control the forces of nature to any significant degree.

The conspiracy theorists who talk about the suppression of the sacred feminine perhaps miss the point, for this is not about men suppressing women but rather mankind seeking to suppress the Great Mother, i.e. the Earth itself.

This is further evidenced by the fact that, in evolutionary terms, there was an octave jump in human intellectual capacity around 10,000 years ago. Humans began to be able to think and act differently. They were now able to think about their world in a new way and plan and control their lives much more than previously possible.

In a sense the rise of brain capacity and technology in those days was the equivalent of stone-age man's industrial revolution.

As a consequence of this intellectual leap humans began to be governed much more by their head than their heart. The brain and mind were much more advanced than their simpler lower systems, and so ancient humans began to rely much more on these advanced brain systems to improve their living conditions and quality of life.

It seems that they also suppressed the side of themselves that had enabled them to live within their various ecologies as a successful species, alongside and in harmony with the rest of nature. As they became more based in rationality and reasoning, this process of departure accelerated and exacerbated over the course of history.

EARTH anagrams to *HEART* and perhaps this is where the renewal of the relationship with the planet on which we live needs to begin. Unless humans have a heartfelt feeling about their planetary home they will continue to treat it and everything on it as commodities to exploit.

In the shift in centre of gravity from the heart to the head, the platform of the heart was relegated rather than built on and the sentiment that humans felt about their existence and their relationship with the Earth and each other weakened. It is not being said that this sentiment applied to all human cultures that existed at this time, but it did apply to many of them. The records that exist in respect of these early cultures indicate that most of them worshipped some form of Earth Goddess and there is little, if any, evidence of them being exploitative upon their environment in the way we are today.

Many, in fact, carried myths or memories of a sacred relationship with the Earth, the whole of their environment and each other, and very few appear to have carried any sense of gender dominance. There seems to have been a sharing of responsibility between the genders, and within this a respect for each other and each other's contribution to the whole.

However, this sentiment between the genders weakened as men sought the ascendancy in their relationships by using their physical strength coupled with this new found brain acumen. In respect of these new mental powers, men developed the left hemisphere more than the right. This led to an imbalance and dominance towards logic, analysis and rationalism. This was done at the expense of the right hemisphere of the brain that governs feelings, intuition and emotions.

As there was no equivalent progression in the development of feelings and sentiment, this led to a self-centred rationalisation of the human race's position in the Universe.

It does not therefore appear to be sensible to try to rationalise ourselves out of the predicament we find ourselves in. These faculties have their role but there is another place to start, and this applies in particular to the relationship between the genders.

The feminine principle of partnership has been suppressed and marginalised over thousands of years of recorded human history. This in turn has led to an imbalance in the human condition and the human race's relationship with the Earth and with each other.

In short, the over developed masculine influence is not listening.

It is not simply a matter of men not listening to women, for although that is true, it is rather a symptom of the human race not listening to its own internal voice and to that of the planet upon which it lives. If it did listen to these rhythms and feelings then even its rational side would see that many, if not most, of the activities that human beings do in the name of progress amount to environmental genocide and self-sabotage on a global scale.

LEARNING TO LISTEN

The human race has forgotten how to listen, and perhaps this hidden side of ourselves has forgotten how to speak to us. We need to remember how to do this before it is too late.

It is a tragedy that the relationship between the genders often gets reduced down to commercial considerations, such as someone being a good catch or that it will help someone move up the social ladder. In times of old the astrologer priests would always look to the couple's spiritual compatibility before anything else. Without that spiritual compatibility everything else pales into insignificance and becomes commodity trading.

Without sentiment things cannot move on in any meaningful way. With it things could progress quite dramatically, for incredible advances have occurred in human acumen and skill. This now needs a legitimate framework and context for it to be applied to optimum effect.

Whether or not a person approaches this issue from a spiritual or biological basis is immaterial for both approaches converge to the same conclusion. This is that it is our moral obligation and in our own best interests to respond from a place of feeling and sentiment rather than from mechanistic analysis alone.

Basing relationships of any kind strictly on a Cartesian approach is fundamentally flawed and fails to touch the higher aspects of human experience.

Men and women do not fall in love solely because their selfish genes think it is a good evolutionary move. This reductionist approach is far too simplistic and narrow to explain who and what we really are. Humans have higher feelings of sentiment and altruism for a reason and if humans come from this place in themselves it provides evolutionary advantage.

In this, the positives of what the genders share far outweigh the negatives, for if that weren't so we would no longer exist.

The future needs to be the era of co-operation. In nature the relationships that work best are the ones that are symbiotic. This requires the parties to see each other for what they are and not for selfish purposes.

It is time for the genders to share their concerns about the problems and opportunities that they face together. With value and appreciation the best of each other can be promoted. This is where qualities become so important for they define who and what we are.

Nature is an endless combination and repetition of a very few laws.

Ralph Waldo Emerson

It gives me a deep comforting sense that "things seen are temporal and things unseen are eternal."

Helen Keller

THE FUTURE OF LAW
AND GENDER

IN THE WORLD TODAY THERE are thousands upon thousands of laws. Having practised as a lawyer for nearly 25 years - and having read more than my fair share during this time – believe me, I know!

There are statutes about every kind of activity that regulate and control what people can and can't do. There are laws stating where a person is allowed to live and where they aren't, which country has what rights over the sea, who owns the airspace above a house, what to do with a person after they die, and much more besides.

Every aspect of human behaviour is governed and regulated, for there are not only written laws but unwritten laws of tradition and custom, which are often more powerful than those passed by the Government.

WHY HAVE LAWS?

Often laws are only passed to ensure a certain standard of behaviour that people themselves cannot guarantee. Why pass a law requiring a certain standard of behaviour if no one has ever gone, or would contemplate going, below that standard? Some tribal societies do not even have a word for 'stealing', let alone a written legal code legislating against it. Because everyone shares what they have the concept of stealing simply doesn't exist. It is not even taboo because it is unknown.

The need for laws enforcing certain standards of behaviour is a sign that human beings have, to one degree or another, departed from a natural and balanced way of living. The greater the departure, the more laws are needed to enforce a basic standard of behaviour. It is perhaps not surprising, therefore, that the supposed developed and civilised West has far more laws than the undeveloped world.

There are laws to protect rights, enshrine freedoms and regulate behaviour, and there are also international treaties and declarations to further address these principles.

The United Nations Declaration on Human Rights is an admirable piece of work and its sentiments about human rights and freedoms are extremely well expressed. Yet, despite the UN Declaration and most of the countries of the world signing up to it, atrocities have continued to be committed in the world and, if anything, have intensified since it was passed. Indeed, the UN itself can hardly be held up as a shining example of practising what it preaches when only 5% of its top posts are held by women!

Fine words on paper do not change a single attitude. It is awareness that changes attitudes and, in turn, changes in attitude cause a change in behaviour. More important than that is the fact that changes in awareness cause changes in relationships, and that is the key where the future is concerned.

Education and awareness are the keys to making real and meaningful changes where all human relationships are concerned, from parents to children, men to women and nations between each other.

A change of internal awareness leading to a change in behaviour is far more powerful than external laws being imposed which seek to enforce behavioural compliance.

NATURAL LAW OR HUMAN LAW?

Humans share the same basic realities about their lives – and there is much more that unites them than divides them. They all share the same planet, breathe the same air and they all need food, water, warmth and shelter to live. These simple needs are much more powerful than the relatively minor differences that make them seem different, such as religious belief, creed, colour, tribe, age or culture. It is just that many choose to allow these lesser differences to be more important than the major samenesses that they share. This leads to the need for man made laws to ensure that the differences don't get dangerously out of control.

Man made laws often seek to give freedoms to people that should already have them.

Even in calling the laws "man made" highlights part of the problem, for most of the laws in the world are made by men. Some countries won't even let women vote or be part of the governing elite, and the vast majority of governments have few women members in positions of power. And when a country like Sweden has a government that has slightly more female members than male it is trumpeted as an amazing and extraordinary fact. But why? Especially when one considers that Sweden has one of the most socially advanced programmes towards the empowerment of its people and its relationship towards the environment and the future.

In most cultures a breach of the law results in some kind of punishment, and this can mean a term in prison or even death. Yet in many ways people can imprison themselves by the roles they play and expect of each other. It can become much like an actor who has become typecast and cannot escape the role that he or she has become identified with.

Much of the change that is needed is therefore to re-evaluate and rediscover the natural relationship that needs to exist between people and not to assume that the patterns of the past should continue into the future. This is especially so when the evidence suggests that most of these roles have historically been based on men assuming power and treating women as second class citizens.

GENDER AND LAW

There is no man made law that can ensure that there is an increase in humanity. Humanity is a transcendent quality that comes from somewhere much higher than any man made laws or declarations. All laws can do is seek to ensure that people won't do certain things, such as discriminate on the grounds of gender, colour, religion or class.

Whilst this legislation helps to enshrine and guarantee certain basic rights it cannot address the core alignments that are needed to facilitate real and meaningful change.

For example, the Sex Discrimination Act in the United Kingdom makes it unlawful to discriminate against women on the grounds of sex, especially in work matters. This appears to be a forward step and in many ways it is because if employers do not follow the law then they face penalties for failing to do so.

However, in effect it treats women as honorary men and extends the benefits that men have to women. As such it still treats women as second class citizens. Further, it doesn't change the core attitudes or the practices, for they simply become more subtle and covert according to the circumstances and locality.

Ultimately, legislating against a negative behaviour pattern is not the way forward. It may prevent certain unacceptable practices from continuing but it cannot change a mindset. For this to be done there has to be a different vision.

A WAY FORWARD – THE VISION

The key to real change, as stated previously, is a change of awareness. When a person changes their awareness they change their behaviour. In particular this need for change applies in the way that men view women. In most cultures it is the men who have dominant behaviour patterns that keep women suppressed. This in turn creates the need for legislation and declarations to try to remedy the imbalance.

Many men regard women as either being something lesser than themselves or even a chattel. This view is even enshrined in their laws and in their so-called holy books or how they interpret them. It is however, most powerfully enshrined in their behaviour towards women, for it cannot be right that in the Global South that women grow between 60-80 per cent of the food and yet they own less than 2 per cent of the land.

If such views are held then either there is a problem in the interpretation of those books or perhaps they are not as divinely inspired as many of their adherents believe. Perhaps they are more mankind inspired, especially as they are almost all written by men to protect the role and position of men in society in the first place.

In creating new life the sperm and the egg are equal partners. It is an absurdity to say that the sperm is more important than the egg in producing this new life. It is equally an absurdity to suggest that if the produce of that union is a boy child then that is more auspicious than if it is girl. Yet the trend is in that direction, for in India there is now a deficit of 35 million women as more and more families are using prenatal diagnostic technology to find out whether the child is male or female, and if the child is female then it is often aborted or even killed at birth. From having 1010 girls for every 1000 boys in 1941 the ratio plummeted to 927 girls for every 1000 boys in 2001.

If one follows that trend through to its obvious conclusion then it suggests that the ideal scenario would be a world of males only. The day that happens is the day that the human race is doomed to extinction because obviously it is only the women that can give birth to new life. Women give birth to so much more than just babies and world history suggests that the only societies that have any chance of long term sustainability are those that have a strong female influence within them based on respect, joint decision making and power sharing with the men. All societies that are based on over male influence tend to suffer from boom and bust.

A VALUE ADDED PARTNERSHIP

A key to success in the relationship between the genders is therefore not equality but partnership, and a partnership that is based on mutuality, respect and friendship. Friends treat each other with dignity and value and it is from such dealings that real equality can emerge, not the other way around.

Partnerships are formed because people want to do something in the future together and they are formed because the partners bring unique individual talents to the partnership. They are also jointly and equally responsible for how the partnership performs its venture/s.

Surely this is a working template with which the genders can approach the future together?

The past is nowhere near as important as the future for there is no profit in what has or hasn't been done. The children of tomorrow would want us to build a better future than what is on offer now.

What better way is there to do that than to work together in making that a reality?

The only alternative is more and more laws about less and less.

All the laws and declarations in the world aren't as valuable as the warmth of a smile shared between a man and a woman who share a common vision and purpose that unites them as companions on the journey through life.

If the human race can redress the balance of the gender relationship then many, if not all, the current problems we face could be remedied. From war, to Aids, to erosion of homelands, to poverty and alienation – all these issues can be traced, to one degree or another, to an imbalance in the relationship between men and women. It is only by healing that relationship that these problems can be seriously and properly addressed.

It is that vital and that important.

Perhaps one day there will be no need for declarations from the United Nations regarding gender equality for the people of the Earth will live it and breathe it as naturally as the air they all share.

It is our birthright as human beings and a thrilling possibility to see ourselves and each other as we really are. Men and women inspired by and inspiring each other and building a home for the future together. What a mission and what a vision to share.

The key to which does not lie in equality, but recognition. And to recognise quality in another a person must have a bit of it in themselves.

With this in mind, what would you want to recognise and champion in the adjacent gender and what qualities would you want to be recognised for by them?

?

THE FUTURE OF GOD

The feeling remains that God is on the journey, too.

Teresa of Avila

God, it seems to me, is a verb.

Not a noun, proper or improper.

R Buckminster Fuller

Oh how we hate one another for the love of God.

Cardinal Newman

GOD:
GROW OR DIE

THE SUBJECT MATTER OF THIS section is perhaps the most enigmatic of all – God. This topic has kept the human race occupied for thousands of years in thousands of ways as the question of God's existence is debated. If there is a God, what is its nature and how should humans think about it in relation to their situation and the future?

Finding a starter location for this research is tricky for after all, there isn't a chance to go down to the local bookstore and buy the book: *God – The Autobiography.*

There is, however, no shortage of opportunity to go and buy countless books about God written throughout history with various views about this esoteric person or thing called God. The He/She/It/ Them of the greatest mystery of all time.

Ready-made answers where matters of faith and belief are concerned, carry their own health warning. For as the world begins to enter an age of new enlightenment, personal religion and personal responsibility will become important features of self leadership rather than the sheep-like following of the dogmas of others.

The Age of Aquarius has always been associated with an arising of greater individuality and humanity, and perhaps it is not possible to have one without the other. The challenge is to allow this new arising to appear naturally whilst letting go of the old fixed holding patterns, especially where religious dogma is concerned. This is not easy for the world's religions are caught between the dogmas of the past and the tide of change that is seeking new insight and perception into the truth of human existence.

Dogma is dangerous, notably because *DOGMA* backwards is *AM GOD*. Anything that preaches dogma denies the truth that humans live in a Universe of constant flux and change. People need to be open to change and adapt their theories, beliefs and practices, otherwise they will end up repeating the practices of the past when they have passed their sell-by date.

Dogma is inevitably a fixing at lesser truth and therefore it will meet other dogmas at its own level. These dogmas will see each other as different and a threat and so they fight over their differences rather than seeing that perhaps they both need to refine their parochial view of life into a more elevated one.

It is difficult for people to escape their preconceived ideas of what God might be for they are lumbered with the views that they have inherited. Humans believe that God created them in the image of himself because they in fact created God in the image of *themselves* so that God could create them in the image of God!

Such arrogance finds difficulty in accepting that we are not at the centre of the Universe but a tiny speck on the outer reaches of it.

Humans might claim to know this scientifically and ridicule medieval religious dogmas as pig-headed and ignorant, but that doesn't mean that there are not similar attitudes at play today. In many ways modern science, with its dogmas and dismissal of anything 'unscientific', often fulfils the role previously occupied by the Church.

How then is it possible to think about God without falling into some classic arguments, from dogma and fundamentalism to atheism and nihilism and everything in between? Even atheism is a belief system that requires faith, for it is not possible to prove that God does not exist any more than it is possible to prove that God does!

It is perhaps more useful as a starting point to consider God as being a process rather than a person or a being in the ways that the human mind is configured. In this GOD could be seen as an acronym for the processes involved. This would give:

GROW OR DIE.

If life works by this method then that process must have originated from somewhere core to the nature of the Universe itself. In life things are either growing or dying all the time. Cells are replaced in the body at an astonishing rate every moment of every day that people are alive without them knowing about it, even whilst they are asleep.

As a person ages this rate of replacement slows down, yet there are other systems that can continue to grow as the person gains more and more experience and wisdom from how they have lived their life and what truths they have managed to distil out from that experience.

What people believe determines what kind of God or Gods they create and then worship. This applies to every religion there is or has ever been from Animism to Pantheism to Gnosticism to Agnosticism to Judaism to Islam to Shintoism to Buddhism and even Atheism, which as stated is a faith system all on its own. It also applies to the very modern religions of capitalism, materialism and the cult of celebrity. What people believe they grow.

There are as many versions of God in the world today as there are people on the planet. All interpret reality through their own filters so it is difficult to separate fact from invention. It is a wise person who sees this firstly about themselves and starts to question certain views they may have built about these areas.

If humans in their journey are unfinished, then could it be possible that God itself is also unfinished and evolving as well? If there is a God then it seems impossible to suggest that God itself is finished when everything else in Creation and the Universe appears to be unfinished and in the process of change.

Perhaps it is not only God that we need to look to in order to find the miracle we need. After all, *miracle* anagrams to *reclaim,* and if we are to reclaim the future from the past we all need to look inside and find that indelible bit of Creation that knows more about the future than we do.

Who knows, perhaps we reincarnated back in time to try and help out here and save us from our current course? This would certainly bring a different colour to the feeling many have of having been here before! A person may indeed have been here before but perhaps it was (or will be?) in the future, which is perhaps why they may have come back now?

Confused? Excellent! Confusion is the mother of good questions!

THE FUTURE OF THE FUTURE

*If you bring forth what is within you, what
you bring forth will save you.
If you do not bring forth what is within you, what
you do not bring forth will destroy you.*

The Gospel according to Thomas

Prevention is better than cure.

Desiderius Erasmus

MEDICINE OF THE FUTURE

THE JOURNEY OF EVOLUTION IS a process whereby things grow, change, mutate, refine and adapt or become extinct. Within this process, some adaptations lead to upgrade and some do not. Those that don't lead to improvements tend not to be taken forward.

If the human race has developed negative adaptations then it becomes vulnerable and threatened as a species.

When a person, group or species is so engrossed in themselves they fail to notice a slow, declentive movement away from the natural process of evolution. The behaviours and attitudes that emerge from this process are often deemed acceptable because they seem to fit with where things are at that time. But given that the last thing to know that it is in the water is the goldfish some kind of external perception is needed to find the truth of the situation before it is too late.

This understanding is important within the whole area of being remedial into the human condition and how to make a difference in the future.

The first thing needed in any such process is diagnosis. Diagnosis is made up of two parts:

Dia – meaning across
Gnosis – meaning knowledge of the broadest kind across the widest range of disciplines.

Modern medical diagnosis has become obsessed with symptom based analysis of conditions and has come up with a number of remedies that will hopefully cure or ameliorate the symptoms. As a result, in modern cultures there has developed a massive dependency on drugs to treat various illnesses. The drug industry is one of the biggest in the world with countless billions spent each year on it, and it seems that the more that is spent on drugs the more is needed to be spent in an ever increasing spiral.

As Ralph Waldo Emerson once wryly observed, the rise of the Insurance Companies led to an increase in accidents.

The more that people use drugs the more they need them.

Why do drug companies exist? Whilst the drug companies might say that they exist for altruistic reasons, which are to help heal and cure people, the truth is somewhat more prosaic than that. They exist to make a profit. There may be subsidiary motives for their activities, which may indeed be humanitarian, but the inescapable truth is that companies exist to make a profit. If they do not make a profit they will go out of business. It's as simple as that.

Drug companies search around for diseases that need a cure and then try and corner the market on a cure and make a fortune by producing it at a huge mark-up. This may appear a harsh or unfair criticism of the drug companies who produce many needed cures for painful and life threatening maladies, but it is a simple commercial reality.

Humans have survived as a species without the massive dependency on drugs that has developed in the last 100 years. Often the medicines people think they need are developed because humans live at distance from the core of themselves and what might be natural.

As humans have grown and expanded their Western attitudes and cultural ethics, they have subsumed and homogenised many of the so called primitive peoples of the world. A side effect of this is that the world is thereby losing much of these cultures' unique knowledge and skills where medical and natural processes are concerned.

The point here is not to seek to romanticise all old cultures as being idyllic and having no problems. Rather it would be better to de-romanticise some of the myths that modern people often have about their own cultures. The height of this arrogance occurred in the 1960's when the consensus was that humans were winning the war against disease and that it would not be long before there was a bug free, illness free world. That was a Utopian myth, the bubble of which has been well and truly burst with the rise of diseases such as AIDS, CJD and Ebola.

The warning signs now suggest that dependence on unnatural remedies sometimes has a spectacular short term benefit. However over the long term it makes the human race vulnerable to attack from the Superbugs that develop immunity to the drugs that are used against them.

WHAT IF THERE ARE NO ENEMIES?

One of the weaknesses of modern culture is its propensity to work by escalation or confrontation rather than by co-operation. This adversarial process tries to win by conquering the 'enemy'. Such brinkmanship leads to a point where there is no super duper whizzo drug to beat the latest super duper, ultra immune bug.

Old world farmers and medicine men knew these rules very well and developed ways of working within the natural order rather than trying to beat it. This in no way suggests that all their systems were perfect or without flaw, but they evolved over thousands of years and have been tried and tested and stood the test of time. They often get dismissed by modern scientists as superstitious hogwash with no basis in scientific fact. Yet modern intensive farming and medical methods have only been around for little over 100 years and already the cracks are beginning to show in this system. The Irish potato famine of the 1840's gives a salutary lesson about the dangers of monoculture farming methods yet the lessons haven't really be learnt for such methods continue today.

In many cases ancient remedies and cures get labelled as being 'alternative' because modern science has declared itself the judge and jury of all matters medical as to what works and what doesn't.

In its pathological desire to cure disease and illness it fails to appreciate their function and purpose. Disease and illness are like a Nature Information Service, both at individual and collective level. The Black Death was a plague with a message that human beings were living in squalid, overcrowded, unhealthy and unhygienic conditions.

As the lesson wasn't heeded, nature took its course and lowered the population levels accordingly until people did get the point of needing to improve their hygiene and living standards in their overcrowded cities.

A modern version of this parable could be seen to be Aids which shows that nature is trying to teach the human race a lesson in terms of its lifestyle and promiscuity. If the lesson is only learnt at shallow levels the problem will resurface later, maybe in a different form but possibly with more devastating results.

The obsession with symptom based cures is creating a time bomb as humans meddle with the natural forces leading towards a possible Armageddon event of the human race's own making.

One has to be careful in interpreting these signs however for many, like the so called End Timers in the USA, use these signs to fuel the fire of their own religious fundamentalist agendas by saying that it is all part of God's plan. It is far better to simply say that it is not a good evolutionary move to wreck one's environment and habitat, regardless of what God may or may not have to say about that fact.

In nature the balance of life is managed or controlled in very subtle and complex ways that have evolved over millions of years because of the complex relationships that exist between species and the planet. Civilised human beings, however, have developed ways of managing nature in the short term and thereby can, to a degree, control the environment they live in. This has led to artificially high human population levels and this in turn creates pressure on the planet's resources.

The proof is illustrated by the speed of growth of human population that has occurred since humans have developed new technologies from the plough to the wheel to the use of pesticides and so on. This has always been matched by a rise in the human population.

As this technology spread and became more sophisticated it created a better short term quality of life on the outside and so populations grew accordingly. This then led to a greater squeeze on resources, which led to more growth, which led to an increase in population, which led to a greater pressure on resources. This spiral continues until it reaches a point of unsustainability where the whole collapses in on itself.

If the West has mainly caused these problems by taking nature away from people, then perhaps not only can they be given back their land, resources and dignity but perhaps the West can help give them back their nature too.

Nearly all countries of the world are running at artificially high population levels, so there is a need to get back to a situation where the balance is more realistic.

It is time to admit to these follies and seek practical means of healing the pain that all endure due to insensitivity, short sightedness and greed. The best medicine for the future is to be natural.

That is the most important research of all – what does it mean to be natural and what does that call for now?

Fear not for the future, weep not for the past.

Percy Bysshe Shelley

How can I be useful, of what service can I be?
There is something inside me, what can it be?

Vincent van Gogh

THE PHOENIXING
OF THE FUTURE

MUCH HAS BEEN SAID THROUGHOUT this book about humans having departed from the line of their spiritual calling. However, that need not give rise to a sense of failure or doom and gloom, for that would deny the dynamic nature of the forces of evolution and the intelligence involved.

History is a great teacher from two standpoints:

1. It shows what works and
2. It shows what doesn't work.

Both aspects can instruct equally as to how to build a better future for all if humans are prepared to learn the lessons of history and not to be imprisoned by them. As Winston Churchill said, "Those who do not study history are doomed to repeat it."

Human beings have all the ingredients they need to salvage new hope from the ashes, if they dare to try.

HISTORY

The Phoenix was a fabulous mythical bird, said to be as large as an eagle with brilliant scarlet and gold plumage and a melodious cry. As its end approached the Phoenix made a nest of aromatic branches and spices, set the nest on fire and was then itself consumed in the flames. Miraculously from the ashes sprang a new and better Phoenix.

The ancient Egyptians linked the myth of the Phoenix with the longings for immortality that were so strong in their civilisation. From Egypt its symbolism spread around the Mediterranean world of late antiquity. At the end of the first century Clement of Rome became the first Christian to interpret the myth of the Phoenix as an allegory for resurrection and life after death.

In Chinese mythology the Phoenix is the symbol of high virtue, grace and power and represents the union of yin and yang.

The principle represented by the Phoenix is one of something reducing back down to ashes then a better form appearing. This is the choice that faces the human race in this pivotal time. It can choose to continue down its current path of materialism, consumerism and depletion of the world's resources until everything is gone or it can reform.

To do this humans need to give up the old ways and admit that no one really knows the way forward, but that they want to try and find it and that they want to do so together. That means sharing. All are part of the old Phoenix; the 'what got us this far'. All can be part of the new world order where the necessary sentiment is one of careful marshalling of the planet's resources and to ensure that the sacredness of all life is respected and revered.

Life is not ordinary. It is truly extraordinary.

There is something deeply wrong with what we *have* become.

There is absolutely nothing wrong with what we *could* become.

The question is – what is it that we would wish to become and why?

?

Fortune favours the prepared mind.

Louis Pasteur

Every action of our lives touches on some chord that will vibrate in eternity.

Sean O'Casey

It's tough to make predictions, especially about the future.

Yogi Berra

Projections For The Future

PROJECTION IS A WORD THAT can mean many things, and in the context of examining who owns the future it is a vital point to consider. Projections can mean anything from extrapolating the data of existing trends in order to see what might happen if they continue; to putting forward new plans and ideas in order to move matters and events in a completely new direction.

In looking at projections from current world trends the future doesn't look that bright. In fact, the prognosis is pretty dire if the human race continues on its current course of wasteful and excessive use of the planet's resources and abuse of the environment. One only has to tune into the news on any given day to find evidence of the ever increasing and worsening trends where the hazardous business of living is concerned.

The warning signs are there for all to see and no one can really say that they don't know what they are. Yet despite countless projections, computer models and goodness knows what else, governments mostly choose to ignore the warning signs and carry on the way they are.

This applies at individual level as well where, for example, people now know that smoking causes fatal diseases yet many people still smoke despite the warnings on the packets. The same principle applies to things like eating junk food and not getting any exercise. People have the information and the data about the possible consequences, but they either don't want to or don't know how to change their behaviour.

People mostly don't realise that the likely result of continuing a certain behavioural pattern will cause specific negative results until those results actually manifest. By the time the symptoms appear it is often too late to make a change to the behaviour pattern or it has reached a stage where the effects are irreversible.

Sometimes people realise that their behaviour is likely to undermine their life and well-being and make profound and life altering changes of direction. It is almost as if they manage at the last moment to steer the ship away from the rocks that are directly in front of them. With so many critical points facing the human race at this time the analogy seems to hold good where the immediate future is concerned.

This is where another kind of projection occurs, for if ever there was a time when creative and generative ideas about the future were needed it is now.

The positive aspect of this is that there is no shortage of talent, bright ideas and creative energy available to find the way forward.

This requires a think tank type of process where the best of the world's minds can be brought together to look at the situation and what might be needed. However, for this to succeed people must be free and not subject to what governments or institutions of vested interest want them to think.

Governments need to follow the lead of what is needed and not try and lead the way to pre-decided conclusions that avoid addressing the real challenges ahead.

Now there's a projection for change if ever there was one.

And if it happened, what would be the first item you would put on the agenda for such a conference?

?

There is a tide in the affairs of men,
Which, taken at the flood, leads on to fortune:
Omitted, all the voyage of their life
Is bound in shallows and in miseries.
On such a full sea are we now afloat,
And we must take the current when it serves,
Or lose our ventures.

Shakespeare (Julius Caesar)

The beginning is always today.

Mary Wollstonecraft

THE PRODIGAL MOMENT

SEVERAL TIMES WITHIN THIS BOOK the parable from the Bible of the Prodigal Son has been mentioned. It is therefore fitting to devote a chapter to this story and its implications for human beings at what is clearly a pivotal time in their history as a species.

There was an instant when the Prodigal Son's journey changed from being one of travelling away from something to turning back again towards that which he loved so much and yet had so nearly thrown away. In modern terms he undertook a U-turn. That moment is something we human beings face individually and collectively in the choices we now make about the future. We need to change direction. It is a very powerful moment when things change their polarity away from the previous lock that they may have been subject to.

This can be felt if a person sits by the sea shore and watches the tide come in. Sometimes it is possible to actually feel or sense the moment when the tide turns and the sensation is a very powerful one. As we know, the reason the tide changes direction is due to the influence of the Moon which is over 250,000 miles away. The forces that move the oceans of the world can't actually be seen and yet they play a crucial role in sustaining life on the Earth.

'Prodigal' is a word that is seldom used in language today, other than to mention the story of the Prodigal Son. It is therefore a very powerful word for it has not become diluted by being incorporated into the vernacular use of language.

What is important about this process is that in a prodigal moment a person doesn't suddenly have a whole set of answers to the problems they face. They simply make the admission that the path they are on is not the right one and that they wish to journey back to the true one. This return journey is a long one, for the road of self-realisation and self-redemption takes time, just as it does for the tide to come in and go out.

The human race faces just such a prodigal moment where it needs to admit that it has become departed from its natural path. This begins with a signal of intention, for inside that change of intention there is a change of state, a change in the molecular and genetic structure even. Slowly things can aggregate around that change of state and grow, compound and accelerate according to the momentum it gathers. As the tide changes, at first the movement is hardly discernible, but it slowly gathers pace as the new force of direction increases in potency.

This can also be seen in the changes of seasons or the lengthening or shortening of the days. December 21st is the shortest day in the Northern Hemisphere and from that point on the days start to grow longer, but very slowly at first. As the Spring Equinox approaches the days are lengthening at their fastest rate. Then slowly the rate of lengthening decreases until the longest day on June 21st when the process then reverses and the days become shorter again.

In mentioning the natural analogies to do with this prodigal process it is important to note that whilst the tide comes in and goes out, or the seasons move from one to the other, they do not repeat what has gone before. No two tides and no two seasons are the same for they themselves are part of the planet's evolving mechanism.

The Prodigal Son returned to a house that had evolved and progressed since he had left. Part of his journey was to admit that he could not assume the position that he had in the house before, not only because he had thrown away his inheritance, but also because things had changed since he had left.

The past is a great tutor for it can instruct as to what works and what doesn't. There is no such thing as an objective view of history, for whilst history may repeat itself historians tend to repeat each other!

DO YOU KNOW WHAT YOU KNOW?

A person reading this probably has the view that the Earth is round as opposed to flat. (There are members of the Flat Earth Society however who still refuse to accept this view.) The question is how does a person actually *know* that the Earth is round? Can they prove it from their own actual experience rather than just repeating what they have been told?

The point of this is not to argue that the Earth is flat. It is simply to challenge assumed knowledge over actual experience.

Consider the view that the planets of the Solar System orbit around the Sun. How does a person know this to be true? Less than 500 years ago this was considered to be heresy.

Or the view that humans descended from apes. The furore that this caused when Darwin first postulated his theory of evolution was enormous, especially from the Creationists whose view of life on this planet was that it was only a few thousand years old. There was even a Bishop Ussher who only 300 years ago postulated that he could date the age of the Earth precisely from the Bible by tracing who begat who back to Adam and Eve. From this he calculated that the Earth began on the 23rd of October 4004 B.C. at 9 am! Makes one wonder what was happening at 8 am!

People were even burnt at the stake for witchcraft up to a few hundred years ago. Today people would say that such ideas were based in fear and ignorance and that society is much more enlightened now. But is that so? The last prosecution in England for witchcraft was during the Second World War barely 60 years ago when Helen Duncan was put on trial for her practices.

Or the view that slavery has been abolished?

It was only in 1838 that slavery was abolished in England, even later in America, yet does that mean it doesn't still go on in overt and covert ways? Estimates indicate that there are 27 million slaves in the world today - more than at any other time in history.

Modern culture has its own myths and folklore as to how it has evolved to its position of pre-eminence on this planet and, indeed, the Universe. Modern humans tend to label everything that happened prior to the rise of civilisation about 12,000 years ago as being *pre-*

history. This implies that nothing much was happening before this as humans in their modern 'civilised' form hadn't yet arrived on the scene.

Yet whilst humans view of their pre-eminence has been challenged by the fact that the Earth is not the centre of the Solar System, or indeed the Universe, nevertheless there is still the swagger of human arrogance that basically asserts that the Universe and everything in it belongs to human beings, and that they can do whatever they like with it. There is even a website where a person can log on and buy their own bit of the Moon if they so wish. When did the Moon decide to sell itself and how are the plots valued?

It was somewhat ironic that the Space Shuttle Challenger blew up as it tried to participate in the conquering of space. Could it be that something somewhere responded to that challenge?

The name Challenger implies that something needs challenging.

Does space need challenging from human beings?

Has it done something wrong?

Does it need regulation and controlling by humans?

Do humans think that they own it?

Do humans not see that an intelligent Universe might resist the expansion of some of their unfortunate attitudes that seriously threaten to turn its own ecology into a graveyard?

Is the invention of the Teflon frying pan really worth all that time, effort and money?

Do humans have the right and mandate to do whatever they like with the Universe and everything in it according to their whims and fancies?

What other kinds of distortions do humans not see about their own view of reality now?

For example:-

What will those of the future make of the current dabbling with genetic engineering?

What will they make of the experiments with cloning?

How will they think about the exploiting of the planet's resources?

How will they think about greed and selfish profit making motives?

How will they assess the dividing up of the planet into territories capable of being 'owned'?

What will they make of the relationships currently portrayed between the genders?

What of the obsession with war and violence and suppression of difference?

What of how women are treated in many societies as being lesser then men?

What of how children are robbed of the opportunity to experience the innocence of childhood?

PRODIGAL IS AS PRODIGAL DOES

The prodigal moment of the Bible was a son returning to his father's house in humility. The prodigal moment humans face now is one of seeking readmission to their mother's house: Planet Earth. Like the Prodigal Son, humans have thrown away nearly everything that she has gifted them, and as such they stand on the edge of the abyss.

This is especially so for the few who think that they have never had it so good. They too will soon join their brothers and sisters who already know the privations and hardships caused by the human race's loss of memory about who and what they are.

There is the saying that 'the heart of the matter can only be seen from afar'. Have humans become so self-absorbed that, like the Prodigal Son, they can't see the truth of their situation? Is it mere coincidence that the human heart tilts at the same angle in the body as the Earth does on its axis? Or have humans disconnected themselves from the pulse of how the planet works and the lives she sustains?

In the story of the Prodigal Son father knew his house could and would go on without the son but that it would be a lesser place without him. The Earth can and will survive with or without the human race in some shape or form, even if it takes millions of years to recover from the profligate spending and wasting of their inheritance by human beings.

Part of the difficulty lies in the inability of human beings to see that they are not the adults of the Universe where the growth of intelligence is concerned, but rather that they are very young children. Humans have only existed as a species for far less than 1% of the life term of the known Universe, and in their so called 'civilised' form for far less time than that. Humans have therefore had little time to mature.

The analogy for this lies in each person's own experience of being a baby. The baby is totally self-centred where its own needs and desires are concerned. This is natural for it can have no sense of a bigger reality whilst so young, nor can it look after itself. At some point, however, it has to be weaned off that state of affairs otherwise it develops a dependency. Could the human race be at that point in its own development as a species? It certainly seems that the human race needs to do some growing up fast before its life support system is cut off, not by the planet but by themselves, by switching the oxygen off on their own space suit.

The only point of leaving this planet in a spaceship would be to look back and see that this is where we belong. The question that naturally follows that is: how is it that we should behave to prove that we really believe that to be the case?

It is the theory that decides what can be observed.

Albert Einstein

Nothing has such power to broaden the mind as the ability to investigate systematically and truly all that comes under thy observation in life.

Marcus Aurelius

You can observe a lot by just watching.

Yogi Berra

THE OBSERVER EFFECT
AND THE FUTURE

THIS CHAPTER REVOLVES AROUND THE fact that people influence the future in many different ways and that it is not possible to be passive about the future. People may think that they don't influence the path of future events, but they do. In fact, perhaps the more they think they don't influence the future the more they do!

Every thought, decision, action, non-action and abdication from freedom of choice gives and grants permission for the course of future events to unfold. Inhibiting one possible pathway for future events creates or allows another route to be followed and creating opportunities does the same.

Many centuries ago people did not ever really consider that they were observers of their reality. They simply thought that they were a part of it and they lived their lives accordingly. They looked for the basic necessities to live and were part of nature in that they were much more subject to its ebbs, flows and seasons.

Slowly over time humans began to perceive their place in the order of things slightly differently. This increased the more they saw themselves as having some degree of power over the forces of nature. They also developed the view that if they could look at their situation from a more powerful place then perhaps there was something else in the Universe that could equally look at them from an even more powerful place.

This led to the development of religion and the idea of there being a God or Gods to worship and follow. There were different ways of viewing how this God or Gods observed humanity with many developing the view that this deity looked upon its own creation with anything from disappointment to disgust to anger. Perhaps this view developed because of the way that human beings began to look at everything they deigned to be below them?

Whatever the case, this deity never seemed to be neutral or entirely objective about its creation and this view of being lesser and unworthy has permeated much religious thought over thousands of years.

The point of being an observer is that a person is meant to be objective and not interfere with the experience that the thing or person being observed is having. Otherwise the observer moves from being an observer to a participant.

This observer principle is important in applying the scientific method and in conducting experiments that seek the nature of truth and reality. If the observer introduces any bias, either knowingly or unknowingly, then the test results will be tainted. The aim in conducting such experiments is to introduce controls and checking systems so that any subjectivity and bias can be removed.

Another feature of the scientific method is that the more objective the test the more likely it is for the results to be replicated if the experiment is repeated.

In this way a greater understanding of how and why things work the way they do can be reached.

As the human race researched its reality it came to view its situation from an increasingly egocentric place. This is where philosophy came to be entwined with science in a volatile and often dangerous mix.

The rise of the rationalisation began to accelerate around the time of the Renaissance when many great advances began to occur in the scientific method with the development of things such as telescopes and microscopes. Inventions like these literally enabled humans to see a different reality, so they had to change or modify their theories of the world to accord with what they could now see.

They became different observers and different interpreters of the reality they were observing.

GET A GRIP!

One of the theories that began to develop around this time was that all other realities revolved around human reality, and that other things only drew their reality when they had been observed by humans. This in part drove much of the discovery movement, for it was felt that by going out and 'observing' other things that had not yet been discovered, more of God's reality was brought into existence and therefore this was a good and noble thing for human beings to do.

It was only when something was looked at that it actually could be said to have come into existence. This may seem arrogant and delusional to us today, but at the time it was a prevailing view and it has not disappeared from modern scientific study.

This process of regarding things as coming into existence only because they had been observed was in turn replaced by the seeking of ever more objectivity in experimentation. The Holy Grail of such experimentation was to completely eliminate any influence from the experimenter in the conducting of the experiment. This was regarded as desirable because the more objective the test the more reliable the results would be.

Many scientists therefore believed that it was possible to carry out totally objective experiments.

In the 20th Century there was not only an incredible advancement in the sophistication of the equipment to carry out and measure test results, but also an equivalent advance in the theories being propounded about life and the nature of reality. Alongside the development of things such as electron microscopes and particle reactors appeared theories such as General and Special Relativity and Quantum Theory.

One of the features that began to develop, however, especially with the rise of Quantum Theory, was what has now come to be known as the Observer Principle. At first scientists couldn't understand how some apparently identical experiments had tiny fluctuations in their results as they now could measure the results attained to a much finer degree than before.

It was then discovered that the experimenter was in fact part of the experiment, and no matter how much they tried to not be part of the experiment they still affected it. This astonished scientists for they had no idea how simply observing an experiment could influence it.

THE UNIVERSAL PLACEBO

An analogous situation exists in relation to the now well known placebo effect in medical science where a person who is given an inert pill can recover if they think they have in fact been given a remedy. This effect is still being researched, but what it does suggest is that how someone thinks about things influences them. This seems to apply not only to one's own internal medical matters, but also to how an experimenter thinks about the experiment they are carrying out e.g. if they want the experiment to work it has a better chance of working.

The mechanics of how and why this happens has scientists baffled and much research is being carried out with fascinating discoveries into things like the nature of electromagnetism, gravity, zero point fields, and so on.

This also relates to the work done by Benveniste in relation to his experiments with water retaining the memory of substances that it had come into contact with, even after those substances had been diluted out.

Benveniste developed a system whereby human involvement in the experimentation process could be eliminated by using robots to carry out the dilutions of the water solution. However, even then he noticed that some of his results contained anomalies that he could not explain.

Then he discovered that the results with anomalies all related to the fact that a particular woman was in the laboratory when the experiments took place, even though she in no way interfered with the actual carrying out of the experiment. Just her presence was enough to affect the results achieved. Similar things happened in other experiments where it was found that the presence of specific individuals could affect the results.

This completely baffled the scientists, for how could a person affect an experiment simply by being present without physically influencing the experiment in any direct way? This caused the scientists to reconsider the whole idea of wave theory and how electromagnetic waves might be given off at different frequencies by different bodies. These waves can travel across time and space and affect the atomic structure and organisation of other bodies without actually coming into direct physical contact with them.

This could mean that once a body comes into contact with another body their wave patterns mix, and to one degree or another, they are changed. The greater the difference in their wave patterns the greater the change that might be caused. This might explain why some people affected the water experiments more than others because of what they were 'giving off'.

This could then mean that even after the introduced substance has been diluted out of the water, it nevertheless retains a 'memory' of it because it itself has absorbed and stored the memory of the introduced substance's wave pattern. It has assimilated it into its own wave pattern and altered its arrangement accordingly.

The hypothesis seems to be confirmed in recent scientific findings that suggest that memory is not held in any particular part of the brain but rather throughout the brain as a kind of wave pattern storage system. Particular parts of the brain might be responsible for specific activities but the memory seems to be stored everywhere and nowhere, a bit like a hologram.

This aspect of wave theory and resonance has been confirmed in many other experiments that have shown that water is affected by music that is played to it, poetry that is read to it, and colours that are stood in front of it.

Other experiments show that plants retain a memory of what they have come into contact with, even though there is no physical contact with the thing they 'remember'. Plants that have been deliberately damaged react when the person who damaged them simply walks into the room.

Classical physics struggles to explain these phenomena but new and exciting theories are emerging to help explain how it might work. This may cause us to re-examine the nature of reality and the laws of physics themselves.

What it seems to suggest is that there is no such thing as the casual observer, for an observer is not merely an observer. They affect and are affected by everything they observe. There is, therefore, no such thing as a passive or neutral experience. This in turn suggests that people affect their reality according to how they observe it.

IT IS NOT POSSIBLE TO SIMPLY STAND BY AND WATCH

This point is crucial in considering the future. Mostly people carry the view that they cannot influence the course of future events and simply observe the changes that happen and react to them accordingly. They believe that they have no major influence in the decision making process other than voting for those in power - if they are lucky enough to even get a vote.

The observer effect principle suggests that a person's involvement begins much earlier than that. How a person observes events does make a difference and how they then think about those events also affects their reality. The level and degree of these matters being influenced may be tiny, but the principle is a very important one for it suggests that many people changing the way they observe world events could make a huge difference to the future.

This may sound easy but people are trained to observe events in a partial and biased way. This suggests that the people in power also have a partial or biased view of reality, which is often short-sighted, local and parochial due to the nature of their policies and decision making processes. Otherwise how can things such as hatred, factionalism, exploitation, tyranny, oppression, greed, bigotry, prejudice, war and terrorism be explained?

More training and education needs to be given to people as to how to observe their reality, and how they can constructively and positively change not only their current reality but also their future one.

Given that it is possible to affect the course of future events just by how one thinks about them, it would make sense to encourage people to make positive changes to that reality, both for their own benefit and for those yet to come. The bigger the context that they observe reality from, the more powerful their actions will be.

People who have closely observed the nature of the human condition throughout history have been able to make a difference to it.

This applies in all great areas of human expression, from art to science to religion and the humanities.

Perhaps it is possible, therefore, not only to observe the future as it occurs, but also to change the predicted observations before they even happen and replace them with a better set?

One final and obvious, but easily overlooked, point about the observer principle is that what a person observes depends upon the location they look at it from. Some vantage or observation points are better than others and some can provide misleading information due to the angle and distance they look at things from.

If a person changes their viewing position, they change what they observe. For example, a person can change from seeing what is wrong about a situation to seeing what is right. They can choose to see that the problems the world faces in the future about such things as resources are not, in fact, about supply but to do with proper management and equitable distribution.

A person sees what they want to see and what they have trained their eyes to see. And what they see they believe.

One thing, however, is certain and that is if a person shuts their eyes then they won't see anything.

I am not an Athenian, nor a Greek, but a citizen of the world.

Socrates

*In order to properly understand the big picture,
everyone should fear becoming mentally clouded
and obsessed with one small section of truth.*

Xun Zi

*Our country is the world, our countrymen are all mankind.
We love the land of our nativity only as we love all other lands.
The interests, rights, liberties of American citizens
are no more dear to us than are those of the whole
human race. Hence, we can allow no appeal to
patriotism, to revenge any national insult or injury.*

William Lloyd Garrison (1838 Boston Peace Convention)

WORLD CITIZENSHIP

WE LIVE TODAY IN AN age of mass communication. Signals and messages fly around the world at breathtaking speed and in innumerable numbers. Life today is vastly different to that of 100 years ago, let alone 1,000 or 1,000,000 years ago.

We live in a time of exponential change.
Think about some of the changes that have happened in the world in the last 500 years: -
The Earth has been found *not* to be the centre of the Solar System.
The Earth has been proven *not* to be flat.
The human race has sent rockets to the Moon and beyond.
The atom has been split.
Jet travel is commonplace.
The Internet has been invented.
The telephone enables people to communicate across the world.
Laser technology has been invented.
Oil has been discovered to be useful for countless purposes.
Weapons of mass destruction have been invented.
Mass printing means books are available freely to most.
The rise of mass media with TV and radio and world news 24 hours a day as to what is going on anywhere on the planet, from earthquakes to riots to wars.
Medical care has changed dramatically.

What can be observed from this is, that for good or for ill, there is a trend away from local living to the world being a global village. 500 years ago it was highly unlikely that most people would ever travel away from their local community by more than a few miles, and some would never travel at all as they were tithed to the land on which they worked. There were far more people living in the country than in cities, and none of the cities were anywhere near the size of some of the mega metropolises of today.

Things were much more local and contained. People were more self-sufficient. They had to live off what they could find in their local area. They had to make appropriate arrangements for storage of food for the winter or, as with the nomadic peoples of the world, follow their food supply during those months.

Whilst there may have been kingdoms and empires, for the ordinary person real life wasn't really so much concerned with those larger realms of politics and church and state. For these people their existence was subject to local ordinance and control and there was a large amount of decentralisation in the administration of local affairs. For example, Germany and Italy didn't come into existence as countries until the end of the 19th Century as they were previously divided up into principalities or states.

A person during this time mostly drew their identity from the institutions they associated with from social class to religious group to profession to culture to language to custom and so on.

IT'S HARDER TO CHANGE THAN CONFORM. OR IS IT?

This propensity towards group identification is very strong, for even if people rebel against one form of conformity they usually replace it with another. This binding and controlling of the individual has been especially prevalent since the time of the rise of city states, yet perhaps at this time of deep and profound change a new kind of natural self government might emerge?

Look at a large map of the world and see how the Earth is divided up into countries and states with their borders and territories. Yet unless a person walks into a man-made structure, such as a fence, then there would be no way of knowing that they were walking from one country to another.

This concept of territory is not unique to humans but the human race's failure to rise above this level prevents it from progressing to its next level of evolution.

Whilst people are seen as separate individuals, nations and states nothing can shift in terms of the human race's perception of its situation now and into the future. The current paradigm is one of divide and rule, the haves and the have nots, the us and thems, the rich and poor, the believers and the infidels, the masters and the slaves, the saved and the damned.

It is time for the emancipation of the individual and the releasing of the shackles of fear and guilt; to emerge as co-responsible people towards a new future possibility. Any attempted unification from lowest common denominators is doomed to fail.

The United Nations missed an opportunity when it was incorporated. Perhaps they went an S too far? Consider the idea of the whole Earth being one United Nation as opposed to many different nations and states all trying to reconcile their differences.

This is where the idea of World Citizenship emerges.

Imagine having a passport that reads: -

Nationality:	World Citizen
Place of Residence:	Planet Earth
Visa:	Free admittance to anywhere where a positive difference to the state of the world will be made.

Or, even better, imagine a world where passports are no longer needed, because fear and control have been removed from the human condition. The separations and differences that exist in the world look to be very powerful and insurmountable, but they are not. It is only because humans choose to reinforce them that they are given any credence and validity. The current paradigm is to believe that there are leaders and followers, but that is an old evolutionary blocking thought pattern that prevents the very change that is needed from happening.

At the core of World Citizenship lies the concept that each and every person is on a journey of discovery into what it means to be human. Each and every person finds themselves to be gifted with a unique and sacred opportunity. Each person therefore has the inviolable right to liberate the genius of their life according to how they choose to live their life.

Humans share a most wonderful and beautiful planet which is both home and holy ground to all. In this vision of the future responsible custodianship and wise investment are essential guidelines in making the future safe.

Is this an impossible, naïve dream? Not when compared to the current ongoing nightmare.

World Citizenship requires a quantum leap of consciousness and belief. The great thing is that human beings are in the right place at the right time to embrace it.

What are you waiting for? Why not apply for your passport today? It's free!

?

Let him that would move the world first move himself.

Socrates

Sweet are the uses of adversity.

William Shakespeare (As You Like It)

DON'T PANIC, IT'S ORGANIC!

THE HUMAN RACE HAS REACHED a critical point in its evolutionary journey and we all have an important role to play in how the future will be shaped on this planet.

It is easy, when faced with crisis situations to panic and look towards solving the problems as soon as possible. However, this 'doing' psychology of humans is one of the main causes of the problems in the first place. There is nothing that can be 'done' to correct things unless it is connected up to some kind of intelligence and therefore pre-emptive, knee jerk responses will only make things worse.

In the world at this time there is, on the one hand, a culture of desperately thrashing around trying to acquire more and more about less and less and, on the other, a rising consciousness and renaissance of human spirituality and purpose. This is not in terms of the emotional or evangelical reinventing of old dogmas, but an attempt to update who and what human beings are and to find their true place in planetary and universal affairs.

It is a time to find the right questions rather than pursuing the wrong answers. The search for truth needs to be undertaken in partnership and friendship, not fear and suspicion.

Humans need to develop the art of knowing how to wait in the right way. *WAITING* anagrams to *GAIN WIT*, and that is a large part of what the human race needs to gather about its situation. Wit is not just being funny, which is largely what that word has been reduced down to today. Originally it had a very high meaning and there was more than one kind of wit. Shakespeare spoke of the Five Wits in his plays, and these are: -

Common Sense
Imagination
Fantasy
Estimation
Memory

It is proposed to consider each of these wits in turn to see how it is they may be able to assist the human condition in looking for the way ahead, but first here is the first known quote where the five wits are referred to, followed by one from Shakespeare:

There are five witts removyng inwardly
First "Common Witte" and then "Ymagination"
"Fantasy" and "Estimation" truly,
And Memory.

Stephen Hawes: The Passetyme of Pleasure (1507)

If thy wits run the wild-goose chase, I have done;
for thou hast more of the wild-goose in one of thy wits than,
I am sure, I have in my whole five.

Shakespeare: Romeo and Juliet, II, I, v.

Traditionally the five wits have been regarded as follows: imagination as being the 'wit' of the mind; fantasy as being imagination united with judgement; estimation estimates the absolute, such as time, space, locality, and so on; memory as being the 'wit' of recalling past events; and common sense as being the outcome of the five senses of sight, sound, touch, taste and smell.

These are five very powerful attributes or qualities and Hawes regards them as "removyng inwardly", which seems to be referring to inner states of being or intelligence rather than matters of external learning. It seems that these 'wits' combine to offer an internal and external intelligence service, that not only registers what is going on in the person, but also enables them to be aware of what is going on around them both locally and universally.

Needless to say, not many of these abilities are taught at University today and so this speaks of a natural training obtained from the University of Life rather than from an institution or some grey, stone building.

IMAGINATION

Imagination is the 'wit' of the mind.

Imagination is a very powerful faculty and tool. It is a gift, and yet humans mostly use it to imagine ways of exploiting the planet's resources, make vast profits, spend the future's time before it is due and prejudice the opportunity of their descendants.

In the modern world impressions are more about image than substance, whilst in the natural world they are one and the same thing.

There is the expression of a person's 'imagination running wild.' This is perceived as being either a good or bad thing depending on whether it is running free or out of control. This imposes a value judgement reading 'wild' as being out of control, but in nature nothing is truly wild in the sense of being out of control as there are laws and rules under which all species exist. There are natural balances so that both diversity and order are kept in check.

It is haunting to reflect that perhaps the most popular song of the modern pop era is John Lennon's *Imagine,* which is full of what its title suggests – Imagination. It imagines there being no heaven and hell, no war, and a world of peaceful co-existence. Yet Lennon says that whilst other people may say that he is a dreamer, he is not the only one, and that maybe one day the world could live as one. The world has lived as one previously and it can do so again.

This is what is referred to in the Bible in the story of Adam and Eve in the Garden of Eden. Prior to the arrival of temptation the Garden of Eden was paradise itself on Earth. But when this was no longer enough humans started to develop other needs.

The Garden of Eden by anagram is: The Danger of Need.

When humans developed needs beyond their basic requirements this fuelled their imaginations, and this in turn caused them to invent things to fill the need.

If a person has everything they need, why would they need to invent something else? This applies to everything from clocks to spacecraft to genetic engineering to organised religion and more. If a person has real religion why would they need to invent something outside of themselves to worship when they are already have the divine inside them?

It is little wonder therefore that most religions have within their central tenets a belief that life is about suffering and the repentance for sin. Or, that humans are all inherently evil and therefore doomed to eternal damnation unless they all repent.

Yet the rise of religion was originally an attempt to help humans connect to their already existing truth and natural way in a deeper and more profound way. It was born out of the human imagination, but mostly that connection has not been sustained and indeed has often been inverted.

We have imagined ourselves into the situation we now find ourselves in and we can also imagine ourselves out of it. We need to remember what it is like to be connected to the Earth, the wind, the seasons, the air, ourselves and each other. From here compassionate, remedial action can begin. Perhaps the Aborigines of Australia knew something when they spoke about the Dreamtime from which the world was born?

FANTASY

Fantasy is traditionally regarded as being imagination united with judgement.

What an amazing coupling these two qualities offer under the overlord cover of fantasy. For imagination carries the sense of an absolute freedom of the mind; yet judgement on the other hand carries the sense of safety and discernment whilst living in that freedom. They offer each other an excellent counter-balance to ensure that the person is at the point in their search for the unknown and yet to be revealed whilst at the same time ensuring that they do not, as Shakespeare suggests, go off on a wild-goose chase and thereby loose 4 of their wits!

As with imagination there are two ends of the spectrum of the theatre of fantasy. On the one hand there is the fantasy of delusion or invention, for why would a person need to invent anything when they have everything they need? On the other hand it has to be fantasy to think that humans can continue to go on as they are and expect to survive.

Somehow a fantasy has developed in the human psyche that they are the centre of the Universe and all of it was put here for their pleasure, for them to do with as they will.

The big is beautiful culture of buy now, pay later is not, and never has been, in any way sustainable. Because of this the edges of this fantasy are starting to bite.

A ray of hope, however, lies in the fact that many are now waking up and seeing that change is needed. What gives hope is that there is far more in the human race's favour than there is against it, if people go with the flow of Creation instead of against it. There is nothing to fight or conquer or beat into submission. Only fanatics do that. Progressive people look for what works and then try and find ways to assist, help and encourage in whatever way they can.

Each person needs to find out what they are good at and do lots of it. It doesn't matter whether or not they become famous for it. What matters is that it makes a difference.

If everybody does this it brings into play the other meaning of fantasy, which is to do with the portent and potential within the human race that says there is nothing to prevent the future from being fantastic in ways beyond our imagination! This is the primary meaning of the wit of fantasy as described by Shakespeare and is definitely the preferred meaning of the two options!

ESTIMATION

Estimation estimates the absolute, such as time, space and locality.

This suggests that this wit is rather large, and rather important, for time, space and locality covers just about everything important within a human being's ken! It implies that the greater catchment area a person has within their sphere of considerations about matters of importance then by direct association the more 'wit' or intelligence they may be able to bring to the reality of their situation.

Estimation has two levels of meaning. The first meaning is that of conjecture or guesswork, where people aren't 100% sure of the outcome of things in dealing with the unknown. It helps a person to know that they don't know and to not expect things to be perfect whilst at the same time helping them to find ways of moving forward.

However, the less well-informed a person is about the situation they are 'estimating' then the more likely it will be that the estimate will be wildly off the mark.

For example, Estimators are often employed in putting contract tenders together, and their role is to price what it would cost to do the job and then add a margin for profit on top of that. If they get it right then they will win the job and all is well, but if they get it wrong then they could cause the Company to either not win the contract at all (and eventually if no jobs are won then the Company can't survive) or, perhaps even worse still, lose a lot of money by badly under-estimating what it would take to complete the job.

From this, perhaps it is possible to suggest that many people don't make good Estimators when trying to win important contracts about important matters in their lives?

The other meaning of estimation is derived from the word 'esteem' as in: to hold someone or something high in one's estimation. What causes a person to hold either themselves or others in high esteem depends entirely on what their value system is. In a world driven mostly by ego, vanity and the cult of the celebrity, it is safe to say that many people's value systems are somewhat shallow and vacuous.

Self esteem of a spiritual order is therefore sadly lacking in a world today that is consumed with outer image rather than inner substance.

On the other hand, where people have a deeper, simpler and more natural value system, then a real sense of appreciation and worth is felt both for self and for others, not so much for what they do or what they say, but for what they are and what they represent. This is where people can become an example of how to live a life of quality and value rather than a role model or some kind of icon that others may seek to emulate or copy.

Two of the major preventions of having a natural esteem for others are competition and cynicism. Unfortunately, these are two of the major fuels that drive the 'outer' world of today and it is hard to resist their magnetic power where much of life is regarded as being cheap, easily available and therefore not much more than a commodity. With this being the general persuasion, it is often hard not to regard self, and others, as being commodities. This can only serve to lower the human race's esteem point rating, and thereby lessen its inner promise and potential.

A true value for each other and our shared opportunity, rather than problems, would go a long way towards healing this situation. For if a person is dying of thirst in the desert, and they meet another person who offers them water to drink to save their life, they will hold that person in the highest esteem possible for the rest of their life.

If we can do that about each other without having to wait for emergencies and life-threatening circumstances then that would be a monumental breakthrough for the whole human race. Some already do. It seems that for this position there are just as many jobs available as there are applicants for the post!

MEMORY

Memory is the 'wit' of recalling past events.

This doesn't simply mean recalling a number of mostly unrelated and isolated facts, but more importantly, their significance and how they inter-relate and inter-connect. It also does not necessarily mean that a person can only have a memory of events within their own lifetime, for the chapter on Epigenetics suggests otherwise. So do processes such as the Aborigines' Dreamtime whereby in the collective unconscious they connect not only to who they are, but what they are, where they have come from and why they are here. In this way they retain their sense of identity and belonging and connection to their spiritual and material world for they are in reality one and the same thing.

Modern humans have lost much of this state of connection and therefore it is little wonder that many of these so-called 'primitive' cultures call modern living – the Great Forgetting. The problem is further exacerbated by the fact that modern humans don't even know what it is they have forgotten and when it is pointed out to them they don't believe that they knew what they have forgotten in the first place!

This declentive journey of departure away from the natural path of living evolution is marked by a change of emphasis from being to doing, from sharing to owning, from connection to disconnection, from integration to disintegration, from consciousness to unconsciousness, from giving to getting. Strangely enough, most of these inverted processes humans today tend to call progress!

The memory of what human beings are lives in their genetic coding and therefore is latent within them. It is something that we all share; it is something we all know. In past times many knew it better than those of today. We can learn from what our ancestors knew, but we cannot go back to where they were and how they lived their lives. In any event, they are no longer there!

The way forward lies not in reverting to a copycat or romantic view of the existence of past times, but in finding what is a natural and integrated way to live our lives today. This might be quite difficult to do given that there are over 6,500,000,000 people sharing the planet today!

The Human Race needs to rediscover and recollect its memory of what is truly important and why. Anything less than that makes us a bunch of half wits and that simply won't do!

COMMON SENSE

Common sense is the outcome of the five senses, which seems reasonable, for what better systems are there to use than those naturally gifted to human beings?

Common Sense is an expression commonly used about individuals today but it has become somewhat hackneyed and diluted in its meaning. It suggests that at some point there was a sense that was common and that it took its references from the five senses of sight, sound, touch, taste and smell.

These senses can be heightened if programmed correctly. They are much more reliable than the brain, for the brain is simply a giant computer that processes the information fed into it and then produces a response to that information. The brain's response is only as reliable as the systems that feed it while the senses are the intelligence systems for the brain.

If everyone's senses were working to their fullest capacity then this would indeed produce a 'common sense' with different people developing different senses according to their natural abilities and talents for the good of the whole. In modern living, however, humans have largely abandoned the use of these faculties and they have become atrophied and even capable of being deceived. Think of all the false smells, from perfumes to chemicals and fumes, or advertising and political propaganda that bombard people, trying to influence the way they think, feel and act.

This process undermines the senses and programmes them to respond in an unnatural way. Most people end up, to one degree or another, with conditioned responses away from their natural selves. Nothing else in nature needs billboards to sell its products, nor does it need to hire marketing executives or spin doctors. It simply takes what it needs in order to thrive and continue.

Humans could begin to re-educate themselves in accordance with these principles for there seems to be a great absence of common sense within the way the world lurches and stumbles forward. It ignores all the signs saying, 'Look out; danger ahead; smell the flowers on the way; touch something deeper in yourself; taste the future and how it would have humans be.'

Humans have all the equipment they need and are their own best computer and laboratory, if they use their equipment in the way that it was designed to be used.

Surely that would be the best common sense of all.

?

It is better to light a candle than curse the darkness.

Eleanor Roosevelt

The purpose of human life is to serve, and to show compassion and the will to help others.

Albert Schweitzer

WHAT WORKS BEST

THIS BOOK ATTEMPTS TO OFFER different ways to think about the human race's situation. It is easy and tempting to try and offer solutions to what appear to be, and are, huge problems that we face. However, there are no solutions to the problems as such, for the 'answer' to these dilemmas lies in the opportunity that humans can do something meaningful with their lives by each and every person living up to the promise and possibility that their life offers.

The way that this works best is to apply compassion and care into the smallest of acts. Big deeds when examined under the microscope are found to be made up of many small acts of kindness and mercy. Constancy and consistency are wonderful cures for hypocrisy.

The reader is therefore encouraged to think about addressing any issue that they may face not in terms of what the solution may be, but rather in terms of what works best and, in particular, in relation to the bigger picture.

This kind of questioning process is very good towards finding a better centre of gravity in respect of any proposed course of action.

Here is an exercise in which there are no right and wrong answers. Simply try to answer truthfully as to what is the case for you, the reader. Sit down with a pen and paper and do the following: -

1.   Write down the 7 best things that money can buy.

Reflect for a moment.

Now read the next page.

2.   Write down the 7 best things that money can't buy.

Reflect for a moment.

3.   Now compare the 2 lists

What does this say about what works best?

?

He who forgiveth, and is reconciled unto his enemy, shall receive his reward from God; for he loveth not the unjust doers.

The Koran

Tell no lies and you then have nothing to forget.

Mark Twain

Forgive, O Lord, my little jokes on Thee and I'll forgive Thy great big one on me.

Robert Frost

FORGIVING AND FORGETTING

IN LOOKING AT THE STATE of the world it is very easy to focus on what is wrong and the peril of our situation as a species. However, it needs to be borne in mind that to have even got this far is a sign of tremendous success, for well over 99% of all species that have ever existed on the Earth are no longer here.

So, congratulations all round!

We ourselves stand at the cross-roads where we may either join the ranks of the 99% of species that are extinct or change direction and not only continue as a species, but thrive, evolve and refine. To a large degree the choice appears to be ours.

In order to change direction there needs to be a forgiving and forgetting of the past that has contained so much pain, suffering and misalignment. We need to be able to let go of these things so that we can grasp the new opportunities that are clear and present before us.

In order that the process of forgiving and forgetting can be more effective, one needs to better understand what has occurred so that one is better able to let go of its negative influences.

The word *FORGETTING* is in fact made up of two words, which are *FOR* and *GETTING*. This suggests that somewhere in their evolving journey humans decided that life was not so much a matter of belonging within the natural order of things, but rather was literally for… getting.

This getting process has become more voracious over time and ever more damaging to ourselves, each other and the planet on which we live. The more one gets the more one needs to get because the idea of getting is very addictive.

Like most addictions it is highly dangerous, for the more a person gets the more they draw their identity from what they have acquired rather than from what they truly are.

We need to remember what we already know before it is too late. This is eminently possible for it already exists in our design and DNA. Unless we remember we may in time be forgotten ourselves.

A key feature in remembering what is important is letting go of what isn't important, especially the attitude of getting, getting, getting. The more people get the less there is to share, and the less of the essential things of life there are then the more endangered as a species we become. The best way to let go of the past is to forgive.

This leads to the second part of the equation, which is to be *FORGIVING* upon the errors and the misdeeds of the past by letting go off them and starting afresh.

Again, the word itself gives great insight into the nature of *FORGIVING*, for it can be seen as *FOR GIVING*. The higher aspects of forgiving are therefore not simply absolving oneself or others of the consequences of actions, but in actually giving something.

What greater forgiveness can there be than giving the best of oneself to any situation, regardless of what may or may not have been done in the past? If a person is constantly in such a process then they have far less to forgive for they do not carry the weight of history or things not done.

It is often said that life is for living, but perhaps it could more accurately be said that life is for giving, for unless there is the ongoing process of giving there can be no living. There can be no better demonstration of this fact than the Earth on which we live, for each moment it gives us all the air that we breathe. It even does this when we ourselves try and make the quality of that air lesser due to our misaligned actions and behaviours.

Yet never is a breath withheld as any kind of punishment for the behaviour of human beings.

The more we realise that life is for giving rather than taking, the more we will realise and remember who and what we are and thereby remedy the great forgetting that has led to our current predicament. In this we can look forward to the great deeds yet to be done.

Generosity seems to be the way that nature says 'thou mayest,' and the more one gives the more there is to share. It is a fool who thinks that they can exploit this generosity for the other side of this law is the more one takes the less one has.

Forgive and forget might therefore take on a new meaning and importance for us all in how we go on in our shared future.

Finally for this section, here is an experiment to try. On the next two pages are written two words opposite to each other. Look at them both and take a few moments to try and feel what the actual nature of each is unto itself.

Then try and feel which is the more attractive.

Then try and feel which you would rather do.

GIVE

GET

If we knew what it was we were doing, it
would not be called research, would it?

Albert Einstein

You've got to be very careful if you don't know where
you're going, because you might not get there.

Yogi Berra

The Unknown:
As we know, there are known knowns.
There are things we know we know.
We also know there are known unknowns.
That is to say we know there are some things we do not know.
But there are also unknown unknowns; the
ones we don't know we don't know.

Donald Rumsfeld

Finding A Map Into An Unknown Future

WHAT A GREAT QUOTE FROM Donald Rumsfeld! If only:

a. He and not one of his advisers had written it.
b. He fully understood what he was saying.
c. That he didn't just apply it in the context of the war in Iraq.
d. That he wasn't based so much in the known knowns when he said it.
e. That he didn't think that the smallest of the 3 categories was the unknown unknowns.
f. That he actually believed what he was saying!

For that reason the quote from Einstein gets much higher marks under the circumstances!

One of the difficulties facing the human race as it faces an uncertain future is trying to find out how to get where no one else has ever been before. Normally when one embarks on such a journey one buys a map and simply follows the directions provided by those who have been there previously.

However, at some point no one knew anything about the land because it had not been explored, let alone mapped. The pioneers and explorers who first went there were going into the unknown for they could never be sure what they might find, from great treasures and wonders to life threatening situations, that they may never have faced before in their lives.

Without their courage and bravery there would be no maps to help others on the journey today.

The situation facing the human race today is similar, except that it is on a much greater scale and the promise and the peril are also much greater. The journey is not to an unknown continent, or even to an unknown planet or galaxy, but rather to a place that no one has ever been before - and that place is called the future.

Whilst the past and the present can give some ideas of what the future might be like, the simple fact is that we just don't know what it is going to be like or even exactly where it is.

Yes, it is true that we can assay what it might be like if this or that happens, but this or that hasn't happened yet and nor have the unexpected, unknown and unaccounted for events happened either.

How, therefore, to navigate one's way into the future?

What kind of map can be followed when all previous footsteps ceased some time before?

Given the nature of the journey there is a map that can be followed; not the physical map of following directions from place to place, but rather a map of what is needed and how to travel into the future. The best thing to do when going into an unknown region is to equip oneself so that one is ready to meet the challenges that appear along the way.

In this regard it is therefore proposed to look at MAP as an acronym for what might be needed in exploring the world of the future.

MAP is therefore taken to be short for: -

M   Movement
A   Alignment
P   Polarity

It is now proposed to look at each of these coordinates in turn to see in which direction they might lead.

M For Movement

It may sound extremely obvious, but anything that wishes to go on a journey needs to move from where it is to somewhere else. The journey into the future is no different, for we certainly cannot stay where we are if we are to continue as a species.

The first evolutionary principle for survival is adaptation by natural selection. The reason that this is so important is that no environment or ecology is static, therefore those organisms that do not successfully adapt end up becoming extinct.

Movement is another word for change, and change is most definitely what is needed by the human race to enable it to move successfully into the future. The human race's situation, however, is compounded by the fact that, over recorded history and beyond, we have made some unsuccessful and life threatening adaptations that places our own future and that of many other species in jeopardy. This needs to change.

Sometimes species are unable to make the necessary adaptations to survive, but it is rare, if not unknown, for any other species outside the human race to make negative adaptations to make their own survival less likely. This is movement of the wrong kind.

The human race needs to find a different kind of movement as it heads into the future. This is the movement away from where we are and what caused us to be in the position we are in. We are badly lost because we have been following the wrong map.

When lost the best thing to do is stop, reappraise, re-assess, re-evaluate and, if necessary, backtrack to where one was not lost before recommencing the journey. Otherwise the tendency is to walk round and round in circles and exacerbate the situation whilst energy and supplies are exhausted. This principle clearly applies to the human race at this time for we have clearly lost our bearings. If this wasn't the case, why would we spend so much time making our own living environment much more vulnerable and increasingly untenable for ourselves and other species?

Part of the journey into the future requires a movement to remember who we are, where we have come from, how we belong, what is important and why. Many of these things were originally on the map that we had but somehow those bits of the map got lost. If we can find them again it will help equip us on our journey into the future.

By moving forward one automatically moves away from things that no longer fit or are dangerous. This kind of movement is vital, for anything that stands still is soon claimed by its inability to adapt. The fight method of survival has been tried by the human race for too long and to its own cost. The future requires flight - not flight away from the past, but flight towards the needs of the future.

Movement of account begins with small, positive changes that aggregate over time rather than revolutionary changes that simply replace one form of instability with another.

This is the kind of movement that is needed, for rather than seeking to change the institutions of the old world order people are waking up to the realisation that they need to change themselves. With this being the case there is much more of a chance of a raising of consciousness, values, standards and principles, and from there the accompanying adaptive behaviours needed will be found.

This is something that we are eminently capable of doing. When they had no maps to follow the early explorers used the heavens as their guide. Is there any difference today? We certainly need to find use of a higher navigation system than the anthropocentric, ego based greed that has got us into the mess that we find ourselves in today.

How does one escape from such a life threatening situation? Move! And even better still – be moved!

The ability to adapt and meet new challenges is supreme and suggests that the right kind of world movement could lead to a future beyond anything anyone could imagine.

A FOR ALIGNMENT

The second co-ordinate on this MAP of the future is that of alignment. Alignment is important on any journey into the unknown, for movement without the right kind of alignment is highly dangerous. Further, if there are diverse alignments within a team as it embarks upon its journey it can only create problems as the journey progresses.

This has been a major problem in the human race's journey to date – increasing differences in alignment causing escalating tensions and conflict, not just between humans and each other, but also between humans, the Earth and other species.

Alignment occurs when two things are in orientation and conjunct. The human race has increasingly developed a selfish, personal and localised orientation as its sense of belonging, connectedness and integration has diminished.

This poor orientation to the bigger, more holistic picture has led to many of the problems we now face, and means that the problems are addressed from symptom level rather than alignment level. This is evidenced by most of the thinking being about what is wrong and how to remedy it rather than asking what is important and why and what changes in orientation that may require.

When looking through the binoculars at the wrong thing one can only see the future in relation to what one is looking at. What is needed is to re-point the binoculars to a far more distant point into the future, and at the same time adjust the focus so that the future can be seen more clearly.

We need to decide what we are a part of, what it is trying to do and why, and what behaviours might fit within that purpose. The point here is not that we necessarily discover what the answer is to these questions, but rather that we ask them. Better questions are themselves aligning, for they will cause the focus and priorities to shift.

This in turn causes unity because difference causes separateness and vested interest.

Unity begins in the mind, and if the orientation is better focused to the truth of our situation then unity will be a natural by-product of this. This in turn brings greater teamwork and co-operation. The question is, however, is this something we *really* want?

The only way that the necessary adaptations can be made is from a change in alignment, for dealing with the symptoms can only ever be like the boy in Holland trying to block the leaks in the dyke with his fingers.

If enough of this alignment change takes place, it can lead to a complete change in polarity, which is the third of the MAP co-ordinates being sought.

P FOR POLARITY

The Earth has two poles- the North Pole and the South Pole. Magnetic North is not where the actual North Pole is because it is constantly shifting throughout the course of the Earth's history. This is due to the fact that the Earth wobbles as it travels around the Sun and this wobble causes a change in polarity. The Earth is currently in the middle of one of these polar shifts.

Such a cosmic event is both radical and extreme in its effects.

If ever there was an analogy to address the human condition this could be it! Due to our own short sighted actions we have caused our affairs to wobble in a major way. Perhaps it is not a coincidence, therefore, that the human race is going through its own wobble at the same time as the Earth is going through its.

This wobble leading to a change of polarity can happen very quickly with a sudden flip to its apparent opposite state, as in magnetic north switching to magnetic south.

To continue the analogy with the human condition, it seems that the human race has developed a negative polarity towards Nature and her laws. Almost all of our technological and scientific advances appear, in whole or at least in part, to work against Nature, or at least have side effects that are damaging.

Could it be that this wobble that we are going through is the harbinger of a profound and seismic change in polarity? There seems to be little or no possibility of the human race surviving in its current form into the future with the dominant polarity that we currently exhibit.

The phrase 'dominant polarity' is used here because there are many people who have and continue to exhibit a polarity that is very much in sympathetic alignment with the ways of the Earth and Nature. This is the alignment spoken of in the previous section and is the one that more and more people need to catch the way of and apply.

This particularly applies to children because they are being born right at the pivotal point of this polarity change. They are also less affected by what they inherit, if they are encouraged to look towards the future and what might be needed rather than looking backwards towards the mistakes of the past.

The trigger in this change of polarity for the human race is a question of values. Our values are a matter of perception, for just as we are trained to think that the Southern Hemisphere is 'down' and the Northern Hemisphere is 'up', our values depend on how we look at any given situation.

Perception is where ideas and ideologies originate, and once they are given birth to they gather force and power and, over time, they develop their own polarity. If they become strong enough they can become the governing polarity and the standard against which all other polarities are measured and judged.

Often these polarities are subjective and biased to one degree or another because they only have a partial connection to the truth.

The most dangerous polarities are the ones that say that they are the absolute truth and that anything that is different is wrong. This dogmatic attitude is one that has dogged the human race and seems to adapt and mutate according to each and every age.

What is needed is not complicated or difficult for it is something we already know very well. It is to have a reverence and respect for Nature and its ways and to live sustainable and moral lives that are in harmony with the rest of Nature.

This needs us to research and discover how to live such a life in these modern times, given what we have discovered on our evolutionary journey to date.

The polarity is not changing *back* to something but rather changing *into* something.

Surely there is more than sheer coincidence in the fact that a polarity carries a charge.

What, therefore, is the charge upon each and every one of us where the future is concerned?

WELCOME TO THE
BEGINNING OF THE BOOK!

YOU HAVE PROBABLY JUST FINISHED reading the book, so thank you for persevering! However, rather than thinking the book is finished the reader is invited to consider that they have just started something. Reading something changes nothing per se, for it is only in the living application of knowledge that real change occurs.

As an example, it is one thing to read the instructions on how to assemble a bookshelf, but quite another thing to do it!

It is hoped that the reader has found it a worthwhile experience to read this book. If only one thing leads to one meaningful change for each person who reads the book then the author would regard that as a total success.

Nothing in this book is claimed to be absolute truth or dogma, for such claims offer closure to new knowledge and perception. The reader is warmly encouraged to seek these processes of revelation and refinement in their own life and discover what is useful for them and works best in serving that purpose.

Contrary to popular belief, the era of the pilgrim is not over, for each and every person is on some kind of journey. The encouraging thing is that many seem to be realising that not only that this is the case, but that they are not alone.

As this chapter says, welcome to the beginning of the book. There is so much more that could and needs to be said and the Earth needs to hear everyone's voice.

The human race needs a miracle to save it. Luckily the future is full of them, and there are over 6,700,000,000 of them alive on the Planet.

Be the difference you wish to make.

There is no better time to be alive.

After all, you did choose to be alive now, didn't you?

Tony Kearney

EPILOGUE

And finally .... honest!

Recently I was travelling back from New Zealand after visiting family there. At one point, on the long flight back to Ireland, I awoke with the thought – 'where does the future actually come from?'

All the way back I kept wondering about this question, for the sense of it was that the future is not simply a continuation of the past. Somehow it has its own reality and originates from somewhere completely different to the past - but from where?

When I arrived back in the UK, for a quick stop over to visit some family there, I took the opportunity to ask three of my nieces from New Zealand and the UK, who were all meeting together for the first time, what their thoughts were on this question.

Here are their responses to the question; where does the future come from?:

"The future comes from other galaxies in the Universe. The future comes through us because we are part of the future."
Jasmine aged 9.
When asked which galaxies the future comes from, Jasmine responded with: **"Well, it depends what we want!"**

"The future comes from the bits that God left behind"
Florence – aged 6.
When asked why God had left the bits behind, Florence immediately responded with: **"So we can see where God has gone next, of course!"**

"Children are the messengers of the future for they are the closest to it. Therefore, we should listen to them. If we listen to the children then we invite more of the future in."
Megan aged 27.

These responses seem to be excellent starters in considering the question, and will certainly suffice until a better set comes along!

?

About the Author

Tony Kearney was born in New Zealand where he grew up and studied at University. Having qualified as a lawyer he then embarked on travels around the world before settling in London where he practised as a lawyer for nearly 25 years.

In his spare time he has travelled widely taking workshops, seminars and giving lectures on many diverse subjects from matters of personal, planetary and global change, to children's education, to gender relations and many other related topics.

In 2006 he moved to Ireland where he now lives and furthers his work in these areas whilst also working as an eclectic mix of writer, consultant, trainer, facilitator, farmer and mediator.

Lightning Source UK Ltd.
Milton Keynes UK
27 August 2010

159073UK00002B/2/P